Facing Black and Jew
Literature as Public Space in Twentieth-Century America

In *Facing Black and Jew*, Adam Zachary Newton couples works of prose fiction by African American and Jewish American authors from Henry Roth and Ralph Ellison to Philip Roth and David Bradley. Reading the work of such writers alongside and through one another, Newton's book offers an original way of juxtaposing two major traditions in modern American literature, and rethinking the sometimes vexed relationship between two constituencies ordinarily confined to sociopolitical or media commentary alone. Newton combines Emmanuel Levinas's ethical philosophy and Walter Benjamin's theory of allegory in shaping an innovative kind of ethical–political criticism. Through artful, dialogical readings of Saul Bellow and Chester Himes, David Mamet and Anna Deavere Smith, and others, Newton seeks to represent American Blacks and Jews outside the distorting mirror of "Black–Jewish Relations," and restrictive literary histories alike. A final chapter addresses the Black/Jewish dimension of the O. J. Simpson trial.

ADAM ZACHARY NEWTON is Associate Professor of English at the University of Texas, Austin. He is the author of *Narrative Ethics* (1995) and numerous articles in scholarly journals.

Cultural Margins

General editor

Timothy Brennan
Department of Cultural Studies and Comparative Literature and English,
University of Minnesota

The series **Cultural Margins** originated in response to the rapidly increasing interest in postcolonial and minority discourses among literary and humanist scholars in the US, Europe, and elsewhere. The aim of the series is to present books which investigate the complex cultural zone within and through which dominant and minority societies interact and negotiate their differences. Studies in the series range from examinations of the debilitating effects of cultural marginalisation, to analyses of the forms of power found at the margins of culture, to books which map the varied and complex components involved in the relations of domination and subversion. This is an international series, addressing questions crucial to the deconstruction and reconstruction of cultural identity in the late twentieth-century world.

1   Ann Marie Smith, *New Rights Discourses on Race and Sexuality: Britain, 1968–1990* 0 521 45921 4

2   David Richards, *Masks of Difference: Cultural Representations in Literature, Anthropology, and Art* 0 521 47972 x

3   Vincent, J. Cheng, *Joyce, Race, and Empire* 0 521 47859 6

4   Alice Gambrell, *Women Intellectuals, Modernism, and Difference: Transatlantic Culture, 1991–1945* 0 521 5568 8

5   Francis Barker, Peter Hulme, and Margaret Iversen (eds.), *Cannibalism and the Colonial World* 0 521 62908 x

6   Kenneth Mostern, *Autobiography and Black Identity Politics: Racialization in Twentieth-century America* 0 521 64679 0

Facing Black and Jew

Literature as Public Space in
Twentieth-Century America

Adam Zachary Newton

CAMBRIDGE
UNIVERSITY PRESS

PUBLISHED BY THE PRESS SYNDICATE OF THE UNIVERSITY OF CAMBRIDGE
The Pitt Building, Trumpington Street, Cambridge CB2 1RP, United Kingdom

CAMBRIDGE UNIVERSITY PRESS
The Edinburgh Building, Cambridge, CB2 2RU, UK http://www.cup.cam.ac.uk
40 West 20th Street, New York, NY 10011–4211, USA http://www.cup.org
10 Stamford Road, Oakleigh, Melbourne 3166, Australia

© Adam Zachary Newton 1999

First published 1999

Printed in the United Kingdom at the University Press, Cambridge

Typeset in 9.5/12pt Palatino [VN]

A catalogue record for this book is available from the British Library

Library of Congress cataloguing in publication data

Newton, Adam Zachary.
Facing Black and Jew: literature as public space in twentieth-century America/Adam Zachary Newton.
p.   c. – (Cultural margins)
Includes bibliographical references and index.
ISBN 0 521 65106 9 (hardback). – ISBN 0 521 65870 5 (paperback)
1. American fiction – Afro-American authors – History and criticism.
2. Literature and society – United States – History – 20th century.
3. American fiction – Jewish authors – History and criticism.
4. Afro-American authors – Political and social views.   5. Jewish authors –
Political and social views.   6. Afro-Americans – Relations with Jews.   7.
Afro-Americans in literature.   8. Race relations in literature.   9. United States –
Race relations.   10. Jews in literature.   I. Title.   II. Series.
PS153.N5N48   1999
813.009'896073 – dc21   98–39339   CIP

ISBN 0 521 65106 9 hardback
ISBN 0 521 65870 5 paperback

For Buster
. . . and other absent presences:

כן לזכר פניך כל מקום בגבה פניך...

Contents

ix

Pre*face*

... why was there so wide a gulf between person and person;
differences so great that to breach them one would have to
cross the world itself ... the Negro, who was quite a way
down the street, why was he a Negro and I a Jew? Why not the
other way around? Or both of us Negroes or both Jews? There
was something between us that neither of us might grasp,
some understanding of which we had only the dimmest
impression; who knew what this was, or what the design was
into which we had been cast? The connections between things
were too fine to be discovered.
... think for a moment, what was it like to be a Negro? I could
only imagine myself to be obsessed if I were one; I should go
about thinking, "I am black, I am black." Everything would
remind me of it: the cover of the loose-leaf notebook I carried
to school, and if it snowed on the way, snow, and therefore
rain too; a chance word heard in the streetcar – "I fell off the
step ladder and my side is black and blue"; any color named,
or the word, "color" spoken, the sight of the pavement, of a
coconut or an eggplant in the grocer's window, a black dog, or
a white dog, the strong sun in summer – everything would
remind me of it. I should constantly be thinking, "I am a
Negro, I am black." And yet, here we were, walking about in
the street and no one gave a thought to it, no one inquired, no
one imagined what the differences were between men.

Isaac Rosenfeld, *Passage From Home*

Old Esau [my grandfather's father] had been a kind of
down-home "Misnagid," but Grandfather signed on with the
Congregational Church.   Darryl Pinkney, *High Cotton*

Can things take on a face? Is not art an activity that lends faces
to things?
The presence of the Other dispels the anarchic sorcery of the
facts.   Emmanuel Levinas, *Totality and Infinity*

This is a book about *facing*, though not in the obvious sense of physiognomy. Here facing refers to the ethical possibilities of criticism: facings between literary texts as well as the way in which they are faced – read and given feature – by readers. The plain sense of the title is: juxtaposed literary fiction by African American and Jewish American writers. As this book's most prominent term, and in concert with a set of others, facing provides me with a critical vocabulary. In a deeper sense, it gives the book a voice, its own *idiolect* – something Ralph Ellison described, appositely enough, in terms of human countenance, a self-created and featured face.

The connection between face and text for me here is thus far more *intrinsic* than a connection – popularly understood – between Blacks and Jews. Perhaps it is exactly because Black–Jewish relations, as a constituted discourse, tends to seal off rather than free up their meanings, that this book has needed to discover terms of its own. In turn, such terms seem to me to make better *discursive*[1] sense of that phenomenon, since they represent critical interventions on the plane of literary discourse. But in order to explain why that is so, I need to clarify where they come from.

The term facing has a double provenance. Primarily, it stems from the work of Emmanuel Levinas, whose chosen figure of "the face" captures the fact of otherness itself, and the ethical drama between persons that it instigates. Just as we ordinarily identify a person by face, the site and emblem of selfhood, so in Levinas face signifies obligatedness itself. It isn't read so much as recognized and heard: perhaps it is best described as an annunciation. It can mean both ethical exorbitancy – "do no harm to me" – and ethical ardor – "do not turn your face from mine." Above all, it means that the self is indemnified to the other, even before freely choosing to be so. Faces that summon, faces in asymmetrical relation with one's own, faces "denuded" or exposed "in their nakedness": this is the hard figural core of Levinas's ethical philosophy.

That also means the subordination of the political to the ethical – or as Levinas might put it, the primacy of alterity over difference, "the face" over its features, a summons behind inflection or timbre. Obviously, that has certain implications for a book about books by American Blacks and Jews, and perhaps even greater ones for Black-Jewish relations. But the face-to-face in Levinas does not describe a symmetry. As Alain Finkielkraut has put it, "*[T]he assigning of difference*, the process of confusing one's neighbor with his attributes" (italics in original) bows to the fact that "our difficulties before the Other, in effect, go deeper than our notions of him."[2] Still, that is a proscription for life not literary criticism, since texts in part depend on such difficulty; they are mediated many times over. The face, contrariwise, *demands* immediacy.

An ethics of the face, then, does not so readily translate into an ethical-politics of criticism, into facing. Consequently, my book, while it may acknowledge the influence of Levinas, attempts no *programmatic* adaptation of his characteristic trope to literary categories.[3] In a Levinasian spirit it eschews a facile symmetry. In any event, texts cannot be made to stand for persons, though they can be made to preserve the strangeness of each other's strangeness. Such call-and-response lies at the core of this book, but it does not model an encounter to be conducted out in the world, except fot the fact that, like Levinas's construct, facing takes place in language.

A parallel genealogy for facing is found in the work of Walter Benjamin, specifically his innovative notion of allegory from *The Origin of German Tragic Drama* and emblematized in the "Angelus Novus" section from "Theses on the Philosophy of History."[4] An arc between the two texts – one didactic, the other lapidary – suggests a fruitful synergy between the trope of face and the workings of allegory. In the *Trauerspiel* book, Benjamin defined allegory dialectically, as a hinge or interface that, while premised upon fragmentation and ruin, can itself "spring over" redemptively. Even if the referent itself signals a dead-end, the play of allegory permits an aesthetic way-out. "[A]llegories fill out and deny the void in which they are presented," Benjamin writes, "just as ultimately the intention does not faithfully rest in the contemplation of bones, but faithlessly leaps forward to the idea of resurrection."[5]

Allegory is representational salvage, a dialectical mediation between history and material culture. It is also, as Benjamin said, a form of expression – like writing or speech. Tropes and figures offer an opportunity to free up meaning dialectically, to display it as produced and therefore movable. Allegory's movement, from melancholy reality to compensatory figuration, is rehearsed by Benjamin's criticism itself, from the Baroque emblems of *facies hippocratia* in the *Trauerspiel* book, on the one hand, to the image of ceaseless facing in the "Theses on the Philosophy of History," on the other. In the latter, Benjamin allegorizes Paul Klee's painting of "Angelus Novus" as the Angel of History, a fecund image critics have not tired of citing. But at the core of Benjamin's text (especially against the background of the *Trauerspiel* book), is the visage of a figure who perpetually faces.

Allegory in Benjamin charts the gap between sign and meaning. As Benjamin's contemporary, Theodor Adorno put it, the aesthetic understood in this sense disenchants an already enchanted world.[6] It breaks the spell that locks figures into ruin or disaster. "As sensuous images and things decay," writes Theresa Kelley of Benjamin, "the effect is akin to phosphorescence – a sensuous because light-full (or light emptying) process whereby things become allegorical signs."[7] There are two connections to make here. One is back to Levinas for whom "the face" dispels the spell cast by persons themselves, and rectifies "a borrowed light" (in his words[8]) with revelation. The other is to Black–Jewish relations itself, trope-haunted, unbound, bewitched by images – a world where, in the Polish writer Witold Gombrowicz's words, persons become "the slaves of each other's faces."[9] In such a *Trauerspiel* world and its semiotic dead-end, the only way-out is to face the Other (ethics), and thereby undo the spell of figures (allegory). And it is in exactly that dual sense – both figurational and ethical – that Black and Jew in this book are faced.

Facing thus also means the relationship between ethics and allegory. Allegory, in Benjamin's sense, and ethics, in Levinas's, have this in common: they both intervene in an inadvertently enchanted world. One could say, therefore, that Black–Jewish relations describes a world where allegory and face both *miscue*, where the one stands in lack of what medieval writers called the clarifying *integumentum* – the allegoresis – between persons, while the other cannot positively *show forth*.[10] By contrast, facing appeals to the aesthetic and the textual as the place where meaning is freed up, but also and at the same time to ethics as the space where distance and difference are at once mediated and preserved.[11]

To call literary criticism allegorical in this sense means that facing texts creates a dialectical interface between them – the crack that constitutes rather than divides.[12] To understand criticism as ethical means that facing texts contrive a space of approach or proximity for them to draw near without coinciding. This tangency between ethics and allegory – but also between Benjamin and Levinas – can be clarified by a small moment in an early essay by Levinas entitled "Reality and its Shadow" (1948). There, Levinas speaks briefly but suggestively about allegory, and by implication, its relevance for ethics and criticism, when he delineates the meaning of an image as uniquely predicated on resemblance – a doubling between original and copy, *already* allegorized from within.

But then to understand an image as such is to see the anomaly it locates in being *itself*.

> Being is not only itself, it escapes itself. . . . Reality would not be only what it is, what it is disclosed to be in truth, but would be also its double, its shadow, its image. . . . Every image is already a caricature. Thus a person bears on his own face, alongside of its being with which he coincides its own caricature, its own picturesqueness. . . . There is then a duality in this person, a duality in its being. It is what it is and it is a stranger to itself. [13]

This other name Levinas gives to the problem of self-resemblance is *allegory*, "an ambiguous commerce with reality in which reality does not refer to itself but to its reflection. An allegory thus represents what in the object itself doubles it up." Art, as he puts it later, lets go of the prey for the shadow. But reality, one realizes, is shadowed too.

While not dialectical in any obvious sense (Levinas at one point says that art stops both dialectics and time), Levinas's allegory implies a twoness not unlike Benjamin's: the tension between visage and caricature. And whatever else the essay says, the relevance here is exactly that doubling or parallax of entity and shadow, self and image: between Black and Jew, and "Black" and "Jew." "The whole of reality bears on its face its own allegory, outside of its revelation and its truth," Levinas writes. Art lends its own terms to the insight, just as "in utilizing images, art not only reflects, but brings about this allegory."[14] The result, however, is that allegory leaves its traces in the world.

Seeing the discourse of Black–Jewish relations as afflicted by its own representational flaw or blind spot is to see it allegorically, figurally, as haunted by shadow and caricature. Black and Jew shadow each other, in the double sense of tracking and obscuring. The title of a vexed essay by Cynthia Ozick, "Literary Blacks and Jews," *already* describes a certain fate American Blacks and Jews have unwittingly assumed: *literaturization* (albeit not in any critical sense). Criticism, on the other hand, poses the alternative of self-conscious and figural facing, unsettling the accidental allegorizations that take the place of facing the Other. (Another possible title for this book had been *Facing Black and Jew: Allegories of Reading*.)

While, as I said, it cannot substitute text for person, it "lends its terms" to the ethical and political exigencies of encounter. It shifts the ground, if you will, from Black–Jewish relations by exploiting "relations" in its most underused sense – tellings, narrative, the call-and-response of novelistic prose. From that perspective as a poetics of recognition, even the epigraphs to this book by Rosenfeld and Pinkney accomplish, in tandem, a minor facing – an asymmetric reconnoiter with otherness, and with each other.[15]

A few methodological signposts, then. The two-part Introduction treats the connection between allegory and Black/Jewish relatedness at greater length. The readings in successive chapters do not pretend to be comprehensive. Some merely pinpoint moments within a particular text (chapters 1, 3 and 5); others follow an entire novel's or story's trajectory, but within a purposefully circumscribed ambit (chapters 2 and 4). All make infrequent reference to socio-historical contexts, and secondary literature generally.[16]

I leave it to the readings themselves to clarify that the method here is not comparativist for comparison's sake alone (for indeed, one can "compare" any number of likely elements that form a pair from among a whole array of literatures). This applies even to the epilogue – the post-face to this pre-face – whose material is neither literary nor strictly textual. Finally, as readers can perhaps surmise already, *Facing Black and Jew* situates itself on the hither side of a cultural studies-based approach (with which it may suggest possible affinities, however).[17]

Levinas says that the notion of the shadow enables us to "situate the economy of resemblance within the general economy of being."[18] And it is that sense of the pathos of self-resemblance, it seems to me, that cultural studies tends to sidestep. Even when it eyes both prey and shadow, socio-historical facts and their ideologization, what it typically does not do is to answer such ambiguous commerce with *allegoresis*, a self-conscious conjuring of its own. To that extent it recapitulates the discourse of Black–Jewish relations, rather than seeking to disenchant through imaginative re-enchantment. If, as an accepted commonplace, culture is fundamentally "discursive," in this book it is the purposeful facing at one another of literary texts and traditions that produces the *counterdiscursive* movement. That would be the face *in front of* feature, or, to blend Levinas with Ralph Ellison once again, a cleaving of shadow and act.

Acknowledgments

In the oral Torah, Jews are told of the importance of greeting those who approach them; the exteriority of a face demands its due regard. The most compelling instance of such a principle I know comes from a Hasidic tale penned in Auschwitz. A rabbi encounters, or rather, re-encounters, a Polish *Volksdeutsche* from Danzig, now the SS officer whose job is to select out those for immediate extermination. To an astonished rabbi, the officer repeats the very formula the two of them customarily performed when they both lived in a very different Europe: "Good morning, Herr Rabbiner." "Good morning, Herr Müller." The SS officer points his baton right, sending the rabbi the way of reprieve.[1] Levinas extends this notion one step further – or back, as it were – by speaking of one's answerability to/for the other person as an always obligatory "After you!" *L'havdil* – in Hebrew, "to mark the distinction" – I am nevertheless reminded of the gravity and humanity inhering in the simple exchange of greeting even amidst the most trying of circumstances, whether face-forward or about-face.

This book has taken a long time to come to light, having weathered trying circumstances of its own. Supervening turns in fortune have attended its unfolding – the private space beneath the public. If I make reference to travail, however, it is simply to lay claim to the wisdom of acknowledgment when the approach of others calls one out of, and to, oneself. It is in such a spirit that I acknowledge all those who in one way or another greeted the writing of this book together with its writer, whom I therefore thank and address in return. I owe a deep material debt to Martin Peretz and Walter Scheuer without whose personal generosity I could have devoted neither the time nor the resources to complete this book, and to Robert King in the same regard. I am grateful to Barbara Solow, Wang Chi, Richard Newman, Henry Louis Gates, Jr., and Randall Burkett of the W. E. B. Du Bois Institute at Harvard for the several roles they played during my fellowship there. And in fellowship's other sense, I wish to express my fraternity with my co-members of the ephemeral Harvard Black–Jewish working group, most especially David Theo Goldberg, Cheryl Greenberg, Laurence Mordekai Thomas, and Patricia Williams.

Back at what still remains improbably home, I thank all those colleagues and friends of mine at the University of Texas for intellectual and salutational exchanges of various kinds, in particular, Susan Sage Heinzelman, Kurt Heinzelman, Itzik Gottesman, Evan Carton, Brian Bremen, Jack Farrell, José Limón, Craig Ackerman, and the students in my classes. Ilana Blumberg, Timothy Brennan, Vasilis Lambrompoulos, James Phelan, Shaindy Rudoff, Jack Salzman, David Suchoff east of Texas; futher east, Ray Ryan and Peter Rea in Cambridge, Avivah Zornberg and Emily Budick in Jerusalem; and Jo Keroes, a beacon in the West, all deserve my deep gratitude for their collective receptivity. Lastly – in echo of a preface by Levinas – I descry again the shadow of that Other too often present to be cited. *¡Oh siempre, nunca dar con el jamás de táno siempre!* (Vallejo).

I thank my parents again, and their parents, and parents all the way back for filiation in its broadest, most encompassing sense – for a religious and cultural tradition that creates the conditions for ceaseless answerability. In my own case that has meant the kind of mind which, in estranging itself toward other particularities, more responsibly affirms the one it calls home; for such air as one's ethnic soul needs to live, I have discovered that the richest oxygen abides somewhere between native grounds and diaspora.

Something very like that tension I have to believe I share also with my readers, according to that "singular and, moreover, providential law of mental optics," as Proust put it, "that our wisdom begins where that of the author ends, and we would like to have him give us answers, when all he can do is give us desires."[2] Positioned at the threshold of the book where preface gives way to face, I extend a final address to readers who turn now to face this text.

Introduction

1. The space between Black and Jew

But then life always makes you choose between two
possibilities, and you always feel: One is missing!
Always one – the uninvented third possibility!
Robert Musil, *The Enthusiasts*

The data of daily use gently but insistently repel us; day by
day, in overcoming the sum of secret resistances – not only the
overt ones – that they put in our way, we have an immense
labor to perform.   Walter Benjamin, *One Way Street*

The task of criticism remains essential, even if God were not
dead but only exiled.
Emmanuel Levinas, "Reality and Its Shadow"

Bright sparks and divine sparkles

From the first section entitled "Of Our Spiritual Strivings," to the last
on the "Sorrow Songs," Du Bois's *The Souls of Black Folk* is framed by
an arresting image of "falling stars." It appears in the spirituals "My
Lord, what a mourning" (whose last line reads, "when the stars begin
to fall"), "Stars in the Elements" (whose first line reads, "Oh the stars
in the elements are falling"), and "Bright Sparkles in the Church-
yard." It also surfaces in Du Bois's prose itself when he writes,
"Throughout history, the powers of single black men flash here and
there like falling stars, and die sometimes before the world has rightly
gauged their consciousness."[1]

At a strictly symbolic level, the trope signifies sacrifice and redemption. Eric Sundquist has pointed to a semantic underground
that discloses African resonances beneath the Christian, notions of

1

race unity and a buried life. "The soul," he writes, "waits not so much to be reborn, as to be discovered as always existing and already engaged in its journey back to the world of the spirit."[2] Du Bois himself remarks of "Stars in the Elements," that it may possess "some traces of outside [non-Western] influence." (213)

From this perspective, "falling stars" – most obviously in Du Bois's theme of dispersed or submerged cultural power – becomes an historicized image for diaspora, for a scattering which awaits future reclamation and integration. As such, like all diasporic narratives, Du Bois's and that of the sorrow songs tells an allegory of fallenness, of damage, of loss, and the link between all of these and *time*. "Diamonds of song, buried deep beneath the weight of dark and heavy years," Sterling Brown once versified.[3] And according to the Yiddish-American H. Leivick, "A song means filling a jug, and even more so breaking the jug. Breaking it apart. In the language of *kabbalah* we might call it: Broken Vessels."[4]

Emboldened by the appearance of the word *traces* in Du Bois's remark about "Stars in the Elements," I want to extend the image of falling stars in a direction that calls up a very different time and culture. I make no argument here for influence or filiation, nor do I want to suggest a common image repertoire. Rather, I want to *create* a correspondence that only takes shape, because, as Harold Bloom puts it, "meaning wanders, like human tribulation, from text to text,"[5] and in this case when human tribulation wanders from people to people, from the sixteenth century to the nineteenth.

After the expulsion of Jews from Spain in 1492, Jewish Kabbalists like Meir ben Gabbai, Moses Cordovero, and above all, Issac Luria Ashkenazi, reconfigured the mystical import of *kabbalah* – the word itself connotes "reception" – to reflect the experience and consequences of exile, the most far-reaching modification being a new theory of creation conveyed through a set of imagistic tropes.[6] *Shevirat ha kelim* (the breaking of the vessels), is one such, and refers to a stage in creation after God has contracted into himself in order to clear a space for the world.

The light resulting from this divine self-limitation was to be precipitated out and resolved through vessels called *kelim* – transcendental 'melting pots'. But the emanations of light were so intense that they shattered two thirds of the vessels, most of the light then falling to earth, and, together with the shell fragments, captured and held fast in a composite form called *klippot*, or husks.[7] Kabbalists called the light *nitzutzot* (divine sparks, or falling stars) and it is the task of *tikkun* (redemption) that all creation strive toward the freeing of these sparkles from their earthly captivity. Indeed, two centuries after Luria, Levi Yitzkhak of Berdichev, one of the early Hasidic masters, claimed, much like Du Bois, that the divine sparks have a role to play in exile, to flash here and there on earth, and in that flashing thereby illuminate creation; like the angels of Jacob's ladder, the *nitzutzot* can rise up to Heaven as well as rain down from above.[8]

Now, apart from its mystical thrust, this re-mythifying of Jewish revelation follows a plainly allegorical design, and tells a dialectical narrative of exile and redemption which, as Gershom Scholem is perhaps most famous for propounding, makes sense *as history*, as the entry into human and *nationalist* time.[9] Scholem's friend, Walter Benjamin called such point of entry the "jagged line of demarcation" whose marks and traces, in the face of a "storm blowing from Paradise," narrate the historicity of individuals and cultures.

But exile is two-faced . . . like allegory: it looks back to catastrophe for its meaning as it finds meaning again by looking ahead towards redemption. In kabbalist tradition, the breaking of the vessels scattered into fragments the light of divinity, but it is the very descent of those bright sparkles that creates a need for human involvement in their re-collection and restoration; the breaking institutes a making. Just as a necessary dialectic links the now-obscured "powers of black men [which] flash here and there like falling stars," to corresponding acts of historical reclamation and restitution, so the exile of the divine and the human in *kabbalah* requires a deliberate and incessant mending.

Something like the African belief in a soul already oriented and laboring towards freedom, the Lurianic concept of *tikkun* signifies acts of mediation that set right the world's imperfectness, acts for which the world could even be said to have been created. What exists, in other words, exists in order that it may be restored.[10] Damaged patrimony, a non-inalienable place in a society, expulsion or captivity: these make up the loss now oriented to a would-be restitution, that bear witness to Levinas's assertion: "The first question in the interhuman is the question of justice."[11]

This is, in part, how Jews generally and African Americans have mutually understood the experience of exile. Their respective narratives of loss and ruin ground and legitimate a substitutive story of spirituality gained through time. That allegorical story of catastrophe, exile, and restitution acquires the sanction of history through its repeated tellings and refiguration in the literatures of African

American and Jewish American writers. *Tikkun*, or the image of restitution has a literary analogue in the concept of *representation*, a word whose very etymology signifies the bringing of something absent into presence. To this extent at least, representation turns wounds into scars, or evinces scars as signs of healing.[12]

Although the literary connections in the chapters that follow require much less of a stretch, and link texts far closer in historical time and space, I began this way for a reason. The interface I have created between an early twentieth-century African-American text and the medieval Jewish tradition of *kabbalah* is purposefully far-flung, a pointed asymmetry. It works, but only because I have allegorically introduced the connection. It creates a *facing* precisely because it preserves both distance and difference. We can call this exercise a grappling with space, where the wide temporal and cultural distance separating divine sparks from bright sparkles becomes bridged *allegorically*, in the adapted sense of the term I have taken from Levinas and Benjamin. What ancient Israel, after its Egyptian captivity, knew as *midbar*, and what Africans *in* captivity endured at one stage as the middle-passage, I want to reconfigure as a conceptual territory – a linguistic interspace where words, as Roland Barthes put it, carry with them the places they have been, where divine sparks find an echo in divine sparkles.[13] This would be a reconnoiter half in shadow as, opposed to the mixed blessing of "rigorously reciprocal relations."[14]

"*Meeting* balances wandering," writes Julia Kristeva. "A crossroad of two othernesses, it welcomes the foreigner without tying him down, opening the host to his visitor without committing him. A mutual recognition, the meeting owes its success to its temporary nature, and it would be torn by conflicts if it were to be extended."[15]

It may be that such meeting ultimately *is* a temporary phenomenon for American Blacks and Jews, yet something *has* conjoined them in public space, and at the very least, they are entangled in American history and culture, complexly thrown up against one another. How such conjunction and entanglement will be imagined or enacted, of course, is the freighted question – the shape, that is, of "relations."

In the chapters to follow, "proximity," "face-to-face," "antiphony," are some of the phrasal cues for this space-in-the-middle, the space marked out by the "and" in *Black and Jew* – the space, quite literally, of conjunction. What is the nature of such linkage? Does it join, coordinate, equalize, span, unify? What *is* the status of the

semantic and pragmatic space it locates: binding, intercommunica-
ting, "rigorously reciprocal?" In the normal course of things, that
space predicts something like the following:

Goodman, Chaney, and Schwerner.
Ocean Hill-Brownsville and Crown Heights.
Hollywood and Castlemont High School.
Louis Farrakhan and the Day of Atonement.
Jewish Roxbury to Black Roxbury
More adventurously perhaps:

More adventurously perhaps:

Edward Blyden and Moses Hess/Leo Frank and Joe Conley.
Zora Neale Hurston and Franz Boas/Billie Holiday and Arthur Herzog.
The Spingarn brothers and the NAACP/Bert Williams and Eddie Cantor.
Naftuli Branwein or Woody Allen/Sidney Bechet or Spike Lee,
Abraham Heschel and Martin Luther King/*The New Yorker* kiss between
    Hasid and Haitian.
Partisan Review and New York Intellectuals/*Transition* and Black Public
    Intellectuals.
Milton Mikelson to Mezz Mezzrow/"Whoopie" to "Goldberg".
Dutch Schultz to Bumpy Johnson/Sandy Koufax to Jackie Robinson.
Irving "Slim" Rose of Times Square Records, The Chess Brother, and
    Blue Note/Frankie Lymon, Muddy Waters, and postwar jazz.

The following section pauses to reflect on such conjunction, and
proposes a different set of spatial relations.

On blackjewishrelations and the space of literature

> For both . . . are victims, big and bitter victims, whatever the
> order of magnitude, whatever the chronology of victimization.
> They have, both these nations, suffered too much and so long
> that they bear their scars grandiosely, as essential features of an
> identity, as relics of a sacred history, as tests of the extent to
> which others represent them as they wish to be represented.
> And so both of them, almost as a matter of emotional and
> cultural course, could let the scars do the work of the wounds;
> and the memory of oppression do the work of oppression. (29)[16]

Let us take this précis as one possible narrative formula for the
historical entanglement of American Blacks and Jews, compelling
precisely because of the accuracy and force of its metaphors ("scars
and wounds" even *sounds* a little like "Blacks and Jews"). Partners in
catastrophe. Crisis as cathexis. In fact, however, these observations
are drawn from an article about the entangled fates of Israelis and
Palestinians, not American Blacks and Jews. I quote the passage not

for analogy's sake (a grossly imprecise one at best), but because the story of competitive scar and wound is such a commonly exploited narrative slot for Black Jewish Relations, and because "Black" and "Jew" so easily plug into it, doing so because the scar-and-wound schema is such a serviceable *American* schema. It is not the only one, to be sure, but it has increasingly become the favored one.

Indeed, despite the restrictive sense of the passage above, out of context, it invites us to correlate the respective fates of American Blacks and Jews, however different and however similar, with deeply embedded instincts of *national* identity and *cultural* character.[17] "The memory of oppression," "relics of a sacred history," "scar and wound": all this can and does describe the *unheimlich* quality that ties American Black to American Jewish experience, that makes them Blacks and Jews vexedly at home but also strangers to themselves and to each other. It is but one instance of the selective narratability and emplottedness of America, "a play within a play backdropped by the peculiar American racial canvas which sets the conditions for the way the play will end."[18] At its most bizarrely ironic (iconic) it stands over the 1995 film *Independence Day* where conjoint Black military prowess (Will Smith) and Jewish scientific expertise (Jeff Goldblum) create the lucky helix that defeats an alien invasion and transfigures Earth into the encompassingly *American* planet in the bargain.[19]

At the time of this book's writing when American Blacks and Jews (differentially) occupy a sideline relative to ethnicities more functionally enmeshed in late modern shifts in immigration and demography, it is, I would maintain, on an enduring *allegorical* not empirical plane that these two storied peoples continue to obsess each other's imagination. Even if the 1991 riots in Crown Heights or what has been dubbed sensationalistically the Harlem Massacre in 1996 answered to the force of inevitability – given local tensions between African American and Jewish American residents – the pre-assigned place these confrontations immediately occupied as symbolic cultural capital attests to the plot function possessed by Blacks and Jews together as particular kinds of Americans.[20] Such *mimesis* needs the disenchantment of a new *mythos*.

A remarkably telling instance of the former can be found in Tony Martin's preface to his broadside, *The Jewish Onslaught*. Martin speaks of finding himself waylaid at the same table in a Jewish archive where Yankel Rosenbaum had come to do research before his death in 1991 during the Crown Heights riots. With perhaps not enough hindsight as could be had, Martin wonders, "what inscrutable fate brought me to this archive, to this conversation, to Yankel Rosenbaum's table, at a time when my authorship of a book called The *Jewish Onslaught* would have seemed a bizarre improbability."[21]

Whether some weird Black–Jewish masterplot could be shown as lying at the root of uncanny coincidences such as this, still the most prosaic of circumstances yoke together Blacks and Jews in ways that call for comment. What one wants an experience like Martin's to do, of course, is what the spirit of Martin's book systematically defies: a critical refraction of some baseline relatedness, not a lock-step re-enactment at the level of ostensible analysis. That Tony Martin and Yankel Rosenbaum sat at the same table independently of one another, and that familiarity – even when accustomed to breeding contempt – failed to bow before the uncanny, presents an opportunity to consider unrelenting discord as no less *constructed* a dynamic than forced concord. Here, however, identification merely reifies difference.

Consider, by contrast, what one interviewee says in a radio play *Can You Hear Me? African Americans and Jews in Coalition and Conflict* about her experience as a summer school teacher in Tuskeegee, Alabama in 1964:

> Everything about being in Tuskeegee was interesting. It's an all black school, and all black community. Most of them are very religious – Baptists, and I'd grown up in New York and never met anyone like them, and they'd never met anyone like me. So I thought of teaching as political work, civil-right's work. I had them read W.E.B Du Bois; I just had them read Black writers. I had them read Ralph Ellison who wrote *Invisible Man* about Tuskeegee. I hadn't read *Invisible Man* either. So we were all discovering what was happening, together . . . And that year there started to be a civil rights' group, and I ended up being advisor to the civil rights' group with really no sense of it being inappropriate really . . . All the planning meetings happened in a church. Being in the churches was so profound to me. It was community, religion, music, warmth, freedom: it was all one, and it was all this one meaning. The main quality for me was just being welcomed. I think that was what was so critical to me. Because I was, in the way that I was Jewish, in the way that I was an immigrant, in the way that I came from a family that didn't identify as Jewish, I was looking for a home, and this was a home to me. Being in those churches was a home to me.[22]

The voice is self-aware, certainly, and place, time, and history determine particular affections and inclinations. But what I find most revealing is the *flow* of identification here, the way newness, other-ness, and all-Blackness lead inevitably not to the *unheimlich*, but to

7

what Jewish vernacular calls *heymisch* and Black vernacular, "down home." Here, the kind of recognition elided or rejected by Martin's anecdote is surplusive, and made iconic: Black Churches house Jewish souls, the secret-sharer as redemptive filler for an originary lack. Crisis speaks to a native susceptibility to disaster.

I see these two narratives as complementary because they respectively understate and overstate the case for *some kind* of relatedness between Blacks and Jews, each distorted by the haze or ambient glow of crisis and disaster. Together, in their cathexes and displacements, the two stories tell a composite story of Black Jewish Relations. They do so, moreover, discursively – as acts of narrative.

Language, of course, is itself an unfailing guarantor of the uncanny in even the most innocuous details, the sheer weight attaching to nomenclature. In his book, for example, Martin was unable to resist castigating Cornel West's suspect orthography that capitalizes "Jews" and diminishes "Blacks," citing the following incriminating evidence: "'a growing black [sic-lower case] antiSemitism [sic-upper case].'" (18) And yet, clearly, words, letters, and even "graphemes" do *make a difference*. Hyphens, negligible punctuation marks that they are, can speak volumes, simultaneously obscuring and disclosing cultural facts of the most salient kind. Is it merely an accident that the hyphen mimics a minus sign? "African+American" and "American+Jew" might be far more linguistically cognate to history and cultural reality, imaging a graphics of deed, not disaster.

Still, with hyphens intact, *African-* or *Afro-American* signify place, typography as topography, the ligature of placename compressing a narrative of travel. The roots of Black America lie in the African continent. By contrast, although American Jews may trace back family lineages to Germany, Russia, Iran, Argentina, *Jewish-American*, like *German-Jewish*, *Russian-Jewish*, *Iranian-Jewish*, or *Argentinian-Jewish*, connotes simply the latest instantiation in a long history of uprooting. Diaspora prove the anomaly of postexilic Jewish peoplehood, a four millenia long migration with a succession of "landings" on multiple shores.

At the same time, however, it must be granted that the hyphen effaces a crucial and obvious difference, functioning like its homograph, the minus sign: Jews emigrated to America by choice; Africans who became Americans did not. If, consequently, we abandon the hyphen, "African" and "Jewish" are still not semantically equivalent; one adjective denotes place of origin, the other transgeographic peoplehood. "African" and "Jew," adjective and noun, do not line up in

8

parallel, even when supplemented (or grounded, some might rather say) by "American." The hyphenless but still equivocal terminology favored by a recent exhibition, *African Americans and American Jews*, illustrates such problems of asymmetry: African Americans are African-inflected *Americans*, but American Jews are, at bottom, *Jews* who happen to reside in America.[23] The subtitle to the radio play, *Can You Hear Me? African Americans and Jews* (produced under Jewish auspices), intimates that "Jews" doesn't even need an accompanying referent: Black Americans are "African Americans" but Jewish Americans are just "Jews."

Perhaps then, polysyllabic nomenclatures should be allowed to go the way of the hyphen, and leave us better served with the plain descriptive force of monosyllables: *Blacks, Jews, Black, Jew,* more compelling markers of otherness as acoustic hard fact rather than demographic expediency. Yet problems surface here, too. *Black* and *Jew* are also not semantically equivalent, the one denoting, simply, race (as color) and the other, religion, culture, and debatably perhaps, ethnicity. If they are understood coterminously, the latter markers of difference are simply conflated and the former marker reified.[24]

Beside, "Black" is only by use a noun; strictly speaking, it is an adjective denoting color. Only by the sheer weight of custom and habit do "a black" or "blacks" signify nonoffensively, though I would still prefer us to detect some residual offense in such terms as proper nouns. Understandably, locutions referring to Africa have come increasingly to replace both "Black" and the more coldly taxonomic "Negro." To defamiliarized eyes and ears, while "black" may objectively designate a certain set of people, it commits a kind of linguistic violence, or in Levinas's more pointed phrase, ethical homicide.

The word "Jew," by contrast, derives from Hebrew *Yehudi* (Judean), which itself follows ultimately from a proper name linked to other proper names in a patronymic chain of familial descent. Its counterpart, however, has nothing ontologically, historically, or culturally to do with the people it selects out and describes: "black" merely discriminates between one generalized color and all the other colors contrasting with it. (Still, the terms are alike in being very loosely moored in reference: there are multiple black peoples as there are multiple shades of black, and "Jew" signifies differently in relation to "Gentile" or "Arab" or "Pole" or for that matter, "Black.")

And then there is the problem of capitalization. T. S. Eliot earned critical censure for the callous antisemitism of the phrase "the jew squats on the window sill" in "Gerontion," sufficient to replace lower case "j" with capital "J," though the word, and its cruelty, remained. But Tony Martin does have a point. If "Jew" is spelled upper case, why is "Black" allowed so often to lapse into lower? Is "black and Jew" an acceptable asymmetry? *Mutatis mutandis*, the accident of word order. Only the book co-authored by Michael Lerner and Cornel West (no doubt by design) prefers the titular sequence, *Jews and Blacks*. Across syntactic time at least, "Blacks" habitually precede "Jews." Is it meaningful that the composite locution is invariably Black Jewish Relations, not Jewish Black Relations?

Are Black Jewish Relations so dependably anchored in empirical reference, anyway? The nomenclature often seems to take on a life of its own, agglutinatively, to become *blackjewishrelations*, like those portmanteau words by Faulkner or Joyce that were meant to evince compression or dissolve boundaries: "mansmell" or "brightwindbridled." As *term* over and above its empirical referents, the phrase is being asked to do too much work, a beanpole on steroids, simultaneously overwrought and underweight.

The discourse of blackjewishrelations itself swells with pregnant, often alliterative figures that attempt to fix the exact nature of the phenomenon: Blacks and Jews are "strange bedfellows," or "stranger and friend," or "ambivalent friends"; they meet in "bittersweet encounter" or "cooperation and conflict" in order to confront "alliances and arguments" or establish "bridges and boundaries" or "let the healing begin," "in the almost promised land." The metaphors are both telling and in their way coercive: they enact rhetorical solutions. "Black" and "Jew" are converted into allegories of the beings they indicate – shadows in Levinas's sense – which are in turn metamorphosed into linchpins for stories and what the narrative theorists call plot functions.

But even ostensibly meta-discursive versions of blackjewishrelations remain caught within the same circuit. In his prefatory remarks to Anna Deavere Smith's performance piece, *Fires in the Mirror: Crown Heights and Other Identities*, Cornel West, for example, supplies a fairly standard rehearsal of blackjewishrelations up to the present time, a condensed version of a history one can find redacted in a number of readily available studies.[25] Two moments, however (both perhaps tangential to West's purposes), stand out for me.

In characterizing Smith's work, West calls it an "example of how art can create a *public space*,"[26] intending this, I think, in the sense we find variously articulated by Greek tragedy, Rousseau, or Bertold

Brecht: theater as communal cultural critique where democratic fear and pity transform what our not-so politely prejudiced culture hero Henry James called an "ethnic cauldron" into a crucible; where *katharsis* carries us out of the melting pot and into the fire. Catastrophe or crisis (as is often the case for Black–Jewish relations), give off a warming glow.

The second moment involves a felicitous collocation around the image of the face; West decries the "faceless universalism" that informs much Black–Jewish dialogue, and which pales in comparison to the "everyday human faces" whose "poignant portraits" *Fires in the Mirror* so powerfully depicts. The distinction between *faces in their representational particularity* on the one hand, and various kinds of facelessness on the other, undergirds both my book's methodology and its thematic focus. The common thread that unites the company of texts in the following chapters is the concrete fact and the moral summons of *face* – variously imaged as a motif or metonym, a theme, or a dynamic of recognition.[27]

Projected as a moral *desideratum*, "universalism," according to its very nature, seeks to melt together, resolve and totalize. A collective and undifferentiated whole awaits the individual ethical beings and their singular, contingent dramas and personal histories that together comprise universalism's universe. The paradox, of course, lies in the necessarily faceless use to which a plurality of everyday human faces is therefore put. Inasmuch as the face of the other includes the vanishing point that leads to "all the others," it connects the political to the ethical. Ethics founds politics, in this view. But in its originary signification, according to Levinas, the face is the event of the facing Other. To say that it represents the site and source of ethical responsibility already misses the point, for the face does not really re-present, but rather *presents*; it is not an image, but a doing, not a sign but a performance. It is "a visitation," it "makes an entry."[28]

> A face, not a sketch, a fleshed-out figure evoking disgust or admiration. A face, not a text in which the soul's movements are inscribed and held out for eventual interpretation . . . The face, or the narrow escape. Its determining characteristic is resistance to definition, the way it never allows itself to be cornered by my most penetrating gaze.[29]

Moreover, face-to-face relation is never an equality but rather a fundamental asymmetry, an original inequality. Conceived in terms of space, or more specifically, height, either the Other commands me from above, or s/he solicits me from below.[30]

Levinas's metaphysics are not impervious to critique. And I do not pretend to reconcile the Levinasian notion of a featureless, contextless ethical face that appears to override cultural and political difference with the empirical realities of Black/Jewish encounter.[31] Not specific qualities or odd customs bring about the other's alterity according to this view, "but the nakedness of his face: a call to my responsibility and a refusal to allow itself to be wrapped in its own exoticism."[32]

But *pace* Levinas, the ethical inviolability of the Black and Jewish face is often exposed through its negative proof – inscribed onto, featured over, the face's ethical plainness and nudity: splayed lips and distended nose, pop eyes and lascivious grin, caricatured brow, chin, and facial tone. The first words ascribed to the face by Levinas are "do not murder," yet at the level of the face outraged, attacked, and wounded, Blacks and Jews share a history of otherness caricatured and defiled. Such perceptual violence, and the answerability to otherness thereby repudiated, are the metaphysical failure of recognition, marking its would-be promise. The face, then, within the context of these pages, signifies the allegorical site of recognition and mis-recognition alike, self and shadow.

Yet, the admittedly complex move of appealing to Levinas's philosophy from this vantage point finds for me a quiet vindication in the choice of a word which Levinas himself uses only in passing. *Le cruset*, "the melting pot," is his preferred phrase to express the englobing and nondifferentiating forces at work when the ethical rupture introduced by the face-to-face is lacking, when the moral particularism of the face is subsumed within a rhetoric of universalism and common transparency.[33] In one of its guises at least blackjewishrelations is just that *cruset*. And while Levinas may be speaking of 'ethicity' over ethnicity, the figure of a melting pot portends not just ethical loss but allegorical: faces become indistinguishable.[34]

On a fairly obvious physical level of course, melting means the obliteration of space, of borders. What is melted becomes no longer discretely recognizable (and historically, the melting pot referred to ethnic or cultural not racial difference, suspending the latter beyond the pale of recognition). As opposed to such non-space, public space of the sort envisioned here remains within the boundaries of recognition; indeed, it articulates them,[35] not as a showcase for *katharsis* – too often the case in Black–Jewish relations – but rather in terms of *anagnorisis* well beyond the confines of its classical function and role, a matter of stoppage and pause as opposed to any climax or rush. All of the chapters that follow give some shape to this idea of human recognition above the plane of mere plot or action. Faces, grimaces, masks within texts, facings between those texts, facing itself as a critical experiment in recognition: that is this book's very burden.

But can literary criticism itself be conceptualized as a venue for recognition? What sense does it make to speak of a text's demand on, or of, recognition, even if it characteristically marks out within itself an inside and an outside, a "mine" and a "theirs"? Asked another way, What do books like the ones I discuss in tandem here want from us, after all? What do we owe them? And what happens when we read the literary traditions they represent dialogically, as interface, with that very facing remarked, comprehended, sanctioned in turn by us?

To ask such questions is, finally, to move from face to text, and from text to canon, and perhaps even beyond to "Blacks" and "Jews" as Americans, a move this book can only gesture towards, or justify in its own readings.[36] Perhaps the one claim worth staking here, is that while different literatures will often stake out different ideological territories, the literature by American Blacks and the literature by American Jews (or versions thereof) look different when juxtaposed, even if precariously. They become strangers to themselves in the light of the other's revelation. And as the face in Levinas, at its most figural, bodies forth the "precariousness of the other,"[37] so might we reconfigure literary traditions in parallel terms of proximity, nearness, approach.

Still, like the borders defining contiguous as well as noncontiguous countries, and which represent the imposition of human will and cartographic convention upon an originally borderless objective datum, perhaps the place of minority literatures, both relative to each other and to a recognized canon, is always something *mapped*. Borders and border crossings, federations, commonwealth: these are the vicissitudes of literary geopolitics, too.[38] And contact between certain regions, whether they share a common border or not, is often frustrated by distance, national pride, failures of will.

And yet it is the contention of this book that the texts by African American and Jewish American authors it couples *deserve* to be positioned thus, whether or not they understand each other as literary influences, echoes, windows, mirrors, or adjacency–pairs within the same field of ethno-racial discourse. They may share a vantage perhaps – as in facing the same way – but more importantly and more interestingly, they refract one another when face-to-face. The *invented* kinship that results, in my view, has as much to tell us about ancestors and relatives (Ralph Ellison's terms for literature's family loyalties) as do the endogamous and consanguineous relations selecting out a given tradition in the first place. [39]

Lateral connections in this sense counter standard notions of literary inheritance, complicating what Richard Brodhead has called the intra-literariness of American literature in general.[40] As the conscious response of one writer to a predecessor's influence, a lineal tradition takes place only partly from within anyway, answering additionally to the dictates of "retro-construction" – the belated organizing into a unified whole of disparate cultural productions.[41] To this degree, literary history is always in some part an historical invention, just as literary criticism's nonreflectionist, allegorizing role creates new possibilities for "relatedness."

In elaborating the schema of facing as the abutment upon one another of texts rather than persons,[42] I am drawing a vector that may or may not ultimately arrive at the point of Black–Jewish entanglement. But as I say in my preface this book is not an exercise in modeling. Unlike blackjewishrelations at its most uncanny, *Facing Black and Jew* does not promise mimetic transfer. Still, I would like to think that vector, if only in a virtual sense, points to an encompassing horizon – a "beyond" in Werner Sollors's sense of non-static notions of ethnicity,[43] a beyond in Levinas's sense of the excess and surplus of difference, signified by the face of the other, and a beyond in Benjamin's sense of redemptive allegory, where human fallen-ness and facing productively intermesh.

Less grandiosely, the call-and-response between texts here means simply that I believe the novels *read well and profoundly that way*. That the Black/Jewish relationship possesses empirical features in time and history is undeniable. That it conduces to a certain story prompting and prompted in return by second-order retellings is perhaps inevitable, as I suggest in the next chapter. That such a story favors the katharses and cathexes of disaster and crisis is lamentable but a matter of record. Yet I believe a more interesting story awaits telling.

To face Henry Roth's *Call it Sleep* and Ralph Ellison's *Invisible Man*, or Bernard Malamud's "Black is My Favorite Color" and John Edgar Wideman's "Valaida," or Saul Bellow's *The Victim* and Chester Himes's *If He Hollers Let Him Go*; to read each of these texts alongside or through the other, beyond the unilinear dictates of literary inheritance; to parse as a conjoint grammar certain ways in which literary Blacks and Jews have imagined and critiqued their symbolic roles in American culture; to display and create nuances of entanglement, connection, proximity: to do so is to imagine public space in a novel way, and to create those self-transcending vectors from ethics to politics and beyond where divine sparks meet bright sparkles. The second part of this introduction rings a final change on this metaphor by tracking the switch-back between history and allegory.

2. History and allegory: a match made in shadow

[Mezz Mezzrow] was not alone in hanging around with blacks, moving physically into the closed black world, marrying a black girl, and having a child with her. But search all the histories of personal "negrification" as you will, you'll never turn up another case of a man who came to believe he had actually, physically, turned black. Mezzrow, after his long years in and under Harlem, did truly think his lips had developed fuller contours, his hair had thickened and burred, his skin had darkened. It was not, as he saw it, a case of transculturation. He felt he had scrubbed himself clean, inside and out, of his origins in the Jewish slums of Chicago, pulped himself back to raw human material, deposited that nameless jelly in the pure Negro mold, and pressed himself into the opposite of his birthright, a pure Black.

Bernard Wolfe's afterword to Mezzrow's *Really the Blues*

At that Gertrude shrieked with laughter, "Claude Jones!" and launched into the story of how he was no longer a Negro or a Christian but had become a Jew. "A Jew!" Clare exclaimed. "Yes, a Jew. A black Jew he calls himself. He won't eat ham and goes the synagogue on Saturday. He's got a beard now as well as a mustache. You'd die if you saw him. He's really too funny for words. Fred says he's crazy and I guess he is."

Nella Larsen, *Passing*

"Are you not like Kushites to me, O Israelites?"   *Amos* 9:7

"For Moses had taken a Kushite woman."   *Numbers* 12:1

In the previous section, I suggested an alternate kind of public space. Here, I want to show its inseparability from allegory, since the allegorical implications of literary recognition in this case already reside, albeit precariously, in grander narratives of cultural formation and deformation, of redemption and disaster. The facing-at-one-another of texts may thus only deepen, and be presupposed by, the already compacted historical fates of American Blacks and Jews. On this historical but also allegorical plane, Black and Jew share a recurrent push and pull towards and against one other. Perhaps the very need to narrate, and compulsively re-narrate, a relationship of one kind or another attests to the density of implication in which the two groups continue to find themselves enmeshed. Such density is partly the work of allegory.

Allegory, as I implied in the preface, might be imagined as wearing two faces, one that faces away, and one that exorbitantly faces. Where the first promises only the spell of a trope-ridden rhetoric and conjures a shadow in place of the Other, the other looks directly at the aesthetic, and comes at otherness obliquely but in a sense more faithfully. The one, in the context of Black–Jewish relations, shows the risk of placing history itself in shadow by allegorizing it improperly; the other demurs at using Grand Narrative as an appeal in itself, and the dialectical syntheses it may consequently invite. That latter face can be glimpsed briefly in the previous chapter's allegorical facing of African American Spirituals and medieval *kabbalah*, a juxtaposition sanctioned by historical gap rather than convergence. Its counterpart will be sketched here.

What follows are complementary narratives about Black and Jew, that, unlike divine sparks and bright sparkles, play off one another in contiguous space and time. Each tells an allegorical story about culture and nation. Told as such, each implicitly marks or "helps to write the other" dialectically, Doris Sommer's pregnant phrase for her deliberate "misreading" of Benjaminian allegory: a "double and corresponding structure" whose terms are "the effects of each other's performance." [44] But if we re-read that misreading in the direction of Blacks and Jews, the question becomes whether it is history that is being reflected dialectically – as usable montage over and against some totalizing schema or telos – or whether the dialectic takes place instead between Black and Jew themselves – halves of a higher (suspended) synthesis, the effect of each other's performance, the source of each other's shadow. [45]

I ask the question because the allegories below are so very tellable and even plausible except for the sleight-of-hand trick each almost invisibly plays. Discerning the trick, it seems to me, is to know the difference between breaking the spell of figures and falling under it, limning the shadow of the other imaginatively, ethically, or colluding in it. It is the difference, finally, between allegorical conjuring and allegorical sorcery. That the short stories below depend on each other to form a composite allegorical whole, thus, is exactly the point; their plausibility derives from that very counterpoint. What Theresa Kelley notes about allegory in Benjamin could *itself* almost as accurately describe the maneuvered impingement here that makes Blacks and

Jews dialectical partners, rival troupes of actors back-dropped by History:

> If the two terms are antagonistic, and to some extent they are, this is so because they are stuck together as they patrol a shared boundary. They may not want to share it, yet each needs the other to say what it is – allegory's need is especially subversive because it requires objects to craft its "other" speech.[46]

My claim, finally, is not that Black and Jew somehow innately lend themselves to allegory, after the fashion of Mezz Mezzrow and Larsen's "Claude Jones" (though Black Jewish relations does put its own spin on allegorizing self or other). Rather, it is to emphasize the obscuring shadow easily cast over "relatedness" in the first place when it reifies what Levinas calls "the picturesque" – the allegorical – aspect of identity. And perhaps, at this particularly hypertrophied moment in Black–Jewish relations, allegory just *is* that relatedness.

Allegory I: Jews as beneficiaries of coil/Blacks as owners of soil

Say that African America is a deeply sedimented place, more topographically anchored than Jewish America has yet had a chance to be. True, only forty years separate the arrivals in the first half of the seventeenth century of Blacks (as slaves) and Jews (as merchants) onto North American soil: a group of Portuguese Jews from Brazil settled in New Amsterdam in 1654; Blacks first arrived in the Virginia colony in 1619. And yet, we may imagine what Du Bois called the "color line" as running not just across this land, but vertically down through it, a crevasse of admixed blood and soil that possesses no real counterpart in the historical record of Jewish America. The directional tropes of African American culture – *Up from Slavery*, "As I Went down into Egypt," an escape *North* and a ritual descent *South* – register just this spatial reality of Black American oppression and striving.[47]

By contrast, the obstacles to assimilation, material success, and acculturation which Jews have faced, seem to belong to some other dimension entirely. Paradoxically, as Africans wrenched from home to toil at the very level of foreign soil, Black Americans appear rooted in America in ways American Jews cannot begin to claim for themselves. There is then no real American Jewish analogue to Du Bois's strain of romantic racialism: the black vitals, the African American viscera, in the bodies politic and cultural.

For Du Bois, for James Weldon Johnson, for Ralph Ellison and Toni

Morrison, the alluvial richness of American soil just *is* its blackness, the "soul of black folks," in other words, having a powerful claim on being considered America's own – not its mask (Ellison's formulation) but its marrow. When, on the other hand, Lubavitch Hasidim build an exact replica of their headquarters at 770 Eastern Parkway, Brooklyn, New York in the town of Kfar Chabad, Israel, that many emigrant Jews saw, and still see, America as a *treyfne medine*, a profane and temporary land. How portable, thus, can American materiality be – like American Jews themselves transplanted eastwards as emigrants to Zion.[48] When Penina Moise, in her 1820 poem "To Persecuted Foreigners," writes, "Oh, not as Strangers shall your welcome be, / Come to the homes and bosoms of the free"; when at the end of Israel Zangwell's 1908 melodrama, *The Melting Pot*, improbably embracing the gentile daughter of the Cossack who ordered his parents' death in the Kishinev Massacre, the hero exclaims, "There she lies the great Melting Pot . . . the harbour where a thousand mammoth feeders come from the ends of the world"; when Jolson dons blackface in order to exchange Jewishness for Americanness[49]: in each of these cases, as adoptive wet-nurse, America gives suck – as *alma mater*, as "Mother of Exiles," as "Mammy."

Or, to shift from domestic to civic spheres, when Alfred Kazin entitles his autobiography, *New York Jew*, he personalizes and Jewifies the project of American literary history he began twenty years earlier in *On Native Grounds*, grounds to which he now has, as it were, squatter's rights. Especially for Kazin and other twentieth-century assimilated Jewish literati, the "New York" in "New York Jew" bestows a kind of global citizenship and proprietorship.

Call this a certain exterior relation to America, a long coil of ethnic "rope" (Angela Davis's image[50]) that seems to allow mobility in any direction. American Blacks, by contrast, have had to answer to a severer force of American gravity; however far a Black presence ascends in this country – "up from slavery" – it is never very far from the landscape itself – profoundly marked, absorbing and constantly exhibiting the physical evidence of black degradation, sacrifice, and triumph. Or else, it produces the corollary observation Bigger Thomas makes in *Native Son*: if there is snow on the ground, it must be because the land is white, if white-men fly airplanes overhead, it must be because the sky is white-owned. Hence perhaps the force of Clarence Thomas's remark about lynching (even if disingenuous) during his confirmation hearing.

But "African American" still signifies a paradox, an allegory of sorts compressed into a phrase. From there, but here. Free now, yet still captive. If we imagine this paradox in terms borrowed from Jewish history – as has been traditional for American Blacks – being Black in America means a Babylonian Captivity that does not portend redemption in any land elsewhere. Though it escapes the fate of effacement (like Biblical Israel's Northern Kingdom), for Black America "Zion" must take place *here*. When James Baldwin writes that America "rescued [the Jew] from the house of bondage; but America *is* the house of bondage for the Negro. What happens to the Negro here happens *because* he is an American,"[51] he articulates the ambivalence of rootedness for African Americans: a land lived in and not yet fully possessed, narrated at the same time as futured, indicative yet optative – the Promised Land *to be*.

By contrast, as Alfred Kazin could say, Immigrant Jews were of the city, even when they weren't in it.[52] The phrase, "New World," perfectly captures what America has historically represented for Jews – from the promise of *einer Goldene land*, a land of "marvelous transformations" (as Abraham Cahan's David Levinsky puts it), to the satisfaction of Podhoretz's *Making It*, from the *weltschmertz* of an enormous, displaced chunk of Eastern Europe to the *schmaltz* of Neil Diamond's updated *The Jazz Singer*. Despite Jewish communities of record in the original thirteen colonies, in Galveston, St. Louis, and New Orleans,[53] the majority of Jewish American genealogies stretch back but two or three generations. Greenhorn or stranger, a figure of mobility who is near and far at the same time, an organic member of the group while still inorganically appended:[54] this is one way to "spatialize" the American Jew.

(One could temporalize the same allegory, as well. Despite the roughly concurrent appearance of Blacks and Jews in this country, African American time appears both longer and deeper than its Jewish American counterpart. The time line of Black American history – indenture, antebellum, postbellum, Reconstruction, Jim Crow, Civil Rights, *Dred Scott, Plessy v Ferguson, Brown v Board of Education*, 1865/1964 – is the time line of post-Jeffersonian American history. By comparison, there seems to be no analogous inflection of "American time" by Jews, notwithstanding the often central roles they have played in many of these same historical moments.)

The problem with such allegorization is not its eliding of the difference between race and ethnicity, although that is surely a patent flaw. Nor is the problem a matter of arbitrariness, although that too is demonstrable. And even if the double narrative converges at points to narrate mutual loss, precariousness, and hoped-for recuperation, the allegory leaves Black and Jew stranded within it, respectively soiled and coiled. The solution of a dialectical synthesis, whereby roots and rope, African Americanness and Jewish Americanness, are sublated into a composite and unified whole, seems just as benighted.

Of course the two stories are not mirrored realities at all, but the product of co-figuration. If they complement one another, it is only because they have been made to do so by a selective complementarity. I have purposely contrived this story, as opposed to, say, one about Black and Jewish political loyalties during the 1960s, because the relatedness here is obvious but at the same time a fiction. Rather than enact Black–Jewish relations by talking about Black–Jewish relations (the customary loop where transference feeds transference), I wanted to suggest how easily Blacks and Jews can be made to haunt and shadow one another. Consider the following inversion.

Allegory II: Blacks: free/Jews: bound

From Paul Cuffe's attempts to colonize Sierra Leone in the eighteenth century, to Edward Wilmot Blyden's attempts to stimulate emigration to Liberia in the nineteenth, to Garveyism in the twentieth; from Ethiopianism to Black nationalism to Black separatism, African America has told a counter-narrative of uplift as *uprooting*, of severance, escape, and redemption from an America which is the House of Bondage. On those same coordinates of space and time, African American history and the Black presence in this land plot the marks of ruin and decay calling for recompense not just memorialization. They announce: it should have been, and may yet be, otherwise: not *of* this land, but, finally, *free of it* – "free at last." This is the arc of African American centrifugality away from this land as *your* land: in exodus from diaspora.

For American Blacks, history and the claims of racial difference summon down to earth the timeless and transcendent theory of justice which is American idealism. By its very presence, African American culture and politics ineluctably hold American democracy accountable by attesting to its failure; in the gap between promise and fulfillment, the collective Black American "will to be" incriminates an America that has yet to deliver. And yet the paradox lies in a necessary presence here. Attestation, witness are secured at the price of a broken-ness between past and present, of an exile and then a captivity still only 150 years removed.

This is one of the permanent ironies of Black/Jewish rivalry over cultural trauma or disaster, uncannily brought home by the popular discussion of Stephen Spielberg's *Amistad* as the African American *Schindler's List*.[55] A "shared boundary line" of suffering obscures perhaps a deeper cleft common to American Black and Jew alike: the gap between present and past. Which of my several pasts? The recent past? The bygone past? The sacred past? Exactly which past do I lay claim to? Which one enfranchises me? Obviously, the questions will be differently answered, but the force behind them in the case of African Americans discloses the fiction of a native American rootedness, and the cordage to an elsewhere.

What, conversely, of the Jewish American romance with diasporism, when abstract citizenship mutes the claims of immanent difference? How do American Jews understand the concept of "free at last?" The counter-allegory here says that Jews in fact hunger, yearn for, are obsessed with, roots in American identity. One form such desire takes is an almost naive patriotism, a gratefulness for American soil and the grounding in it which stems not from a take-it-or-leave-it luxury of estrangement but from an overwhelming gratitude for a land of tolerance and democratic freedom.

If postwar American Jewry could be confident and almost cavalier, if Jewish lawyers in the ACLU defend the legal rights of American Nazis, it is because they have adopted America's Bill of Rights, Constitution, and Declaration as secular counterparts to the collective texts of Jewish law. "A world-historical event," Philip Roth calls the sheer comfort that greets American Jews in *The Counterlife*: "flourishing mundanely in the civility and security of South Orange, more or less forgetful from one day to the next of your Jewish origins." This very unselfconsciousness is, for Roth, what it means to "stand . . . in time and culture."[56]

A concomitant cultivation of roots seeks involvement in the ethnic life of the nation's other minorities, providing one way to read the intermittent Jewish identification with Black America. Through the engine of transference, Warsaw, Nizhni Novgorod, and Vilna slide across to New Orleans, Chicago, and Harlem, ghetto cathects onto ghetto, rich Old World Jewish culture crosshatches rich New World Black culture, at its worst a cultural secret-sharing, at its best, the coiling of rope that is really strong and vital roots. In Spike Lee's *Jungle Fever*, when the architect's druggie brother tracks him to the Village only to discover with surprise that his white lover is not even Jewish, local knowledge discloses that from this side too, the tacit bridge or hinge between white and black in America is *Jew*.

Inflected toward race, Leslie Fiedler's ecumenical model of Jewish American desire – the Jew "woos" the American *shikse* and thus becomes American – possesses an analogue if not a re-expression in Jewish cathexis onto Blackness.[57] In the 1993 film *Zebrahead* by Anthony Drazan, when a generational line connects Jazz and Blues-loving Jewish father with rap and house-music loving Jewish son, each romantically involved with African American women, the *eros* of Black–Jewish relations becomes palpable. Michael Rogin's illuminating analysis of the surplus value of blackface for Jewish entertainers of the 20s and 30s – one solves Jewishness by donning blackness – really explains only the particular historical moment in American popular culture that it studies.[58] The continued, almost libidinal attraction for Jews of Blacks, while it may sometimes seek grounding, ultimately expresses groundedness.[59]

Suspending a synthesis, these allegories too depend on one another as much as they subvert each other. And as before, the problem is their very allegorical co-dependency, the way in which they marshal history by pushing off each other for balance. One obviously non-redemptive result of such storytelling is that the stories can lead to competition, the sort of scar-rivalry on display in Norman Podhoretz's "My Negro Problem – and Ours" and Harold Cruse's "My Jewish Problem and Theirs," or Toni Morrison's vexed dedication in *Beloved*, "To sixty million – and more," and the defensive totemicizing of urban Black life in Cynthia Ozick's "Literary Blacks and Jews." Such reciprocal cathexsis, even at this ostensibly self-conscious level, is the very stuff of blackjewishrelations.[60]

Readers may have noted the absence of "facing" in this entire discussion, a term I use so liberally in previous pages. That is because, very simply, it represents an ethical criticism possible only between individual texts. It cannot really be made to speak to collective entities, where face, of necessity, morphs into the crowd. If, consequently, the turning of the other into shadow – by multiplying and diffusing him – has been the allegorical mis-step here, perhaps another figure is called for entirely. In Levinas's work, happily enough, such a figure can be found that not only rhymes (in English) with face, but is also one of his most important formulations: the trace.

For Levinas, the contact with transcendence evinced by self and other is a rupture, a break in ordinary phenomenal experience, the epiphany of face through which the other makes an entry outside of any shared horizon. Levinas uses the dramatic image of someone opening a window on which his figure is outlined, and the recurrent construct of "the trace" to underscore how the other clandestinely leaves a mark, disturbing and calling into question the luxury of self-presence.[61]

> [The trace] insinuates itself, withdraws before entering. It remains only for him who would like to take it up. Otherwise, it has already restored the order it has troubled. Someone rang, and there is no one at the door: did anyone ring?[62]

Levinas also calls this rhythm between approach and departure, "proximity," a constant drawing nearer of the other without ever arriving, for to arrive means to coincide, to grasp and take hold, to make one's own or make insufficiently other.[63] The allegories narrated above, and indeed the customary discourse of Black–Jewish relations generally, by contrast, *arrives* with a vengeance, as the characteristic rhythm tends to be impatient with either fermatas or caesurae. The Other, after all, must be my double, or my partner.

If the preceding cautionary tale about allegory's (mis)match with history succeeds, then a construct like "the trace," I think, more profoundly captures any *allegorical* relatedness between Black and Jew – at once more modest and more oblique. Adapted to the special features of literary criticism, instead of a clandestine proximity – "no one at the door" – this sort of allegoresis requires something more like a mail delivery slip instead, announcing that someone *has* in fact been there. For a trace remains, signaling limited but not full disclosure: a "partial post." The following chapter, on Ralph Ellison's *Invisible Man* and Henry Roth's *Call It Sleep*, suggests how such delivery is made, by looking at – and listening to – the trace as embedded in language. The novels may or may not need one another, but each *reads* the other surprisingly. Each, in W. E. B. Du Bois's own uncannily Levinasian formulation, becomes more visible through the other's revelation.

"An antiphonal game" and beyond: facing Ralph Ellison and Henry Roth

That's the way I've torn on through,
Torn my way, and bitten, too,
With my head as through a wall
Cross-country, over roads and all.
Break the stone
With tooth and bone!
Dog & bum, clod & wind so wild:
Reckless and free, on alien dirt,
I have no coat, I have no shirt
I have no wife and I have no child
So as if to break
The drum, I bang
And then I make the cymbals clang
And round and round about I spin –
Boom! Din-din-din!
Boom!

אט אזוי זין דורכגצדיסן,
דורכגצדיסן, דורכגצדיסן
סיטן קאפ ווי דורך אוואבט,
איבער שטעג או ן וו עג או ו לאבד
סיטרי ציין –
האק רצם שיין!
האק רצם שטיין און גייב אליין!
הובט און פלעפּעד ,לומפּ אונווינט.
הפקר דורן דער פּרעמד!
האב איט קיין דאק ,קיין העמד
האב אין ביט קיין יוייב ,קיין קיבד.
פויק אין אז הי פויק זאל פּלאצד,
און אין דשיבדושע אין די טאצן
און אין דדיי זין הובד–אדום –
דזשין ,דזשין ,בום–בו ס–בום
דזשין דזשין בום!

MOYSHE-LEYB HALPERN

I lie down in the shadow.
No longer the light of my dream before me,
Above me.
Only the thick wall.
Only the shadow.

My hands!
My dark hands!
Break through the wall!
Find my dream!
Help me to shatter this darkness,
To smash this night,
To break this shadow
Into a thousand lights of sun
Into a thousand whirling dreams of sun!

LANGSTON HUGHES

I myself was a public square, a *sook*; through me passed words,
tiny syntagms, bits of sentence . . .   Roland Barthes

In this chapter I will trace out some implications of facing as an encounter in sensibility – an antiphony or call and response in sound and sight. What develops over its chapter does not, however, pretend to efface the differences that make Roth's novel *Roth's* novel and Ellison's, *Ellison's*. But I want to stress at the outset that the aggregated differences distinguishing these texts from one another – ethnic, racial, literary-historical, and intentional differences – do not therefore inhibit a dialogic facing between them. On the contrary, the resulting antiphony, I hope, makes them sound (and look) fresh in a way only vis-à-vis one another.

I would prefer, then, to let the texts themselves speak before I intervene, but of course it would be disingenuous to pretend that their dialogue precedes my intervention. As with Du Boisian sparkles and kabbalist sparks, *Invisible Man* and *Call It Sleep* wake and become visible to one another because of an encounter contrived between them, beyond the confines of what Ellison's novel calls a mere "antiphonal game." As a general guide, however, the following analysis looks primarily at these texts' linguistic plenitude – a novelistic property, certainly, but perhaps more importantly, the allegory that is narrated by "African American" and "Jewish American" writ large in African American and Jewish American Imaginaries.

An allegory of antiphony

"I am an invisible man."
"He shut his eyes."

Hear them in call-and-response, the first sentence of Ralph Ellison's *Invisible Man*, and the last sentence of Henry Roth's *Call It Sleep*. Each keys into the title and a governing trope of its particular text; each locates its subject precisely. Ellison's protagonist speaks to us from within a state he calls "hibernation."[1] Roth's David Schearl takes leave of his readers by entering into a similar state, what the penultimate sentence of the novel says we "might as well call . . . sleep."

"I am an invisible man." – an announcement, perhaps a self-description, or maybe just an invitation – the speaker's "Call me Ishmael." As plain assertion, Invisible Man's words bear witness not to ontologic defect but phenomenological crime: others simply refuse to see him, "a matter of the construction of their *inner eyes*," he explains, "those eyes with which they look through their physical eyes upon reality."(3) Through his place of hibernation, by contrast, Invisible Man acquires a kind of second sight. In his "hole in the ground," refulgent with the light of 1,369 light-bulbs, he turns his invisibility to

advantage; light confirms his reality, it gives birth to his form, he is able to feel his vital aliveness. (6)

This heightened vision – these new-found sightlines which, as the Langston Hughes epigraph puts it, "break this shadow into a thousand lights of sun" – is but the first of a series of metamorphoses the narrator undergoes underground. His story begins anecdotally with a scene of accidental violence. While ambiguous as to whether an anonymous white man had bumped into Invisible Man, or the other way around, (cf. 4 and 14) the text uses their "encounter" as a pretext for a disquisition on dreaming, sleepwalking, recognition, responsibility, and most polymorphously, "the Blackness of Blackness," (9) "the blackness of my invisibility," (13) and "the music of my invisibility" – all made correspondent.

"He shut his eyes." – a valediction: forbidding morning. An observation. Or perhaps another sort of invitation, this time, a "Call *it* Ishmael." Here too, we become privy to a set of marvelous transformations the protagonist undergoes by retreating from the world, each a loss which is also a gain. And, once again, the first of these transformations involves a "peculiar disposition" of the *inner eyes*. But unlike the ones Invisible Man describes, these belong to the protagonist himself; they bring reality into sharper focus, and – far from deadening or neutralizing or effacing it – enhance and make it vitally alive:

> It was only toward sleep that every wink of the eyelids could strike a spark into the cloudy tinder of the dark, kindle out of shadowy corners of the bedroom such myriad and such vivid jets of images – of the glint on tilted beards, of the uneven shine on roller skates, of the dry light on grey stone stoops . . . [2]

The passage goes on to describe a change in hearing, as well (as, indeed, does *Invisible Man*). In sleep, David's ears have the power to "cull again . . . all sounds that lay fermenting in the vats of silence and the past." Likewise (with the help of a reefer), Invisible Man tells us that in the music of Louis Armstrong he becomes aware of time's *nodes*, "those points where time stands still or from which it leaps ahead," through which he can "slip into the breaks and look around."(8)

In a counterpart to Invisible Man's street-fight, David has himself just survived a scene of accidental violence, precipitating rather than precipitated by, a riot of jostling. But here it is a riot of the foreign tongue, a multi-ethnic chorus of one's own accented word relative to all the others'. The narrator's summary statement on behalf of David's consciousness also predicates dreaming and sleep, and may be read in its own right as a disquisition on recognition and responsibility. And while Invisible Man riffs on Blackness, David, for the last time in the text, enters a similarly polymorphous domain of "darkness."

Each character, at the beginning of one text and the end of the other *feels* his world more intensely, and therein finds a kind of consummation. "Strangest triumph, strangest acquiescence" is what Roth assigns to David Schearl's sensate (though unconscious) grasp. A world "concrete, ornery, vile, and sublimely wonderful as before," but better understood, and more importantly, *articulable* – spoken into shape for us while *our* eyes "look through" – becomes Ellison's bequest to Invisible Man.

> "I am an invisible man."
> "He shut his eyes."

With their tonalities counterpointed, "Invisibility" and "shut eyes" become doublevoiced and composite. Without violating either text overmuch, we could even transpose the two motifs' sight- and sound-lines, altering the discursive strategies to make David a first-person in the present tense, and Invisible Man a narrated third-person. Invisible Man now shuts *his* eyes, and it is David Schearl who assumes the status of an Invisible. As primary figures in the fictive worlds of each novel and despite all their differences as characters and culture heroes, this Black and this Jew can be made to *face one another* even if they do not "see" or "hear" each other.

I have not arbitrarily selected a sentence from each novel in order to pair them this way, of course. Yet *Call It Sleep* and *Invisible Man* do engage one another along lines of correspondence, threading back and forth a common concern with recognition which the short dialogue I have constructed fortuitously illustrates. No, Ellison's sophisticated troping on *invisibility* – a figure by turns for racism, and for race consciousness – has no counterpart in Roth's novel's far less politicized rendering of individual consciousness. And to be sure, a narrator who wants, Armstrong-like, "to make music of invisibility," (14) while at the same time, marshaling considerable rhetorical powers "on the lower frequencies" to "speak for" us, (568) cannot be equilibrated with a narrator chiefly concerned with turning a small boy into a lightning-rod for epiphanic sensation and visionary synthesis.

On the plane of critical currency, obviously, "ethnicity" and "race" do not easily commensurate. But that is only to emphasize again the obvious fact that it is as *Ralph Ellison's Invisible Man* and *Henry Roth's Call It Sleep* that these two novels stake their respective claims. I do not wish to ignore such difference, nor do I wish it fixed in amber. Besides, "race" and "ethnicity" are non-native terms for both these novels, however much they figure in their stories narratively, conceptually. They are *critical terms*, and when one looks especially at authorial comments by Ellison (in *Shadow and Act* or the most recent preface to *Invisible Man*) and Roth (in various recent interviews), each expresses a legacy of critical inflation apart from any burden as self-understood. Each goes on speaking in the liberally inflected, artistically mobile patois of "human values" athwart more critically efficacious categories.

In the world of the novel, Ellison's racial identity or the topic of race, Roth's ethnic identity and the topic of ethnicity are placed in the service of other ends, a mutual communion discovered in the facing of their novels. While vicissitudes of race and ethnicity propel them, the novels resist being reduced by or to them. To put this in terms familiar to Ellison, the respective timbres of clarinet and saxophone, indeed the very material of the instruments – wood and brass – yield a "third possibility" of sound when heard in duet. And for the clarinet of ethnicity and the saxophone of race alike (as Langston Hughes said of the latter poetically), the "vulgar tone" of *mere* metal or wood – critical constructs – sounds more musically within, and between, the texts themselves.

A lesson from literary history

Certainly one can select almost any pair of novels, place them in parallel, and draw up a list of columnar affinities. But novels like Roth's and Ellison's can be understood as *themselves* inviting such a linkage – an elective affinity as opposed to a merely selective one. Let us consider that complementarity for a moment in the light of each text's separate standing and respective difference, a matter of how books tell stories of literary history.

If we grossly simplify the case for similarity between Roth's and Ellison's novels, each announces a highly self-conscious departure from its own local "tradition." In program as well as style, in topic as well as structure, *Call It Sleep* (1934) and *Invisible Man* (1947) ask to be read not just as exemplary American fiction (with or without the outrider, "ethnic"), but as "literature" – whatever such category status connotes: (international?) (world?) (classic?) – in a broad sense. Both, in other words, are permeated by that "Galilean" spirit Mikhail Bakhtin ascribes to modern narrative in general, "a certain linguistic homelessness of literary consciousness" informing all aspects of a given text.[3] Such "literary consciousness" originates from inside the Novel, apart from any claim for literariness staked on a particular text's behalf. This centrifugal impulse, according to Bakhtin, but with particular reference to Roth and Ellison:

> . . . erodes that system of national myth that is organically fused with language, in effect destroying once and for all a mythic and magical attitude to language and the word. [Such a] deeply involved participation in alien cultures and languages (one is impossible without the other) inevitably leads to an awareness of the disassociation between language and intentions, language and thought, language and expression.[4]

That disassociation, as I have argued for dialectical allegory, creates the conditions for a corresponding *pull* by alien cultures and languages for each other. Novels like Roth's and Ellison's may ransack a national past, but they do so in each other's presence as well as against a background of composite nationalisms, of ethnicity and race entangled. Their dialogue with each other is also a chorus with other literatures, a polyphonic antiphony.

While the kind of generalized porosity and openendedness Bakhtin describes is not identical to the more specific "decentering" impelling texts like these to reach beyond their own ethnic literary traditions (indeed, one might argue, beyond race and ethnicity *per se*), the two processes still do not operate entirely independently of each other.[5] Indeed, such lability underpins Bakhtinian dialogism *tout court*, a more sensitive barometer of language's auto-critique and comic sense.

For "minority literature," the complex relationship between group identity and language is, of course, anything but *minor*. Ellison's and Roth's novels *immerse* plot and character in a literary-chemical bath of collectivity and individuality where it remains ambiguous just which element is reagent and which precipitant. *Call It Sleep* and *Invisible Man* at the same time purposely *alienate* themselves from constrictive and ideologically onerous nativisms, an impulse not easy to square with the *critical* impulse that champions these same texts as representative or culturally emblematic – the ethnic-clarinet or racial-saxophone solo.

As authorially *willed* discourse, the novels internally campaign for resistance to theory.[6] Indeed, rather than try to mitigate such putative dissonance, perhaps we should see such programmatic homelessness as an external coefficient to the internal dramas of dislocation each text enacts. Or to state the same case differently, both novels' interest in mobile identity can be viewed in the light of a certain impatience with static notions not only of ethnicity, but of literary history and literary tradition as well.

It goes without saying that such a claim does not gainsay the plain fact that Roth and Ellison write as a Jewish American and a Black American, respectively. Moreover, each writes from within a particular cultural milieu. How else, after all, could they write? In tersely unsaying itself, for example, William Faulkner's "plaudit" for *Invisible Man* – "[Ellison] has managed to stay away from being first a Negro, he is still first a writer"[7] – could not better expose the fatuity of any universalist argument for independent literary "value" here.[8]

Any claims I advance here rest therefore on two, interrelated assumptions: (1) on the broadest level, the modern novel rehearses (and often anticipates) a decentering movement that governs the very "socio-ideological evolution of languages and society"[9] within which literary texts take shape. In this respect, Roth's and Ellison's novels make their bids for *representative* status. (2) These same texts "territorialize" themselves within the widest inter (or better, multi-) cultural ambit. They self-consciously keep company with Kafka and Melville as well as Jean Toomer and Charles Reznikoff, which is to imagine a whole constellation of ancestors and relatives.

But focusing on how these texts position themselves in literary history, in relation to anterior texts both foreign and domestic, would seem merely to highlight a crucial *difference* between them – only the first of many. The question of both novels' "singularity" needs to be referred to the fact of each novel's singleness in relation to the other, the standing fact of their disparity. When one text in question is a first person novel and the other third-person, when that first person is an adult, and that third person a child, and when that child's drama is confined primarily to the interior spaces of mind and inchoate signification, and that adult's exploits the dimensions of physical space and signifyin(g) out loud, obviously, strictly *narrative* form and structure will not permit a facile correlation. Yet I would argue, bracketing such divergence does not necessarily distort the case for comparison, but may free us instead to explore certain thematic parallels otherwise obscured.

To take simply the matter of divergent literary inheritance. African American and Jewish American literary histories do not neatly align in anything close to exact congruence, Ellison's "anxiety of influence" being a far more densely populated entity than Roth's. Twentieth-century African American fiction (in the form of the first-person novel) has a precursor history in nineteenth-century slave narrative, both traditions comprising that "vast, multivolume project of Narrating the Negro"[10] for which no analogue really exists in Jewish American fiction.

In an extremely sensible essay, Robert Alter expresses a wise diffidence about translating "vague intuitions" of (in this case) characteristically Jewish attributes "into clear descriptive statements about what actually goes on in the literary works."[11] Using Leslie Fiedler's archetypal model as foil (the Jew as *Master of Dreams*), Alter observes,

> [U]sing the same mythic touchstone to identify characteristically Jewish literary inventions, one might justifiably conclude that the most remarkable American Jewish novel is neither *Call it Sleep* nor *Herzog* but Ellison's *Invisible Man*.

He even quotes an Ellisonian axiom: "Archetypes are timeless; novels are time haunted." And so, of course, are the histories we construct around them.

The retro-construction of post-war Jewish American writers like Malamud, Bellow, and Roth into a "school" (something each held at bay) does not describe the Jewish twin to a *sui generis* movement like the Harlem Renaissance.[12] The parity here would have to be invented. Very different kinds of cultural politics dictate the formation of a canon in each case. By the 1950s in American literary history, the task of gathering under the same sign of the hyphen widely disparate ethnic sensibilities and modes of cultural self-understanding as we find in Jewish American literature alone, becomes simply elusive. (A similar argument could be mounted for Black fiction as well, something both Ellison and James Baldwin spelled out, in different ways, at the time.[13])

Roth's text, in fact, only prefigures these developments. Hardly in the same class as Mike Gold's *Jews Without Money*, and despite its Joycean ethos, the book was typically read – when it *was* read – through the lens of proletarian fiction (with which it has little but locale in common) and ghetto narrative. Neglected as it was for years or more recently claimed as definitive, Roth's novel still remains anomalous, a notoriously tough act to follow (even by its own author).[14]

The fiction of Yezierska, Lewisohn, and Mary Antin (certainly of Cahan and Sidney Nyburg) bears only the dimmest relation to it. *By the Waters of Manhattan* (Reznikoff), *Aaron Traum* (the brothers Cohen), *Bottom Dogs* and *From Flushing to Calvary* (Edward Dahlberg) may constitute its modernist peers, but Roth's novel does not really rub shoulders with any of them. Nor from a subsequent vantage does *Call It Sleep* haunt Daniel Fuchs's *Williamsburg Trilogy* or Rosenfeld's *Passage From Home*, each of which stands in only the most tenuous of "agonistic" relations to it. Paradoxically or not, for such an Oedipally driven text, *Call It Sleep* does not seem particularly fixated on predecessors or forbears: if Roth has a strong-poet precursor or a literary descent-rival for cultural consent, it is Joyce or Eliot if it is anyone.[15]

By contrast, if we cluster together the likes of Langston Hughes, Claude McKay, Zora Neale Hurston, Jesse Fauset, Nella Larsen, and Rudolph Fisher (not to mention Wright or Himes, given the ten-year discrepancy between Roth's novel and Ellison's), we get some idea of the densely endogamous kinship network that surrounds *Invisible Man*. Ellison's novel consciously *thematizes* its lineal relation to Black culture: to slave narrative, to folk vernacular, to *The Souls of Black Folk*, to William Dunbar's *Sport of the Gods*, to Johnson's *Ex-Coloured Man*, to Richard Wright. *Call It Sleep* is an orphan by comparison, and calling it an "ethnic novel" certainly poses more questions than answers. Yet, Ellison's text too (together with its author) resists the narrow and received confines of "race" as its ancestral and native home.[16]

Clearly, this direction will not really take us very far if we remain bent on charting discrepancies between the two texts since it caps the energies of intertextual reach and full extent of literary influence each novel wants to claim for itself. As regards *Call It Sleep* and *Invisible Man*, any antiphony between them takes place *inside* a polyphony, a public space of heterogeneous literary relations. The opening sentence from Ellison's novel together with the framing conceit it initiates, sets the novel in deliberate relation to Dostoyevsky and Melville. The penultimate chapter of Roth's, with its contrapuntal, multilingual structure (and the novel's play with consciousness and narrative voice in general) makes a similarly conspicuous bid for high culture status "beyond ethnicity." *Call It Sleep* attempts a Judeo-Christian synthesis; *Invisible Man* forces African American "Invisibility" and "blackness" into the horizonal space occupied by American "Optic White."

Both writers' anti-realist sensibilities – Ellison's preference for allegory, Roth's play with symbol – gesture forward to a *transnational* modernism, a full blown heteroglossia of the Novel, just as they simultaneously reach back to usable forms of nineteenth-century American literature. "I am in the great tradition of American t[h]inkers," says Invisible Man.[17] But to view literary texts in this way calls for a critic's version of the kind of unbound sensibility and tinker's sense that Roth's and Ellison's novels license in themselves. Literature often corrects for criticism's blindnesses, just as criticism endeavors to supplement the literary with its own insights. Thus, in Invisible Man's and David Schearl's stories, Bakhtin's concept of literary "homelessness" paradoxically discovers its obverse: each novel latently keeps the company of the other, as well as that of other traditions, times, and places. Exile becomes an ingathering, as the ethnic modernist shares public discursive space with, if not fellow cosmopolites, then literary kinsmen. As Ellison puts it himself in *Shadow and Act*, "Unlike a relative, the artist is permitted to choose an ancestor." (162)

Lessons in object-relations: the wearing and absorbing of words

Invisible Man and David Shearl are human synechdoches – not only in the predictable ethno-racial sense as novelistic heroes, but also as stand-ins for a general verbal overload, for a fulness of discursive space. In excess of the many scenes of eye-contact rife in both novels,[18] recognition takes place as, or against, an expressive *landscape*. The novels are determined to get themselves heard, against and within other sheets of sound. That metaphor (from Gunther Schiller's description of John Coltrane) points to the way *Invisible Man* and *Call It Sleep* possess their own musicality, their own *time signature*, the forepulse of personal, present experience over the insistent beat of familial and cultural freight. In Bakhtinian jargon, to be a human synechdoche is also to be a human chronotope – "where the knots of narrative are tied and untied," in time.[19]

Recognition thus underwrites the material content of each book not as a drive towards knowledge (the basic premise of literary realism) but as a filter through which to perceive and sort culture; recognition, in this sense, does not so much pierce the mystery of experience as preserve it intact.[20] Finally, and as the heading to this chapter makes clear, in the tangled dealings each protagonist has with other characters, recognition in these novels "verbs" in the imperative: *call me/call it*. That is a demand for visibility and audibility made of insiders and outsiders alike, as my epigraph from Halpern's "The Street Drummer" suggests: the clamor of an isolated and dispossessed self venting a personal *I am! See me! Hear me!* by harnessing at street level the cultural debris – and particularly the *noise* – that collects around him. "Look at me! Look at *me*," (494) Invisible Man demands of the Brotherhood. "Whistle, mister! WHISTLE" (431) David unconsciously vents at the culmination of his final and dazzling act of synthesis.

But the texts make their own like demands on our attention, even above the heads of their heroes; in their materiality, the discursive landscapes of *Call It Sleep* and *Invisible Man* function only partially as "backdrops." For they are also themselves kinetic, strewn with junk, brimming with thing, sight, and sound. The very book divisions of Roth's text – "The Cellar," "The Picture," "The Coal," and "The Rail" – for example, narrate a spare progression of brute object facts. So does the entire plot of Ellison's novel – Brother Tarp's chain-link, the broken pieces of a toy bank, a sambo doll, various documents. As these texts fairly soak in their own linguistic plenitude, such object-facts are at the same time, perhaps even primarily, facts of *language*, separately and altogether a kind of summons to readers' eyes and ears.

Additionally, each novel invokes language and other symbol-systems by turns coded, opaque, and *politically* charged, selecting out insiders and outsiders.

> Then later [my grandfather] told me to open my briefcase and read what was inside and I did, finding an official envelope stamped with the state seal; and inside the envelope I found another, and another endlessly, and I thought I would fall at weariness . . . "Now open that one." And I did and in it I found an engraved document containing a short message in letters of gold. "Read it," my grandfather said. "Out loud!" "To Who It May Concern," I intoned. "Keep This Nigger-Boy Running." . . . at that time I had no insight into its meaning. First I had to attend college. (Ellison, 33)

> "How d'*you* play bad?" she asked.
> "Bad? I don't know," he quavered.
> "Yuh wan' me to show how I?"
> He was silent, terrified.
> "Yuh must ask me," she said. "G'wan ask me."
> "Wot?"
> "Yuh must say, Yuh wanna play bad? Say it!"
> He trembled. "Yuh wanna play bad?"
> "Now, *you* said it," she whispered. "Don' forget, you said it."
> By the emphasis of her words, David knew he had crossed some awful threshold. (Roth, 53)

And later David will say of language that does not stay put, "Everything changed . . . They [words] were something else, something horrible. Trust nothing." (102) In both novels, linguistic plenitude is also a torrent through which one either swims or sinks, holding on to the odd bit of solid object or solid that comes to hand. Each novel embeds a "secret" narrative – the inset story of Trueblood in *Invisible Man*, and of David's mother's romantic past in *Call It Sleep* – that trade between them themes of transgressive sexuality, family violence, and cultural overconnectedness. Just so, as a symbol system, or as the consciously ordered linguistic artifact known as "a novel" for that matter, discourse possesses the capacity to make and unmake, expose and conceal, usually doing one in the service of the other.

Both novels exemplify the modern novel at its most metonymic: a clothes-line, a rosary, a chain, telephone poles in succession, a carom of objects and emblems and words. In chapter 14 of *Call It Sleep*, for example, David's mother's nervousness, translated into haphazard object-relations, translates itself all over again into David's metonymic behavior, the whole sequence a model for the novel's obsession with associativeness, contiguity, and unmoored signifiers:

> She went from the sink to the window and left the water run-ning and then remembering it was an odd overhastiness, turned, missed the handkerchief she was pegging to the clothes-line and let it fall into the yard. A few minutes later, separating the yolks from the whites of the eggs . . . she cut the film of the yolk with eggshell, lost it in the whites. She stamped her foot, chirped with annoyance, and brushed back her hair . . . . [David] occupied himself in a score of ways – now frightening himself by making faces at the pier glass, now staring out of the win-dow, now fingering the haze of breath upon it, now crawling under beds, now scribbling. He spent an hour tying himself to the bed post with a bit of washline and attempting to escape, and another constructing strange devices with trinkets. (117)

Or again, true to its immodest allegoricalness, *Invisible Man* holds out a chain-link as (along with its narrator-protagonist) one of its most prominent *running* motifs.

> I looked at the dark band of metal against my fist, and dropped it upon the anonymous letter . . . . I felt that Brother Tarp's gesture in offering it was of some deeply felt significance which I was compelled to respect. Something perhaps like a man passing on to his son his own father's watch, which the son accepted not because he wanted the old-fashioned time-piece for itself, but because of the overtones of unstated seriousness and solemnity of parental gesture which at once joined him with his ancestors, marked a high point of his present, and promised a concreteness to his nebulous and chaotic future. (380)[21]

Like Roman Jakobson's famous linguistic model of an axis of "substitution" (metaphor) projected onto an axis of "combination" (metonymy), cultural continuity comes about through a crossing of paternity and patrimony (hence, the sequence of father figures in the novel through whose hands Invisible Man passes, as their varying stock of symbolic capital reciprocally passes through his).

The chain link's semantic heft correlates exactly with its object-function: it burdens, it shackles, it connects, it narrates. It serves as mnemonic, as token for re-cognition:

> Perhaps from the shock of seeming to see my grandfather looking through Tarp's eyes, perhaps through the calmness of his voice alone, or perhaps through his story and his link of chain, he had restored my perspective. (381)

The most important word in these two passages for me is not "father" "grandfather" or even "parental," but, rather, *concreteness*. Even if Invisible Man's future (like David Schearl's present) stays "nebulous and chaotic," culture and his participation in it weigh in with incredible density – unremittingly concrete . . . and concretized. The classic instance of this in the novel is the eviction or dispossession scene in chapter 13, an event framed explicitly in terms of *anagnorisis*. From the display aspect of the "scene" to the audience of bystanders assigned to witness it ("witnesses of what we did not want to see"), a tableau of recognition is staged, tracked by Invisible Man's methodical inventory of household objects. His soliloquy becomes redemptive, gathering-in what has been so shamelessly dishevelled in the public space of stoop and street.

Appropriately enough, the inventory begins with a pair of faces – a portrait of the evicted couple – described as "looking back at me"; it continues for a page and a half – a demotic, decidedly un-homeric, catalogue.

> . . . a useless inhalant, a string of bright glass beads with a tarnished clasp, a rabbit foot, a celluloid baseball scoring card shaped like a catcher's mitt, registering a game won or lost years ago; an old breast pump with rubber bulb yellowed with age, a worn baby shoe and a dusty lock of infant hair tied with a faded and crumpled blue ribbon . . . a fragile paper, coming apart with age, written in black ink grown yellow. I read FREE PAPERS. (266)

In the set piece immediately before this scene, Invisible Man plays sidewalk Proust, awash with remembrance of things past through the taste of an al fresco "hot, baked Car'lina yam." Thus already *located* in the grip of memory – "I yam what I am" – (260) he responds to the dispossession scene by being repossessed by the slipping-inside-the-breaks sensibility tripped off in the prologue by dope and Louis Armstrong's horn.

> I turned and looked at the jumble, no longer looking at what was before my eyes, but inwardly-outwardly, around a corner into the dark, far-away-and-long-ago, not so much of my own mem-

ory as of remembered words, of linked verbal echoes, images
heard even when not listening at home. And it was as though I
myself was being dispossessed of some painful yet precious
thing which I could not bear to lose . . . And with this sense of
dispossession came a pang of recognition: this junk, these
shabby chairs, [etc.] all throbbed within me with more meaning
than there should have been. (266–267)[22]

Invisible Man finds himself idling here in the realms of the *neighbor*
and of *everyday language*, the novel's superior versions of kinship-
relations. And yet he shifts right away into the high gear of elevated
rhetoric in one of his many spokesman set-pieces (prompting
his immediate recruitment by the propagandistic "Brotherhood"),
that "eloquence"-above-the-everyday-exchange circumscribing his
aloneness in language, and his solitude generally. While his linguistic
sense may be Galilean and centrifugal, his characteristic predicament
in social relations is to remain Ptolemeic and self-centered.[23]

To turn analogously to David Schearl, the crowded world of
"junk" that comes to hand, and eye, and ear in *Call it Sleep*, likewise
throbs with more meaning than it should perhaps otherwise contain,
independent of the general agglutinative style of the novel's discourse. As befits a small child's more inchoate and broken chain of
association (more interior and individualized but at the same time
markedly ineloquent and unrhetorical), David's also swings bivalently between connection and dispossession. And as in Ellison's text,
this is ultimately experienced as a problem of disentangling self from
world, of negotiating filial responsibilities both bound and free.

But where Invisible Man assembles, David sponges, profoundly
permeable to the impact . . .

> . . . of the glint on tilted beards, of the uneven shine on roller
> skates, of the dry light on grey stone stoops, of the tapering
> glitter of rails, of the oily sheen on night-smooth rivers, of the
> glow on thin blonde hair, red faces, of the glow on the out-
> stretched, open palms of legions and legions of hands hurtling
> toward him . . . the perpetual blur of shod and running feet, the
> broken shoes, new shoes, stubby, pointed, caked, polished,
> buniony, pavement beveled, lumpish, under skirts, under
> trousers.   (Roth, 441)

He seems able to reconstitute the press of humanity, of top-to-bottom
physicality, as something more than merely *proximate* but almost
engrossed. He absorbs others. Invisible Man tinkers with them. The
two characters do not mirror each other according to how each lives
in, or through, language; but they do bend each other's light.

If we think of Brother Tarp's link of chain bequeathed to Invisible

Man as the perfect image of the embodied and binding past shackling the present-tense self to family and history, its complementary counterpart in *Call It Sleep* is a pair of bull's horns. In chapter 6 of the section entitled "The Rail," David is greeted by the sight of bull's horns lying on the dinner table, a wall-mounting purchased by his father, and ostensibly a reminder of days tending cattle for his own father in Austria. David fixates on this most unusual adornment to a Jewish home at the same moment as he notes a strange look in his mother's face, the text's oblique nod to the afterglow of his parents' lovemaking.

In the previous relevant scene, David's mother greets him still wet from her bath, forcing the painful realization that she and a naked woman espied at her bath from the rooftop by a gang of neighborhood boys are one and the same. Immodest in *its* Freudianism too,[24] Roth's novel positions the horns next to another pair of phalluses, "a new white handled whip and the butt of the old broken black one" (297) (the latter the result of one of father's splenetic rages vented on an anonymous man in the street). Libidinally charged by a series of sexualized scenarios, David is not inclined to accept at face value his mother's explanation of the horns as being merely a "memento."

> Somehow looking at the horns, guessing the enormous strength of the beast who must have owned them, there seemed to be another reason. He couldn't quite fathom it though. But why was it that two things so remote from each other seemed to have become firmly coupled in his mind? It was as though the horns lying on the washtub had bridged them, as though one tip pierced one image and one tip the other, that man outstretched on the sidewalk, that mysterious look of repose in his mother's face when he had come in (299).

A physical sign themselves of disjunction within connectivity, the horns are made to "bridge" male sexuality and aggression (perhaps with an ironic nod to cuckoldry). They also conjoin paternity, the upswell of cultural memory, and the associative process of "bridging" itself.[25] But as with *Invisible Man*, it is, I would argue, the concrete object itself which is a sum greater and more palpable than its combined parts. Invisible Man will muse upon his mother's imagined hands and gray head, *"why were they causing me discomfort so far beyond their intrinsic meaning as objects?"* (267) which seems to hint at his greater allegiance to symbol-systems instead of the disparate signifiers David prefers.

The horns in *Call It Sleep* may not cognitively solve the problems posed by its several associative parts, but it certainly *resolves* them in a chemical sense, binding together a whole nexus of meanings. Thus, while the novel as a whole beckons psychological readings (David's negotiation of Imaginary and Symbolic realms, of mother and father, of mirror and language, of oral and phallic signifiers), it stubbornly insists on the brute facts of its bits of the Real as its densest semiotic currency, as its most material basis for, and version of, language. In this way it fore-echoes *Invisible Man* as *Invisible Man* echoes it in turn.

Each of the objects introducing the major book divisions in Roth's novel performs the same function: "the picture" (a corn field that bridges family history, illicit tryst, and courtship); "the cellar" (bridging fear, clandestinity, and sex); "the coal" (bridging speech, taint, and purification); and "the rail" (bridging energy, light, and "marvelous transformation").[26] Towards the end of the novel, David gives vent to his own manic expression of this, the text's penchant for "bridging" and coupling. Having blurted out a confused story about his own origins (patched together from conversations overheard but half understood and from his own imagination) he bolts into the street. As at other moments in the novel when internal confusion breeds flight, the text metonymically tracking him against a succession of telephone poles or sidewalk cracks, David now propels himself forward, punctuating his racing thoughts by wishing for a "potsee" so that he could "kick it here . . . and kick it there . . . and follow where it went" (378) – the very image of serial, though random, progression. He pauses before a store window.

> Only his own face met him, a pale oval, and dark, fear-struck, staring eyes that slid low along the windows of stores, snapped off from glass to glass, mingled with the enemas, ointment jars, green globes of the drug store, snapped off, mingled with the baby clothes, snapped off with the cans of paint, steel tools, frying pans, clotheslines of the hardware store, snapped off. (378–379)

The fragmented montage created by his own reflected movement in the window-glass provides David with an intermittent haven. In between the succession of objects "snapped off," David discovers a kind of non-space of, let us say, invisibility.

> On the windows how I go. Can see and ain't. And when I ain't, where? Ain't nobody. No place. Stand here, then. BE Nobody. Always. Nobody'd see. Nobody'd know . . . Carry, yes, carry a looking glass. Teenchy weenchy one, like in a pocket book, Mama's. Yea. Yea. Yea. Stand by house. Be nobody. Can't see. (379)

"Can see and ain't" is one way of putting the novel's central theme, an ethnic identity problem as well as a personal one, the disappearing act of a self facing sensory and *cultural* overload. Superficially at least, that problem resembles a parallel theme in *Invisible Man*: how to disentangle a self, how to find a voice, how to *individuate*. On one side, Homer Barbee, the blind seer of Invisible Man's university, a paean to knowing one's place. On the other side, the utter dissociation and displacement Rinehart, the novel's final allegorical figure, turns to advantage; Reverend and runner, "dark-glass boy," he is the master of chaos and possibility, of fluidity, of ethnic *jeu* as con.[27] Both figures dissemble, both see opaquely, one blind and the other wearing dark glasses – an overload of defective seeing that Invisible Man ultimately counters by means of 1,369 lightbulbs in his refuge underground.

Invisible Man's antiphonal rejoinder to David Schearl would be therefore "Can see and am!" If, the figure of Rinehart demonstrates the most obvious instance of self-identity and verbal play as *wardrobe* – words donned, acquired, exhibited – any parallel with *Call it Sleep* halts at the brink of David's interiority, the difference between Roth's "Can't see" (i.e., "He shut his eyes"), and Ellison's triumph over "Monopolated Power and Light."[28]

Another difference: unlike Ellison's novel which is all headlong rush, Roth's adds a contrapuntal retrograde to its potsee leaps ahead. In the midst of the drivenness narrated above, the text has David *retard*; he keeps moving, but on "tottering, rebellious legs," this time using the series of poles to impede rather than impel.

> His eyes glazing with panic, he crept toward his house, and as he went, grasped at every rail and post within reach not to steady himself, though he was faint, but to retard. And always he went forward, as though an ineluctable power tore him from the moorings he clutched. (379)

Such stop-time within motion is a rhythm announced in the very first pages of the novel, where the steamer that carries David and his mother to the Golden Land nearing its dock, "drift[s] slowly and with canceled momentum as if reluctant." (3)

Both ethnicity and personhood are matters of push-and-pull for David. He cannot fit the contours of *Invisible Man*'s picaresque because he is so obviously labile and unfinished a character; he is, after all, not yet ten years old. It is David's very unfinalizability that gives him depth and dimension, a matter of language as well as consciousness. By contrast, Invisible Man appears more *figure* than character, more rhetoric than exchange, his function within the novel almost entirely allegorical, reveling in "the 'enthusiasm' of eloquence."[29] Thus, from the dream of pursuit that begins his account to the flight underground terminating it, Invisible Man answers to a single prime directive; "Keep This Nigger Boy Running." Moreover, Invisible Man himself, as an effectively finished protagonist, does not develop, as much as become exposed to the dialogizing influence of other characters and their "discourses," the better to perform his own.

In the novel's first chapter, just as Invisible Man has begun to narrate autobiographically, his dying grandfather bequeaths to him the linguistic legacy, "overcome [white people] with yeses . . . agree 'em to death and destruction," (16) words, our narrator confesses (for "the first time . . . outside the family circle") which "were like a curse." (17) "On my graduation day," reads the next sentence, "I delivered an oration in which I showed that humility was the secret, indeed the very essence of progress." (17)

Two secrets revealed through two palpably different language-games, each, however, idiosyncratically warping public and private, authoritative and inner-persuasive discourses. Two speech-acts whose sequencing models the rest of the text's ensuing concatenation of rhetorics. While one might want to distinguish here between, say, "home speech" (familial, vernacular, authentic) and "away speech" (alien, distanced, and distancing), it may be more plausible to read these simply as two versions of the same linguistic problem. *Language*, Ellison's novel says, is always the not-self, the exterior – coerced and imposed, taken up or discarded, the container or form for identity.

By contrast, when David blurts out to two Rabbis the garbled sense he makes of the story that passes between his mother and his aunt (part in *mameloshn*, part in alien Polish), of his mother's past liaison with a gentile, he publicizes a family secret whose import and selective vocabulary have a felt, almost organically mutating effect on him. Language happens *in* him whereas it happens *to* Invisible Man.

> And what was it all about he wondered. What did those Polish words mean that made his mother straighten out so. Intuition prompted him. He divined vaguely that what he had just heard must be linked to the sparse hints of meaning he had heard before, that had stirred him at first so strangely and afterwards scared him. Now perhaps he might learn what it was about, but if he did, something might change again, be the something else that had been lurking all the time beneath the thing that was. (193)

"Like mica-glints in the sidewalk" (196) the text calls the word and phrase fragments David cobbles together: "Benkart," "organeest," "corn field," "goy." In this novel, "Words here and there, shimmering like distant sails tantalized him, but never drew near." (197) Eventually, however, he pieces things together to his own satisfaction. Although David's initial fears prove unfounded, as the text proceeds, all this coded linguistic information proves so much provender, ingested, stored, transforming, and transformed.

The converse of *Invisible Man* in this respect is its donning or wearing of words, the habiliment to *Call It Sleep*'s aliment. All kinds of "junk" may come to hand for Invisible Man, but they get systemically absorbed by David Schearl.

Sorting sounds and posting signs

Above I chose examples from both novels that make language mobile while mobilizing it. *Call it Sleep* and *Invisible Man* commonly evince a drive towards flux and motility: in the shared predominant chronotope of "the road," in the Odyssean thrust of the main character, in the metonymic quality of the prose, the migration of word and object. A more interesting implication for each text, however, would seem to be the problem of *sorting* thus foisted onto the protagonists and their spectator-readers in the bargain. Roth's and Ellison's texts very consciously stage that sorting maneuver in a public space outside of their internal plots, in front of a readership *external* to the eviction scene in Ellison's novel or the multicultural tableau at the end of Roth's.

While each text may idiosyncratically organize both the sorting and the staging, my point regarding both is that when cultural identity becomes an *affair de bricolage*, things, words, and people are randomly distributed, freely associating according to that peculiar Quixotean novelistic habit of letting metonymy run rampant. That Ellison's and Roth's novel both do so, suggests to me that they are comparably interested in the ways that culture sorts persons and persons, culture. Moreover it illustrates how for both texts (in Ellison's words from *Shadow and Act*), "a writer did not so much create the novel as he was created by the novel."

"Boddeh," "Poddeh," "Potter," "Bodder," "Pother an' Body an' Powther," "Bahday": does it really matter, finally, which of these names most closely approximates the name of the Schearls' street in Brownsville, as Irish policemen try to decipher the name David pronounces? As long as "Cocaine" can blur briefly with "kockin" (Yiddish for defecate), or "molleh" (*molar*) superimpose itself on "molleh" (Yiddish for circumcision), (160) we understand the Sassurian trick of language being exploited here. Or the similar manipulation in *Invisible Man* that splits "responsibility" into the separate phonemes, "respon" and " – sibility." (30) The desire for communication compromised – "respon . . . " – by language as pure sound – "sibility" (like "sibilance"?). Or simply a reminder of invi-sibility? Responsibility does rest on recognition, as the novel claims, but in multiple senses.

A certain pressure on the social identity of the ethno-racial self could be said in these texts to undergo a strange process of lexicalization and dissemination. What is usually twoness – the hyphenate condition – becomes multipleness, as personhood proliferates into image and language. As a claim on identity linking persons, recognition here ends up being honored more in the breach than in the observance. Misfires *prove the rule*, in a double sense; they predominate, and they confirm, if negatively, the centrality of recognition as expression, to choose and be chosen by language. "It is through our names," writes Ellison, "that we first place ourselves in the world. Our names, being the gift of others, must be made our own."[30] And as with names, so with faces – the uncreated features of the self's own face, the created and decreating faces of others. Recognition undoes or is itself undone by failures of recognition, suggesting both David's sexual mystification as well as his father's own violence implicit in such perceptual alteration.

> Faces [David] had seen so many times he scarcely ever glanced at any more were twisted into secret shadows, smeared, flattened, whorled, grotesque grief and smirking never before revealed. (Roth, 283)[31]

> . . . seeing him above me and the others behind him as suddenly something seemed to erupt out of his face . . . . A glass eye. A buttermilk white eye distorted by the light rays . . . . I stared into his face, feeling a sense of outrage. His left eye had collapsed, a line of raw redness showing where the lid refused to close, and his gaze had lost its command. (Ellison, 463)

Invisible Man is forever asking "what?" "what did you say?" just as David continually conflates (and confuses) different languages. But abscesses in intersubjective space do not thus remain empty; they are taken up and filled in by language, itself a border zone (a term favored by Bakhtin and Invisible Man alike) between public and private worlds. Ethnicized and racialized billboards, Invisible Man and David Schearl advertise themselves in the process of being layered over by language and culture. Differently put, they "will" recognition, but only in the sense of serving as lightning rods for it.

For example, in the prologue to Roth's text, a multi-leveled recognition scene constitutes readers' port of entry into the novel as it simultaneously narrates the arrival of David and his mother into "the Golden Land." The "throb" of humanity the narrator describes as continuing from steerage to tenement (suggesting, perhaps, that similar terms and conditions carry over unmediated from Old World to New) sets up, two paragraphs later, the first of the novel's many "catalogs" of accumulation.[32] In this case the material clutter is human, to be sorted out as so many new Americans, but at this point sorted *through* in order to locate David and his parents, the inventory proceeding from person to thing to sound.

> . . . her decks had been thronged by hundreds and hundreds of foreigners, natives from almost every land in the world, the joweled, close-cropped Teuton, the full-bearded Russian, the scraggly-whiskered Jew, and among them Slovak peasants with docile faces, smooth-cheeked and swarthy Armenians, pimply Greeks, Danes with wrinkled eyelids. All day her decks had been colorful, a matrix of vivid costumes of other lands, the speckled green-and-yellow aprons, the flowered kerchief, embroidered homespun, the silver-braided sheep-skin vest, the gaudy scarfs, yellow boots, fur caps, caftans, dull gabardines. All day the guttural, high-pitched voices, the astonished cries, the gasps of wonder, reiterations of gladness had risen from her decks in a motley billow of sound . . . . All those steerage passengers . . . had already entered except two, a woman and a young child she carried in her arms. They had just come aboard escorted by a man. (9)

Structurally, the scene can be broken down into a set of intersecting visual planes. As the trio is "eyed curiously" by bystanders (one woman "continually squint[ing] her eyes in their direction"), so it in turn comprises three distinct sightlines.

> . . . the man staring with aloof, offended eyes grimly down at the water – or if he turned his face toward his wife at all, it was only to glare in harsh contempt at the blue straw hat worn by the child in her arms, and then his hostile eyes would sweep about the deck to see if anyone else were observing them. And his wife beside him, regarding him uneasily, appealingly. And the child against her breast looking from one to the other with watchful, frightened eyes. (11)

But "recognition" is also the point at issue among these three, the common theme they mechanically rehearse. In the confusion of arrival, David's mother fails to recognize her husband who has come to fetch them both. "You refused to recognize me," he berates her. "You don't know me." A botched attempt to deceive the authorities as to

David's real age introduces a tension between deception and recognition that hangs over the entire novel: David himself will become the focus of persistent mis- or anti-recognition by his father as the possibly bastard son of another man; "a fine taste of what lies before me!" is Albert Schearl's unwitting remark. Plot dynamics, such as they are, however, turn out to be more a function of random accretion and coincidence of detail than any teleological necessity, with plot more plausibly serving the dictates of "recognition" – as thematic prime mover – than the other way around.

Almost imperceptibly, the affective vacancy yawning between family members asks to be filled. Human silence creates a cavity immediately compensated for by random noise.

> They were silent. On the dock below, the brown hawsers had been slipped over the mooring posts, and the men on the lower deck now dragged them dripping from the water. Bells clanged. The ship throbbed. Startled by the hoarse bellow of the whistle, the gulls wheeling before her prow rose with slight creaking cry from the green water . . . (14)

Likewise, the text draws our eyes from the lattice of bridge cables and pillars – an iterative background-filler – to the small but pregnant metonym of David's provincial child's hat; object this time, not sound, takes up the slack in human intimacy, and redirects to itself, faces which should be eyeing each other.

> "Will you take that off when I – " A snarl choked whatever else he would have uttered. While his wife looked on aghast, his long fingers scooped the hat from the child's head. The next instant it was sailing over the ship's side to the green waters below . . . .In the silvery-green wake that curved trumpet-wise through the water, the blue hat still bobbed and rolled, ribbon stretched out on the waves. (15)

A floating signifier in the truest sense, the hat initiates a novel-long progression of objects and images detached from their native contexts, bobbing, rolling and, coursing within the text.

As recognition in a prosaic and ordinary optic sense is often undermined and imperiled in *Call It Sleep*, so *Invisible Man*, hardly subtle about its constantly circulated motifs of sight and vision, almost always introduces them only to have them negated or sterilized. " . . . that I may not-see myself as others see-me-not" (466) is how Invisible Man rebukes Brother Jack before the novel's climactic descent into chaos and invisibility. "They were blind, bat blind," he observes soon afterwards, "moving only by the echoed sounds of their own voices." (497) Listening to the blind griot Homer Barbee, "the students move with faces frozen in solemn masks." (111) Voice or speech, on the other hand, turn out to be far more reliable conduits for personal and transpersonal recognition within the text.

When Invisible Man is accosted by Pete Wheatstraw, he has to field a barrage of nitty-gritty, a jazz-palaver of riffs and verbal cues catching him off-guard. "I'd known the stuff from childhood, but had forgotten it," he says. Such vernacular rebop is the street's answer to earlier tests of recognition to which he has been subjected. Only in this instance, language plays and dances and slips through the breaks as the very counter-offensive to institutional ordeals of civility.[33] "Well, git with it! My names's Blue and I'm coming at you with a pitchfork. Fe Fi Fo Fum. Who wants to shoot the Devil one, Lord God Stingeroy!" (173)

But even more than the capacity to sort, what is being called upon here is the willingness to *con*sort, to *talk that talk* in the kind of accidental fellowship the street makes possible, and thus the very matter of recognition: "Why you trying to deny me?" Wheatstraw asks, after Invisible Man fails to take him up on his initial query, "What I want to know is, is you got the dog?" As in *Call It Sleep*, language floats free, simultaneously consolidating a more or less freely floating self. Taking on a life of its own, it serves as a recognition-machine sorting experience and letting the self – even if unaware – send roots down into public space.

> She's got legs like a monkeeee/Legs/Legs, Legs like a maaad/Bulldog . . .
>
> What does it mean, I thought. I heard it all my life but suddenly the strangeness of it came through to me. Was it about a woman or about some strange sphinxlike animal? Certainly his woman, no woman, fitted that description. And why describe anyone in such contradictory words. Was it a sphinx? Did old Chaplinpants, old dusty-butt, love her or hate her; or was he merely singing? What kind of woman would love a dirty fellow like that anyway? And how could *he* even love her if she were as repulsive as the song described? I moved ahead. (174)

As the woman in the blues bodies forth composite, multiform reality, so language and personal identity themselves intersect and combine in *Invisible Man*, each a composite and patchwork process.[34]

David gets arrested by song, too, in the early pages of *Call It Sleep*. He falls into a reverie that finds its consummation at novel's end in the "sleep" described by the final paragraph. Fiddling with a stray cog that has come to hand, he becomes diverted by a chant raised by a group of neighborhood girls (also, coincidentally, the vehicle for some obscure erotic content): "Waltuh, Waltuh, Wiuhlflowuh, Growing up so high; so we are all young ladies, an' we are ready to die." (23) The song reminds David of Europe, dimly remembered fragments of his early years, "a world somewhere else." He "yields" to it (as the text puts it), and like the novel's initial substitute for him – the prologue's discarded hat – he seems "to rise and fall on waves somewhere without him." (23)

> Within him a voice spoke with no words but with the shift of slow flame . . . . From the limp, uncurling fingers, the cog rolled to the ground, rang like a coin, fell over on its side. The sudden sound moored him again, fixed him to the quiet, suburban street, the curbstone. The inarticulate flame that had pulsed within him wavered, and went out. He sighed, bent over, and picked up the wheel.

Here, too, word (and object) mysteriously cathect the self, mooring it while unmooring it from itself. They seed it with meaning to fructify later on. Like the Sambo doll Invisible Man carries in his briefcase or Brother Tarp's chain-link or the street-corner yam he eats all catalyze a set of recognitions; like the blues about the sphinx-woman or the jingle about "pick[ing] poor Robin clean" or the linked verbal echoes that come to him and tap into "frequencies" both higher and lower than the individual self; so David's cog and the "Wildflower" song function as but two siphons into a constantly replenished cistern of *expressive or discursive material*.

The most compelling instance of this mechanism in Roth's novel is also the most daring for its melding of sacred and profane: the random sorting of Isaiah 6–7 (the reading from the Prophets accompanying that week's Torah portion from Exodus – the revelation at Sinai) with the slangy detritus of street life in chapter 4 of Book III, "The Coal."[35] The resulting unlikely compound appears in two forms, an antiphony created by the text itself[36], and the imagistic alchemy that is David's own incessantly febrile consciousness.

The Babel of voices on the text-level is witty and virtuosic.

> [a boy in *cheder*] "You hea' me say it. You hea' me! Shid on you. C'mon Solly, you hea' me. Yuh did push! Mendy's god a bendige yet on –"
> [the rabbi] *"Said whom shall I send?"* [quoting Isaiah] The rabbi's words were baffling on thickening briars of sound. *"Who will go for us?"*
> "Izzy Pissy! Cock-eye Mulligan! Mah nishtanah halilaw hazeh – Wanna play me Yonk?"

[David] – **Couldn't ask him though** (David's eyes merely rested
    on the page) . . . .**where Mendel read, you were saying that
    man saw God. And a light –**
"How many? I god more den you. Shebeechol haleylos onu
    ochlim. I had a mockee on mine head too. Wuz you unner de
    awningh? Us all wuz. In de rain."
"And tell this people, this fallen people – "
"Yea, and I'll kickyuh innee ass! Halaylaw hazeh kulow mazo –
    So from t'rowin' sand on my head I god a big mockee. I seen a
    blitz w'en I commed in."
– **Where did he go to see him? God? Didn't say. Wonder if the
    rabbi knows. Wish I could ask** . . . .
"C'mere Joey, here's room. De rebbeh wants – Fences is all
    slippery. Now wadda yuh cry?"
"Nor ever be healed, nor even clean." . . .
– **And why did the angel do it? Why did he want to burn
    Isaiah's mouth with coal? he said, You're clean. But coal
    makes smoke and ashes. So how clean? Couldn't he just
    say, Your mouth is clean? Couldn't he? Why wasn't it clean
    anyway? He didn't wash it, I bet** . . . .

While such questions as David's uncannily recall Invisible Man's
own in trying to puzzle out the meaning of the "sphinx-woman," it is
a less fortuitous coincidence between protagonists that intrigues me:
David, like Invisible Man, functions as the generalized and sometimes unwitting smelting pot for family, history, and culture.

As modernist fiction, *Call It Sleep* has commonly been read for its
synthesizing ethic: religions (the hyphen between "Judeo" and
"Christian"), the psyche, and quotidian life all assembled in moments of visionary, transcendent clarity. That may indeed be Roth's
overt intention for his novel, and yet the novel's own often auton-
omous thematic of recognition skews interpreting such synthesis at a
slightly different angle, as the way in which ethnic identity can be
understood itself as a drive towards recognition: both the problematic of "double consciousness" that is the minority self, and the curse
and blessing of the "composite consciousness" which is cultural
legacy. As Ellison put it more plainly, the staking out of name-as-
place for name-as-self.

To take two small examples of Roth's piecework: 1) he segues
improbably from the Prophet's "And the whole land waste and
empty," to the vernacular chime that follows, "T'ree [meaning 'three'
but sounding like 'tree'] is a lie, mine fodder says," and back to the
Prophet again, "And-not-a-tree – " (230–231). The entire linguistic
process pivots on a preternaturally transportable *tree*. 2) the sound a
blacksmith makes early in the novel, *Zwank*, creates a palimpsest later

in the text with the Yiddish word for tong, "Zwank" becoming mere sound once again in the novel's climactic apotheosis, *Zwank! Zwank! Zwank!* This is minority discourse as "deterritorialization" with a vengeance, a wandering at the mouth that cleaves between sound and sense. [37]

When he reads the words of Isaiah's vision on his own (and attempts fitfully to explain their resonance for him to his rabbi), David gives himself over to the inspiriting power of scripture, their sense somehow intuitively grasped, his own "senses dissolv[ing] into the sound." "The lines, unknown, dimly surmised, thundered in his heart with limitless meaning, rolled out and flooded the last shores of his being." (255) Despite the fact that Rabbi Pankower dismisses David's childish domestication of the text – "God's light is not between car-tracks" – he also recognizes an exceptional synergy at work: "If I weren't sure . . . I'd think he understood." (366) Such interpenetration of self and culture James Joyce called "the smithy" of transformative personality (in David's case, of course, neither self-willed nor fully self-aware).

Coincidentally or not, Joyce's *Portrait of the Artist* is the very same text Ellison signifies on along these very same lines when Invisible Man's college teacher tells him, "Stephen's problem, like ours, was not actually one of creating the uncreated conscious of his race, but of *creating the uncreated features of his face*." (346)[38] And this is that same fate of becoming "one yet many" which by the end of his story, Invisible Man describes as "description not prophecy" (564) because he discovers it to be absolutely unavoidable. If culture is burden and curse, it is also possibility – the double edge Invisible Man comes to appreciate in his grandfather's death-bed words: "I want you to overcome 'em with yeses." (16) To be a picaro, says Ellison's novel, is to slip inside the breaks to look around, hear, and also do cultural work.

"Something strange and miraculous and transforming is taking place in me right now . . . " (337) observes Invisible Man during his first performance as orator. "What had come out was completely un-calculated," he muses afterwards, "as though another self within me had taken over and held forth." (344) But whether involuntary or willed, the fate of becoming one yet many (or becoming both "more human" (337) and "someone else" [327]), yields a *forged* self whose only claim to recognition – to a created, featured face – is that power to configure or shape haphazard features of experience into momentary coherence and form.

In the most shamelessly allegorical part of *Invisible Man* – the

Liberty Paints section – disoriented and amnesiac, "fretting over his identity," Invisible Man is tested for his powers of recognition. WHO IS BUCKEYE THE RABBIT?, he is asked. "Somehow I was Buckeye the Rabbit . . . or had been, when as children we danced and sang barefoot in the dusty streets: Buckeye the Rabbit/Shake it, shake it . . ." (236) (as in an earlier instance of self-recognition, when he realizes that his story has already been encoded in the "who-what-when-why-where of old Poor Robin" (190)). Scoring a small rhetorical victory upon leaving the factory hospital, he lays claim once again to a self possessed:

> I had the feeling that I had been talking beyond myself, had used words and expressed attitudes not my own, that I was in the grip of some alien personality lodged deep within me. (243)

If identity begins in both these texts as, in the Bible's Genesis, a *tohu vavohu*, something unformed and void, it ends as a finished face – not a realistic or particularized face, for this is allegory after all (analogous to the realm of ruin in things, says Benjamin), but rather like that children's toy whose object is to assemble disparate eyes, mouth, nose, and so on into a random but still recognizable countenance.

But what keeps this from lapsing into mere "facework" or ethnic legerdemain? Why are *Invisible Man* and *Call It Sleep* both more than simply textbook exercises in ethnic semiosis? What genuinely catastrophizes[39] them from within? To return to this chapter's opening juxtaposition, it is the threat of invisibility on the one hand, and the redemptive but still artificial and almost counterfeit power of "sleep" (or dormancy), on the other.[40]

Difference and language

From the chapter's current vantage point, those two modalities appear far less congruent than they may have at first; such is the benefit of a cumulative facing. But they remain very different novels. *Call It Sleep* comes by its alienation somewhat romantically, after all, its ethnic consciousness in this respect closer in spirit to Joyce than to Ellison. The harmless ethnic slurring of David's Catholic chum Leo's – "Dat's Chritschin light . . . Bigger den Jew light" (322) – and a few cameo indulgences in street-prejudice comprise all the novel has to say about Jewishness as stigma. *Call It Sleep* is not even obliquely about antisemitism.

And despite all its archness and skeptical ad-hocing, on the contrary, *Invisible Man* rehearses an irreducible (if still allegorical) story about blackness as social death – as the "unmaking" of self if not community to be understood within a historically and culturally embedded politics of race. *Necessity* makes Invisibility a virtue, creating possibilities for slipping inside the breaks which, if not quite amounting to negative freedom still permit a kind of "positive bondage," nevertheless.

"My problem was that I always tried to go in everyone's way but my own," Invisible Man confesses.

> I have also been called one thing and then another while no one really wished to hear what I called myself. So after years of trying to adopt the opinions of others I finally rebelled. I am an invisible man. Thus I have come a long way and boomeranged a long way from the point in society toward which I originally aspired. (560)

Hibernation, exile, and invisibility are self-chosen to the extent that anyone can actively "choose" or embrace such fates. For catastrophic subjectivity looks like a bonus only from the outside peering in. The affirmation of negativity one dramatizes by stepping outside reality into chaos (563) does not necessarily differ in consequence from what was earlier decried as the decision to "plunge into nothingness, into the void of faceless faces, of soundless voices, lying outside history." (428)

For it is the bitter fruit of invisibility to have to create anew (or rather, decreate) the already created features of a face. Invisible Man distinguishes between two contexts for invisibility: "Before . . . I lived in the darkness into which I was chased, but now I see. I've illuminated the blackness of my invisibility and vice versa." (13) But an inversion of terms does not constitute a free act of definition (as Frantz Fanon showed in *Black Skin, White Masks*). Perhaps that is what Invisible Man means when he acknowledges at the end of his story the more pressing distinction between revolutionary solitude and the obligatory "next step" of disinterment.

On the most facile level, what persuades him finally to emerge from his hole in the ground, is, simply, the cessation of his story: in narratological terms, discourse and story have converged at their common still point, and there's nothing left to tell. And for the sort of alluvially rich narratability a text like this demands, one needs communicative others. And not just listeners or readers. Invisible interlocutors – those faceless faces and soundless voices that lie outside the story to and for whom Invisible Man speaks – will not in the end suffice. Even if the narrative voice remains privileged in its aloneness,

African American fiction like *Invisible Man* depends on human density in its commitment to representation in a double sense. Invisible Man does "speak for" a community of others in a way that David Schearl simply cannot.

One way to see Tod Clifton's Sambo doll or the vet's earlier characterization of Invisible Man as a "mechanical man" (92) or other images of automata in the text is as the novel's internal critique of individual autonomy – up to and including manipulating the Invisible. (Such a critique would thus represent the obverse to the text's ongoing satire of organized, institutional artificers like Liberty Paints or *faux* communalism.) That is, insofar as it constitutes an optical defect in others, invisibility remains a white man's burden.

The "fine, black thread" causing the Sambo doll to jiggle up and down, Invisible Man later discovers, had been "invisible." (435) What is visible, on the contrary is the long black line threading from Invisible Man's grandfather through Trueblood and Pete Wheatstraw to Mary Rambo, Brother Tarp, and even Rinehart: lifeworld, legacy, the "marrow of tradition," in Charles Chesnutt's resonant phrase. "Even an invisible man has a socially responsible role to play," (568) as the novel's send-off, may mean simply that sociality itself constitutes a necessary and enlivening responsibility – the generative and generational burden of cultural adhesion. Call this the hyphen not as minus sign but rather chain link.

> Or was it, did [my grandfather] mean that we should affirm the principle because we, through no fault of our own, were linked to all the others in the loud, clamoring, semi-visible world . . . . Weren't we part of them as well as apart from them . . . ? (561–562)

In what way does such a "principle" inflect the question of difference in the text – the "blackness of blackness" (as it is called in the prologue)? And is the blackness of blackness, in fact, the novel's central topic, its phenomenological point of departure or fulcrum for critique? Would it be fair, moreover – to retrieve Roth's novel and bring it back into view at this point – to apply the same principle to *Call It Sleep* where the "Jewishness of Jewishness" seems to weigh out as such a different phenomenon? Does the problematic of race, in other words, sunder these texts finally and definitively from one another, and moot any comparison beyond thematic points of contact?

Above, I comment on the more or less benign atmosphere of ethnic accord that prevails in Roth's text; the book limits its "conflicts" to the familial and the linguistic. Indeed its unapologetic point on so many levels is, as we know, redemption through synthesis. And yet I have also maintained that we need to refract that point at a different angle than is customary – hence my reference above to the "counterfeit power" of sleep as the novel's consummating image for visionary experience. True, as many of its contemporary readers felt, *Call It Sleep* betrays a certain indifference to political realities, if "politics" is configured strictly in terms of the conflict between competing populations or class interests. Should we shift to the text's mental landscape and call purely psychological vicissitudes "political" by way of redress, we only vitiate the force and sense of the category and find ourselves becalmed in no less depoliticized waters.

And yet if angled alternatively, Roth's text exemplifies the kind of political tension Deleuze and Guattari attribute to the deterritorializing power of minor literature, the way its "cramped space forces each individual intrigue to connect immediately to politics."[41] If the allegories narrated in the previous chapter outstrip such an argument complicating its abstractions with concrete realities, the same argument with reference to *Call It Sleep* possesses real merit since its very *denouement* is Deleuze and Guattari's own: "there isn't a subject; *there are only collective assemblages of enunciation.*"

> This is the problem of immigrants, and especially of their children, the problem of minorities, the problem of a minor literature, but also a problem for all of us: how to tear a minor literature away from its own language . . . Kafka answers: steal the baby from its crib, walk the tightrope. [42]

That may be Henry Roth's and Ralph Ellison's answer as well.

For counterpart to the mechanizing implications of *Invisible Man*'s Sambo Doll surfaces in *Call it Sleep* through the brilliant stroke of making a lifeless automaton the occasion for a politics of language. Like Kafka, like Ellison, Roth kills metaphor in order to make room for metamorphosis.[43] After the extended conversation above between David's mother and his aunt as overheard (and undercognized) by him, David looks out the window (a recurrent figure in the text for interpretive autonomy) for something to "distract curiosity from himself." At first he notices a "Negro," and wonders (much like the speaker in the Rosenfeld epigraph) whether he should ask "Why does he breathe white if he's black?" (205) He opts instead to concentrate on two boys playing with an object, "a headless, stove-in celluloid doll with an egg-shaped bottom, the kind that when they are pushed, bounced upright again." (206). The doll is lit on fire; all that remains is the metal armature. David tells his mother and aunt to observe the resulting "mejick" (magic). "There's a little piece of iron," he explained. "In that kind of doll. That's what makes it stand up when you push it over. And the doll burned. And only the iron is left." (207) The chapter ends with David's satisfaction: "Easy fool them. But they didn't fool him. Didn't scare him either."

Like Tod Clifton's, this doll works its magic by dint of being a manipulated sign, a diversionary tactic that, while compressing all sorts of symbolic content – it prefigures David's own climactic trans-figuration through fire and metal, it rehearses a ritual of violence in the text, it comments on Genya's guilt – performs the greater "mejick" of David's *expressive* sleight-of-hand. Not only has he "cap-tured" some part of the story of his origins from a coded language-game played by adults, and knows that he knows. But also the text conjures for him a kind of sympathetic magic over an object lain bare by stealing the linguistic baby from its crib, by becoming nomadic, immigrant in relation to language itself, "abandon[ing] sense, ren-der[ing] it no more than implicit . . . retain[ing] only the skeleton of sense or a paper cutout."[44]

A "drick" is what David calls the trick, a word which pronounced the same way in Yiddish means "kick." "A drick," Aunt Bertha asked grinning . "Where? In the pants?" (206) Well, one might reply, Yes, of a sort: a kick in the pants to territorialized language, tearing it from sense, conquering sense, which therefore "no longer finds its value in anything but an accenting of the word, an inflection."[45] The text plays this particular language game often, as the ground of mediation through which culturally inscribed differences (if indeed, difference can ever be prised apart from language in the first place) have to pass marked in a whole new way, as a place of contestation, of double and triple voices. Here is the public space where Roth's and Ellison's texts reconverge. Even beyond the specificities of race or ethnicity, *Invisible Man* and *Call it Sleep* keep their eye on politics through their common focus on *language* as the primal force that "makes" and "un-makes."

Face and voice

His Master's Voice, on the red seals of the Victor rec-
cords! But his young uncle played different voices,
Al Jolson sang for them of going to the sunny South,
where the Negro, the enslaved peasant, and Dixie, the de-
feated nation,
Furnished for the immigrant Jewish genius metaphors for his
maternal emotion,
And reached to touch the fusing boy with the lyricism

flowing from the profoundest sources,
From the Ghetto, from the Civil War, from the warmth
of Nature in summer,
Of the suffering nations and people who had made him a living
child!⁴⁶

The child in these lines from Delmore Schwartz's unfinished long poem "Genesis" is obviously not David Schearl, nor are the "profoundest sources" touching him the ones which, while replenishing, cost Invisible Man so dearly. And yet in imaging one aspect of the peculiar entanglement which binds nonliterary as well as literary American Blacks and Jews, these verses offer both a conclusion, and an implicit answer to the questions about race and politics raised immediately above.

The gesture towards antiphony here – the Black American voice as a harmony both *heymisch* and *unheimlich* for the immigrant Jew's – is not one that Roth's novel makes, nor one that Ellison's would necessarily endorse. One could, I suppose, ironically collocate the phrase "his master's voice" with a sentimentalized slavery as mediated by a Jew in blackface, but such a move would be too clever by half.

The black speech, black faces, and black Americans of *Invisible Man* do not figure within Roth's text whose immigrant tensions are, in turn, not what Invisible Man understands by "going up" or "going down." But, in the ligature between these books that criticism makes, with and against the grain, and which the books themselves may silently petition, a shadow is cast. An oversound is heard, slipped "between the breaks" by a surplus of language, of identity, of difference.

And short of an argument for commensurability, this interpenetration – the fugal trajectory of counterpointed voices – is what unites this chapter's "Black" and "Jew" in call and response. *Invisible Man*'s "Blackness" and *Call It Sleep*'s "Jewishness" call and respond to each other precisely as correspondences from inside the *text*, not as theory or programmatic intent from without – hence the power, for each, of what Schwartz calls voices, any putative master for which presides in the polyphonic diaspora of ethnic "American-ness."

2

"Jew me sue me don't you black or white me": The (ethical) politics of recognition in Chester Himes and Saul Bellow

We were the end of the line. We were the children of the immigrants who had camped at the city's back door, in New York's rawest, remotest, cheapest ghetto, enclosed on one side by the Canarsie flats and on the other by the hallowed middle-class districts that showed the way to New York. "New York" was what we put last on our address, but first in thinking of the others around us. They were New York, the Gentiles, America; we were Brownsville – *Brunsvil*, as the old folks said – the dust of the earth to all Jews with money, and notoriously a place that measured success by our skill in getting away from it. So that when poor Jews left, *even* Negroes, as we said, found it easy to settle on the margins of Brownsville . . .   Alfred Kazin, *A Walker in the City*

I want to talk about the first Northern urban generation of Negroes. I want to talk about the experiences of a misplaced generation, of a misplaced people . . . These were the poorest people of the South, who poured into New York City during the decade following the Great Depression . . . They felt as the Pilgrims must have felt when they were coming to America. But these descendants of Ham must have been twice as happy as the Pilgrims, because they had been catching twice the hell . . . The children of these disillusioned colored pioneers inherited the total lot of their parents – the disappointments, the anger. To add to their misery, they had little hope of deliverance. For where does one run to when he's already in the promised land?

Claude Brown, *Manchild in the Promised Land*

Certain pairings of texts from different literary or cultural traditions – say, Conrad's *Nostromo* and Marquez's *Hundred Years of Solitude*, or Gogol's "The Overcoat" and Melville's "Bartleby the Scrivener" –

make a natural kind of sense, marriages born of more than just creative matchmaking. But Saul Bellow and Chester Himes? A high-cultural Nobelist and a no less driven and willful expatriate and ex-con, the one a living testament to the creed of literary man as humanist, the other to writer as raw *force*?[1] A novel that traps consciousness in Jewish minds, and one that makes it indivisible from Black bodies?

Imagine a line segment bounded by the totemic fiction of Bernard Malamud's *The Tenants* on one end, and the polemic friction between Blacks and Jews as replayed by Harold Cruse and Cynthia Ozick on the other,[2] – a belletristic narrative of blackjewishrelations, short but bitter. Have the organizing structures of fiction and journalism, then, not already beaten literary criticism to the punch? Where is any space left on that line for another "point," another story?

With its hypertrophied Jew and its elementalist Negro, Malamud's novel alone would seem to consign the unlikely conjunction of real-life writers like Saul Bellow and Chester Himes to the twilight zone of the uncanny. Or at the very least, as unironic and biased social commentary, as both dystopic and dyspeptic, doesn't *The Tenants* render the whole convenient dichotomy between the "Jewish mind" and the "Black body" ludicrous, the very worst sort of stereotypified polarity? Ozick's and Cruse's (albeit dated) analyses of the cultural politics pitting Black against Jewish intellectuals, only make this chapter's Black/Jewish authorial coupling the more implausible. Conceivably, Bellow and Himes (were he still alive) would themselves chafe at being so associated, even on the accessory, ad hoc plane of "representational thematics."

Nevertheless Chester Himes's *If He Hollers Let Him Go* and Saul Bellow's *The Victim* supply a most apposite pairing of "Black" and "Jew," for *in conjunction*, they uncannily convert exegesis into political, and ethical, exigency, criticism into criticism as ethical-politics. If Ellison's Invisible Man and David Schearl are ethnics "on the run," juggernauts for mobile cultural accretion, Himes's Bob Jones and Bellow's Asa Leventhal *desire to run*, having been arrested and fixed by a certain paralytic power endemic to race-prejudice. Accordingly, this chapter's texts treat *space* – personal, social, verbal, and especially recognitive – differently. Moreover, reading these novels together deeply unsettles the customary selecting out of Jewish intellectuality and Black physicality as "natural" planes of text-topic and reader-response, let alone of everyday condition. Extending the previous chapter's opening counterpoint, then, let the novels' titles model an interchange: Bellow's *If He Hollers Let Him Go*, Chester Himes's *The Victim*.

Earlier, I spoke of literary history and criticism as venues of "social space" *formed* by the ligatures, the binding ties willed into being by reading. Itertextuality then becomes as much a critical task as a latent property of texts themselves. Whether the lived realities of antisemitism and racism can be doubletracked (and I do not gainsay the need to do so, if I remain not entirely sanguine about the outcome), an identity politics cordoning texts like these from each other, or else backlighting them against the separate horizons of "African American" and "Jewish American" literatures, makes for a pinched and hamstrung criticism. In the present readings, I aim for something less flattened. But as recognition becomes the shared optic for reading these two novels, so literary criticism, by the same token, cannot therefore be *merely* academic.

Unlike *face*, my own application of Levinasian vocabulary to criticism, Levinas himself does not speak of "ethical-politics." While the two terms may inform each other, they do not sit on either side of the same hyphen in his work, and do not bear equal weight (unlike, say, "African-American" or Jewish-American"). In common usage, the qualifying adjective "ethical" supervenes upon an already familiar noun phrase; politics, accordingly, would be the more anchored term, ethics its lexical dependent. In these pages, by contrast, the compound phrase signifies a politicizing of specifically Levinasian categories, much as socio-politics creates the opportunity in this book for ethical criticism.[3]

If the title of a Levinas essay, "Politics After!" be read as exemplary, it is *politics*, rather, which is seen as supervening on an already ethical situation. For Levinas, the political moment however crucial arrives phenomenologically (though not temporally) *late*.[4] Even if we grant, with Roger Simon, that the politics of recognition is "based on the assumption that the public assertion of the collective history to which one belongs is supposed to serve as a corrective to some deficit in self-esteem," nevertheless "the articulation of identities . . . cannot be reduced to a personal desire for cultural acknowledgment. What's at stake must be written in different terms."[5]

My version of such terms begins by sketching a Bellow/Himes face-to-face, backlit by Kazin's and Brown's epigraphs above. A consideration of certain thematic implications about particularism and group identity in Levinas's work follows. The balance of the chapter will then be taken up by close reading in tracking the recursive transit between ethics and exegesis. Any "voiding" of history as the backdrop for Himes's and Bellow's respective careers and concerns should be seen on the order of selective focus, to be redressed in any event by the chapter following this.

Victims

Asa Leventhal, one of several candidates for the titular condition of Bellow's *The Victim*, comes – not even from Brownsville – but Hartford, Connecticut: closer to "middle class districts that showed the way to New York," than to something truly impoverished. Still, having for a time drifted on New York's East Side, "starved and thin," (21) he has learned what "getting away from it" means. As he puts it, "I was lucky. I got away with it." (21)[6]

> He had almost fallen in with that part of humanity of which he was frequently mindful (he never forgot the hotel on lower Broadway), the part that did not get away with it – the lost, the outcast, the overcome, the effaced, the ruined. (27)

In Kazin's terms, Bellow's protagonist has come to mark a division between a "they" and a "we," and yet, at this point in the novel, "that part of humanity" with whom he shares a kind of solidarity does not designate *other Jews*, as indeed Asa's Jewish identity has not so far emphasized any personal past. The text makes sure we note his Jewish features – large nose, coarse hair – and its action begins with Asa's recalcitrant visit to his brother's family on Staten Island because of a sick nephew, but apart from an ethnic slur directed at him by his boss, we do not sense a *palpable* Jewishness in him. Still, with Kazin, we conclude that "to settle on the margins" promises a less than happy ending for Asa, tantamount as it is to being set apart, singled out, enclosed.

Even, *pace* Bellow, for "Negroes," as for instance, Bob Jones, the titular, though elided, "nigger" in Chester Himes's *If He Hollers Let Him Go*. Like Leventhal, conversant with the dilemmas of marginality, of the "end of the line," of *they and we*, he too learns hard lessons of misplacement. He also knows what getting away from/with it means. But his fate remains far more penumbral than Asa's, and he catches "twice the hell," since for him, *place* much more than accidentally rhymes with *race*. Framed for rape at the end of the novel (a trumped-up charge with the court's collusion), he catches "a break" from the judge and is allowed to enlist in the Army rather than be incarcerated:

"If I let you join the armed forces – any branch you want – will you give me your word you'll stay away from white women and keep out of trouble?" I wanted to just break out and laugh like the Marine in my dream, laugh and keep on laughing. 'Cause all I ever wanted was just a little thing – just to be a man. But I kept a straight face, got the words through my oversized lips. "Yes sir, I promise." . . . Two hours later I was in the Army. (203)[7]

That is how Himes's novel ends, the mood of *eminence grise* and scene of escort reminiscent of the last paragraph in *The Victim*, though far more consequential, since Jones gets packed off to the Army where Leventhal merely sits down to watch a play:

"Wait a minute, what's your idea of who runs things?" said Leventhal. But he heard Mary's voice at his back. Allbee ran in and sprang up the stairs. The bell continued its dinning, and Leventhal and Mary were still in the aisle when the houselights went off. An usher showed them to their seats. (Bellow, 256)

"Who runs things" for Bob Jones, within the claustrophobic machinery of an unhappy "occupied" consciousness at the beginning of the story, and a swift succession of institutional entrapment – police, law, military – by the end, signifies something much less speculative. Even the title of Himes's novel betrays imperativeness.[8]

How it feels to be colored (or *Jewish*) me.[9] *We*, in contradistinction to *you*, *you* in relation to *they*. That most durable device in the syntax of ethnic auto/biography: a grudge match among pronouns, the contest of surplus identities. Kazin and Brown sketch it as the difference between identity's home and its beyond. Bellow's and Himes's texts, however, begin *in situ*, taking the otherness of place for granted as merely preparation for the otherness of person . . . or of self. Even a matter as ostensibly benign as pronominal deixis – the marking out of *your* or *those* or *my* "people" – in their novels demonstrates both an underlying politics and a poetics. Pronouns and proper nouns could accurately be said to be their twin theme – the "attack-words," as Elias Canetti put it, of antisemitism and racism.[10]

Yet, related but even more embodied thematic pattern in the novels not intimated by Kazin's and Brown's epigraphs propels *The Victim* and *If He Hollers Let Him Go* from their very first pages: a persistent and obsessive concern with the human face as subject, object, and field, finally, for politicized recognition. And by this I mean an ethics that becomes necessarily "troubled" by political conditions and consequences.[11] To illustrate briefly: Bellow's novel itself has two epigraphs, the first a parable from *The 1001 Nights* about accountability, the second drawn from Thomas De Quincey's *Confessions*:

> Be that as it may, now it was upon the rocking waters of the ocean the human face began to reveal itself; the sea appeared paved with innumerable faces, upturned to the heavens, faces imploring, wrathful, despairing; faces that surged upward by thousands, by myriads, by generations . . . [12]

Himes's text also begins with a series of hallucinatory visages. In the first of five dream set-pieces which correspond to the five days of the story's action, and block out in shorthand the novel's propulsive anatomy of racial animosity, the narrator imagines a black man given the task of "look[ing] at the dead body of Frankie Childs in the face." (2) Jones turns over on his side and conjures up a second tableau of humiliation centering on his own excruciated fascination with two white faces that persist in laughing at his. Upon waking, Jones laments that he typically greets the day with a persistent fear and trembling he assigns to with the "handicap" of race, brought home to him (more powerfully than by anything else) by recalling "the look of people's faces when you asked them about a job." (3)

In fact, the *differentia specifica* of figure, physiognomy, and hue run absolutely riot in Himes's novel.

(1) The first [colored fellow] to be called was a medium-sized, well built, fast walking dark brown man of about thirty-five.
(2) She was a full-bodied, slow-motioned home girl with a big broad flat face, flat nosed and thick-lipped; yellow but not bright.
(3) He was a thin, wiry nervous Irishman with a blood-red, beaked face and close set bright blue eyes.
(4) A short, dumpy, brown-skinned girl with slow-rolling eyes and a tiny pouting mouth let us in.

These are only four out of perhaps two dozen. At the same time, the novel compulsively stages scene after scene of face-to-face "recognition."

(1) Something drew her gaze and she looked up into my eyes. We held gazes until I stopped just in front of her.
(2) Looking up, I caught a young captain's eye. He didn't turn away when our gazes met; he didn't change expression; he just watched us with the intent stare of the analyst.
(3) The white woman next to me stopped talking and looked

around. I could feel her gaze on me . . . Our eyes met . . . She
looked away after a moment and I looked into the mirror and
met the eyes of the man on the other side of her.

(4) We both jumped back from pure reflex. Then recognition
came into his eyes and his face turned greenish white. It froze
him, nailed him to the spot. For a moment I was stunned. I'd
never seen a white man scared before, not craven, not until
you couldn't see the white for the scare.[13]

In Bellow's novel, the entire narrative and imagistic tension of the
plot follows from the traded looks and prolonged "studying" passed
back and forth between Leventhal's and his nemesis Allbee's two
faces – one *Jewish* the other *non-*.

(1) Some such vague thing was in Leventhal's mind while he
waited his turn at the drinking spout, when suddenly he had
a feeling that he was not merely looked at but watched.
Unless he was greatly mistaken a man was scrutinizing him,
pacing slowly with him as the line moved.

(2) "Well, now you've found out that I still exist and you're
going home, is that it? . . . I mean that you just wanted to have
a look at me . . . wanted to see me."

(3) But now and then, moving from cage to cage, gazing at the
animals, Leventhal, in speaking to Philip, or smoking, or
smiling, was so conscious of Allbee, so certain he was being
scrutinized, that he was able to see himself as if through a
strange pair of eyes: the side of his face, the palpitation of his
throat. . . . Changed in this way into his own observer, he was
able to see Allbee, too . . . his raggedly overgrown neck, the
bulge of his cheeks, the color of blood in his ear . . .

(4) He had a particularly vivid recollection of the explicit recognition in Allbee's eyes which he could not doubt was the
double of his own.[14]

While these passages may suggest merely descriptive contours for a
poetics of face as opposed to something more politically edged (and
while they do not take into account each text's equally characteristic
investment in acting and performance), I turn to Levinas's ethics for
profounder interpretive ballast, extending the limits of recognition by
tracing another sort of path (in Levinas's own phrase) from ethics to
exegesis, this time mediated through politics.

From ethics through politics . . .

In Levinas's philosophy, "ethics" means more than an account of norms for human sociality. It declares itself *first philosophy*, preceding ontology, because "to be" already means to be obligated to other persons. Levinasian ethics sees "in justice and injustice a *primordial* access to the Other beyond all ontology."[15] Justice here does not signify fairness, as in John Rawls' moral philosophy in the Anglo-American tradition, where a hypothetical "original position" bestows a veil of ignorance that guarantees each person a similarity of position to, but no vis-à-vis with, all the others.[16] Nor does it correspond to the moral law I impose upon myself in the Kantian tradition vis-à-vis objective norms of social relation. Nor, finally, does it express the communitarian ideal of a society rooted in communal attachments, a collective vis-à-vis.

It is instead, simply and radically *vis-à-vis*. In Levinas, the drama of face-to-face encounter between an obligated self and a summoning other *accomplishes* justice. To meet the face of another means to approach without empty hands. Ethics is featured and bodied forth by *visage*, manifested before it can be cognized. In Levinas, ethics is always *event*, which the ethical subject undergoes, and the ethical other produces. Rupture, upsurge, shining, visitation, denuding: this is the language Levinas commonly exploits in describing what ultimately exceeds formulation because its very condition is surplus and transcendence.

Alongside its power to show form – its phenomenal character – the face is defined by expression. It speaks, from above me, and so enjoins responsibility.

> "Thou shalt not kill" or "Thou shalt love thy neighbor" not only forbids the violence of murder: it also concerns all the slow and invisible killing committed in our desires and our vices, in all the innocent cruelties of natural life, in our indifference of "good conscience" to what is far and what is near, even in the haughty obstinacy of our objectifying and our thematizing, in all the consecrated injustices due to our atomic weight of individuals and the equilibrium of our social orders.[17]

The Biblical topos here does not appear merely coincidentally, for Levinas has particularized the metaphysical thrust of his own work – independent of his philosophical writings – through a body of essays on Jewish identity, and Talmudic commentary. Yet this *particularism* introduces a real problem, and not just for the consistency of Levinas's philosophic/religious project. On the one hand, Levinas typically identifies "the particular" with privileged – that is, seated – positions of autonomy, a positionality he accuses, in the same essay quoted above, as:

> The original perseverance of being in its being, of the individualism of being, the persistence or insistence of beings in the guise of individuals jealous for their *part*, this *part*icularism of the inert, substantivized into things, particularism of the enrooted vegetable being, of the wild animal fighting for its existence, and of the soul, the "owner and interested party" Bossuet speaks of, this particularism exacerbated into egoism or into political "totalities," ready or readying themselves for war . . . (110)[18]

Differently put, the narcissism of little differences (Freud) simply picks up where primary narcissism leaves off.

On the other hand, Levinas just as consistently privileges the specific textual and prophetic traditions of Jewish peoplehood which, in their particularity ground a universal drive towards justice. "Israel" becomes "a *figure* in which a primordial mode of the human is revealed" (110). Monotheism is the bearer of justice in relation to the nations. Judaism becomes "a rupture of the natural and the historical." Jewish destiny means "a crack in the shell of imperturbable being" where political necessities are "and no longer excused by their universality."[19]

Levinas typically favors the term "universalization" (a making general) over "universality," in the sense of universalizing the unique, in this case, Israel: "Don't be shocked!" he writes. "The authentically human is everyone's Jewishness and its echo in the singular and the particular." Israel, Judaism, the Torah: tropes mobilized for ethical personhood and courage: exemplary, iconic, standing (in) for the human. The notion of Israel, Levinas writes, "must be separated from all particularism, except for that of election . . . a surplus of duties."

Consider, however, a similar argument about "race," as made for instance by Ellison and Morrison when they speak of African-American history's *moral* exemplarity, or by Fanon, in capturing the logic of racism: "[The Jew] and I may be separated by the sexual question, but we have one point in question. Both of us stand for evil." As even the sexual distinction here is perhaps debatable, the unifying point is *symbolic capital*, the capacity to "stand for," to represent both particularly *and* universally. And indeed, Levinas expressly concerns himself with the pre-symbolic or the pre-cultural. Ethics is a dimension of height that arrests and contests the laterality, or mutual translatability, of independent realms and nationhoods. Height, the face, the

proletarian, are all ethics, but they are also, more vexedly, "Judaism,"
a perpetual instance of social justice and answerability, not merely
their figure or emblem.[20] Yet ethics is also nearness; "proximity"
indicates an *ethical* relationship not a consanguineous one, approach
not resemblance.

Even from this brief foray into the Levinasian image repertoire, I
hope that certain tensions between Jewish election and Jewish universalism become evident.[21] That is to say, I do not think that Levinas has
fully clarified in his work a particularism which is sometimes universalist and sometimes . . . Jewish for Judaism's sake. History, cultural
expression, moral perfectionism, religious experience, emplacement
in nationhood, displacement in land and state: all of these human
modalities become Judaized for Levinas to a profound degree. Indeed, while he himself distinguishes rhetorically between his philosophical texts and those he calls confessional (Judaic), I do not think it
overstates the case to draw a direct correspondence between the
ethically transcendent and the Jewish.

But certainly, other narratives of cultural and ethnic misfortune can
claim a similar privilege to define collective identity. Passion and
persecution are not Judaism's and Israel's alone, nor are election and
obligation. Other peoples testify to their own versions of an answera-
bility-for-the-others, a moral purpose understood in terms of sacrifice, service, peace to the one who is near and to the one far off. Surely
a *universal* moral indemnity vibrates through, and rescues, human
history. Need the Law as given to Israel to reveal what it means to be
essentially, ethically human be the only medium for such revelation,
the only instance of it, a transhistorical, transcultural light unto all the
other nations?[22]

Obviously, these sorts of questions call for deliberative, considered
reasoning, and are hardly answerable in any short form. Nor do I pose
them to be answered, really, but merely framed, reflecting the ethical
and political stakes of Levinas's concepts of universality and election.
To paraphrase the title of one of his collections of Jewish essays, his is a
difficult particularity. And yet if I accentuate one dimension of Judaism's multiform meaning over and above the others in Levinas's
writings, it also, quite practically and empirically, signifies text and
interpretation – the portability of Torah and its creative extension as
elaborated through the Talmud in diaspora. It means study in the
sense of discourse with God conducted in the company of others,
anywhere in the world. It means an extreme consciousness, attentive-
ness, insomnia – a close reading, if you will, that precisely takes the
particular, the featured, the differentiated into account.

It is in this sense that I think Levinasian themes become pedagogically and hermenutically useful, and offer a wider applicability than the strictly philosophical or "Judaic." Although I do not believe Levinas can transcend territorialism as easily as, say, Philip Roth (whom we will meet in the next chapter) – which perhaps just marks the difference between philosophy and the Novel – and while I want neither to truncate and simplify the complexities here nor extend Levinas's meanings imprecisely or too freely, an ethical-politics of encounter (as opposed to identity) offers real value for criticism. At the very least, Levinas's wrestling with particularism in the broad context of social amity, of universalized ethical primacy, points the way to a politics beyond the "merely," political – if not a politics wholly 'after,' than one at least co-extensive, proximate, like the shadows of alterity that fall on Asa Leventhal and Bob Jones.

. . . to exegesis

Which returns me to Himes and Bellow. Each of their novels in the early pages fortuitously dramatizes Levinas's own metaphor of awakening to an insomnia as an image for the monadic, self-limited self. Every one of the five days comprising the action of *If He Hollers Let Him Go* begins with an awakening from disturbed sleep to the greater nightmare of everyday racism, and throughout *The Victim*, Asa Leventhal either interrupts his sleep only to be visited by his nemesis, or else feels "threatened by something while he slept." Apart from such coincidence, however, can the two novels be plausibly glossed by tracking their particular, ethnically specific "cases" after the fashion of Levinas's paradoxically transcendental and exceptionalist model of human relations?

Let me suggest an approach that has the virtue of unifying the texts, and extending, challenging Levinas's work as well. Two obstacles in Levinas's thought, then, would hamper its usefulness for a criticism-as-ethical politics: (1) "particularity" vacillates between difference per se, and *uniqueness*, an ambivalence attesting to Levinas as (generalizing) philosopher, and Levinas as (specific) Jew.[23] (2)"face" is identified not with culturally marked features, but with rather "abstract man disengaged from all culture."[24] The first obstacle is broached in the preceding section. The second I will negotiate by re-emphasizing a point I made in *Narrative Ethics*.[25] If "violence can aim only at a face" – the emblem and core of humanity, the exterior feature that is interiority *par excellence* – then violence that aims at

Black or Jewish faces limns the Black and Jewish masks of humanity, respectively. Racially motivated ethical homicide (in Levinas's sense, "the indifference of 'good conscience' to what is near and what is far"), means the murder done to *black* faces by *white* eyes. The failure, or abrogation of, recognition devolves upon an impaired moral faculty that directly sees, and dehumanizes, faces racially and culturally *particular*. Or, in *The Victim*'s terms:

> Leventhal's figure was burly, his head large, his nose, too, was large. He had black hair, coarse waves of it, and his eyes under their intergrown brows were intensely black and of a size unusual in adult faces . . . . They seemed to disclose an intelligence not greatly interested in its own powers, as if preferring not to be bothered by them, indifferent; and this indifference appeared to be extended to others. He did not look sullen but rather unaccommodating, impassive. (20)

Conventionally, such physiognomic information in fiction is the establishing material of *vraisemblence*.[26] This, the text tells us, is a fully featured "character." Yet, in *The Victim*, Bellow renders faces and face-to-faces with an exactitude, unremarkable in itself perhaps, but gathering piquancy in light of the ambient air of mystification hovering about the plotted circumstances of recognition. *Something* here is flagging our attention.

I say this, fully aware of Bellow's eye for the discrete particular, because this text (whose burden is being "summoned" to account) works *in particular* by soliciting directly *our* looking at its dynamics of looking concentratedly.

> The park was even more crowded than before, and noisy. There was another revivalist band on the corner, and the blare of the two joined confusingly above the other sounds. The lamps were yellowed, covered with flies and moths. On one of the paths an old man, sunburned, sinewy, in a linencap, was shining shoes. The fountain ran with a green, leaden glint. Children in their underclothing waded and rolled in the spray, the parents looking on. Eyes seemed softer than by day, and larger, and gazed at one longer, as though in the dark heat some interspace of reserve had been crossed and strangers might approach one another with a kind of recognition. You looked and thought, at least, that you knew whom you had seen. (Bellow, 31)

Immediately after this description, Kirby Allbee (Leventhal's antagonist in the full classical sense), accosts him. Leventhal muses, "My god, my god, what kind of fish is this? One of those guys who wants you to think they can see to the bottom of your soul." A dance of eyes, faces, and recognitive looks fills out the episode, reaching its acme in the following passage:

> Leventhal grimly looked at him in the light that came through the leaves. He had been spying on him, and the mystery was why! How long had he been keeping watch on him and for what reason – what grotesque reason? Allbee returned his look, examining him as he was examined, in concentration and seriousness . . . And in the loom of these eyes and with the warmth of the man's breath on his face, for they were crowded together on the beach, Leventhal suddenly felt that he had been singled out to be the object of some freakish, insane process, and for an instant he was filled with dread. (36)

Alternative phenomenologies of "the look" can be brought to bear here – as plausibly from, say, Hegel or Sartre or even Goffman, as from Levinas. But, in the context of the notion that "strangers might approach one another with a kind of recognition" – *l'approche du prochain* – and the sensation of being "singled out," what Levinas will call "the subject . . . unseated by a wordless accusation," the recognition scene at this juncture in the text seems nothing short of uncanny . . . as, in truth, Asa observes himself.

> Any derelict panhandler or bum might buttonhole you on the street and say, "The world wasn't made for you any more than it was for me, was it?" The error was to forget that neither man had made the arrangements, and so it was perfectly right to say, "Why pick on me? I didn't set this up any more than you did." Admittedly there was a wrong, a general wrong. Allbee, on the other hand, came along and said, "*You!*" and that was so meaningless. For you might feel that something was owing to the panhandler, but to be directly blamed was entirely different. (77)

In fact, the plot progressively indicates to Leventhal and readers alike that he does bear a certain irrecusable responsibility – that the unfamiliar betrays more than a little familiarity through one of life's inveterate *unheimlich* maneuvers, direct "blame" or not. Irrespective of its xenophobic pressures, life, by definition of its open spaces unsafe from the claims of responsibility, forces a kind of ethical agoraphobia, an always about-to-be-accosted: fingered, touched, faced.

Face-to-face interactions in *If He Hollers Let Him Go* lend themselves to a more flagrant polarization, and in that sense appear more "political" (material? immediate? raw?). But they illustrate only another and analogous kind of agoraphobic, or better, diaspora-phobic, harrowing:

The red light caught me at Manchester; and that made me warm. It never failed; every time I got in a hurry I got caught by every light . . . . When the light turned green it caught a white couple in the middle of the street . . . . But when they looked up and saw we were coloured they just took their time, giving us a look of cold hatred . . . I sat there looking at the white couple until they had crossed the sidewalk giving them stare for stare, hate for hate . . . . My arms were rubbery and my fingers numb; I was weak as if I'd been heaving sacks of cement all day in the sun. (12–13)

Here especially, the ambient pressure of arrest *arrests*: the light *caught* me; it *caught* a white couple. The pained weight of scrutiny (something that Bellow's text also figures), charged and contestatory gazing, is absorbed *into the body*. As in Fanon's repeated motif of specular aversion in "The Fact of Blackness," – "Look, a Negro!; Mama, see the Negro!" – being black in this novel means fundamentally *to be seen* as any face-to-face takes the shape of *stare-for-stare* – swapping looks instead.[27]

Levinas's favored trope marshals its power from the conjoint ethical urgency of speech and vision in the human face, each signifying both entreaty and command. But its peculiar relevance for this novel centers on the way in which faces act as weapons or targets of racism's negative proof (or political corrective) for the ethics of encounter. In the concrete, physiognomic facts of Blackness and Jewishness (or any *particularized* humanity, for that matter), Levinas's transcendental ethics discovers its political objective correlative.[28] Fanon's distinction between antisemitism as an attack on Jewish history, religion, ancestrality and posterity, and white racism's direct focus on black *bodies* on the other – culturism vs. biologism – becomes less tenable when it is the Black or Jewish *face* that is held out for contemplation and consequence.[29]

I have invoked Levinas *thematically* here, borrowing against the rich and capacious pledge of imagery and figure that enriches his argumentation throughout. I take his own ever-more intense drive toward the material content of ethical encounter as legitimation for my own restricted focus on trope and image (admittedly at one remove from the strict sense of Levinasian ethics). Levinas often adverts to the Biblical formula, *hineni* (or "here I am"), *me voici*, – to emphasize what he cleverly terms the "accusative" aspect of subjectivity. Selves assume a place already marked out by obligatedness, and thus occupy an ethical *terminus ad quem*. Instead of the "merely" ethical pointing expressed by *here I am*, however, the stigmatized subjects of Himes's and Bellow's novels might be said to exclaim, rather, *let me go*, a different trope of accusation altogether (which, however, has its own Biblical precedent in an archetypal narrative of bondage and culturally legitimated persecution).

To be protagonist in these texts means to *agonized* and *agorized* – out in the open, the victim of unreasonable and yet unaccountably personalized prejudice.[30] This is not classical but rather the most modern of cultural tragedies: American Jews and African Americans as the objectified subjects in the unreconstructed grammar of racism, trapped ("let him go"), outraged ("if he hollers"), ontologically slotted ("victims").[31] Yet they tell different stories from each other, whatever their points of tangency. The title of Bellow's novel, for example, names no referent, and so it just as plausibly designates Allbee, the text's putative malignity, the sub-plot of Leventhal's sister and dying nephew, and an assortment of urban anonyms all of whom fail to "get away with it" – a bum (33), a peddler (95), a dishwasher (96), a Filipino busboy (119), a dying man on the subway tracks (198).

By contrast, the anonymous third-person "captured" by the title doggerel of *If He Hollers Let Him Go* draws ironic attention to Bob Jones's *singular* non-person double-bind as first-person subject and second-person object alike, in each case the only and unequivocal victim of his story's plot. To paraphrase Bakhtin, since Bob Jones cannot simply be himself, he must cite himself, as much a self-catching as a letting-go. Moreover his very name bespeaks a kind of already-namedness, nondenominational in the sense of totally public property: "Bob Jones" is anybody's name.[32]

> I wanted to tell him I didn't want to go to bed with her, I wanted to black her eyes; but just the idea of her being a white woman stopped me. I felt flustered, caught, guilty. I couldn't realize what was happening to me myself. It was funny in a way. I couldn't tell him that I *didn't* want her because she was a white woman and he was a white man, and something somewhere way back in my mind said that would be an insult. And I couldn't tell that I *did* want her, because the same thing said that that would be an insult.
>
> Every white person I come into contact with, every one I have to speak to, even those I pass on the street – every goddamn one of them has the power of some kind of control over my own behavior. Not only that but they use it – in every way. (Himes, 119, 17)

As the second passage describes a textual dilemma, too – the seizure-like quality of Jones's narrative – the first conveys a communicative paradox from which that same narrative does not remain exempt. Is the narrator's "penning" (to recycle Stanley Cavell's bon mot) release or just another kind of incarceration?[33] The novel's answer is finally equivocal, but of the two texts certainly, *If He Hollers* draws a far bleaker picture of the racialized subject-as-prison-life. Indeed, Himes's novel exhibits racialized social life as, more than apparatus, even *machinery*. This is perhaps the significance of Bob Jones's Buick Roadmaster as the site of so much freedom denied, cabined, cribbed, confined, and the role played by industry in the novel generally – a fact ironically driven home by the very names "Road*master*" and "*leaderman*" (Jones's job title). On the heels of an argument with Alice, for instance, Bob says, "I felt crushed inside as if a car had run over me and left me lying there," (99) capturing perfectly the text's hemmed-in quality – simultaneously external, objectified, machine-powered, and interior, cognitive, in the bones and blood.[34]

Bellow seems to work off of the more broadly Levinasian premise that an indefeasible guilt attaches to selfhood *ab initio*, even though Allbee may assuredly *aim* his violence at Asa's specifically Jewish face. Despite being singled out through or better perhaps, along with, antisemitism, Leventhal comes face to face, with an obligatedness and answerability in excess of it. It is precisely this very polarity of surpluses – the "remainder" of selfhood which is ethnic particularity and the extra weight which is the Other – that defines the thematic tension between both novels, also finding its counterpart in Levinas's philosophy of recognition: the self alienated by *its own* exorbitant otherness from within while still pledged outward.[35]

Towards the pole of "ethical responsibility," then, is where *The Victim* seems to cluster its sequence of events. (Seen against the backdrop of long-standing metaphysical and allegorical veins in American fiction, especially in its play with figures of substitution and doubling, Bellow's novel legitimately sanctions a recourse to the "transcendental" here.) The very first time Allbee descends upon Leventhal, for example, the two fail initially to make contact – conspicuously so:

> He had already taken off his shirt and was sitting on the bed unlacing his shoes when there was a short ring of the bell. Eagerly he pulled open the door and shouted, "Who is it?" The flat was unbearably empty . . . . There was no response below. He called out again, impatiently. (29)[36]

When Asa and Allbee finally meet shortly afterwards in the park, the vector from summoning to facing is drawn and scored: " . . . suddenly he had a feeling that he was not merely being looked at but watched. Unless he was greatly mistaken a man was scrutinizing him, pacing slowly with him as the line moved." (31)

Allbee's second visit even more obviously lays bare the metaphysic of "intrusion" on which the novel can be said to turn:

> "Now who in the name of hell would ring like that?" he said. But he already knew who it was. It was Allbee . . . He knew that he had come in; nevertheless he controlled his desire to turn . . . To enter without a knock or invitation was an intrusion. Of course the door was open, but it was taking too much for granted all the same not to knock. "I *owe* him hospitality, that's how he behaves," passed through his mind. (66)

What the novel rehearses is precisely Leventhal's indemnity, irrespective of any actual impact he may have had on Allbee's life, and the latter's antisemitism – as the text formulates it in its final chapter, "something very mysterious, namely a conviction or illusion that at the start of life, and perhaps even before a promise had been made." (249) Here we learn the significance of Bellow's other epigraph, drawn from *The Thousand and One Nights*, about agency and unforseen consequences, including, perhaps, an intimation of Leventhal's nephew's death later in the story.

But what has happened to the *politics* of recognition? What of the pole of ethnic, racial, religious surplus, of "particularity?" Surely Allbee's antisemitism, its content and motivation, is not incidental to *The Victim*'s "metaphysic of intrusion," its plot of target, pursuit, and capture.

Hollerers

> "I wanted to talk. I didn't think there'd be any physical violence. That's not how you people go about things. Not with violence."

> "Why do you sing such songs?" he said. "*You* can't sing them . . . You have to be bred to them . . . Sing one of the psalms. I'd love to hear it . . . [Or] any Jewish song. Something you've really got feeling for. Sing us the one about the mother."[37]

> "And try to imagine how New York affects me. Isn't it preposterous? It's really as if the children of Caliban were running everything . . . I go into the library once in a while to look around, and last week I saw a book about Thoreau and Emerson by a man named Lipschitz . . . A name like that?" Allbee said

this with great earnestness. "After all, it seems to me that people of such background simply couldn't understand . . . "

"You people, by and large – and this is only an observation, nothing else, take it for what it's worth – you can only tolerate feelings like your own."[38]

Allbee (the name portentously "ontological," or simply an exclamation of surprise) bears down on Leventhal throughout both as the imagined cause of all his misfortune, and as a Jew. The two contingent facts, the accidentally particular and the peculiarly particular, intertwine. Allbee never approaches, reproaches, or designates Leventhal apart from the "stain" of peoplehood. But does the text? What measure does it assign to ethnic difference in its own discomfiting of Leventhal's subjectivity?

Toward an answer, I turn to Chester Himes. The crux of *If He Hollers Let Him Go* involves the extended face-off between Bob Jones and Madge, a white co-worker at the wartime shipyard which the narration inaugurates thus: "face to face with a tall white girl in a leather welder's suit." (19)

> We stood there for an instant, our eyes locked, before either of us moved; then she deliberately put on a frightened, wide-eyed look and backed away from me as if she was scared stiff, as if she was a naked virgin and I was King Kong. It wasn't the first time she had done that. I'd run into her on board a half-dozen times during the past couple of weeks and each time she'd put on that scared-to-death act . . . But now it sent a blinding fury through my brain. Blood rushed to my head like gales of rain and I felt my face burn white-hot. It came up in my eyes and burned at her; she caught it and kept staring at me with that wide-eyed phoney look. Something about her mouth touched it off, a quirk made the curves change as if she got a sexual thrill, and her mascaraed eyelashes fluttered. Lust shook me like an electric shock; it came up in my mouth, filling it with tongue, and drained my whole stomach down into my groin . . . When she turned out of my stare I went sick to the stomach and felt like vomiting. I had started toward the ladder going to the upper deck, but instead I turned past her, slowing down and brushing her. She didn't move. I kept on going, circling. (19)

Behind the lurid and hard- or pot-boiled style[39] (though sexualization of racial difference is hardly unimportant here), Himes has warped Levinas's "rectitude" of the face-to-face relation in a very interesting way: *the face* has become *the look*. The rules of engagement cede to the rules of performance.

The scene of recognition, in other words, overtly dramatizes its always-latent potential for theatricality. And with the novel's "investment in performance," a dimension of the text neither "ethical" nor "political" (though potentially both) merits a discussion in its own right – as, will in turn, be the case for Bellow's novel. Several pages after the passage above, the narrator and his new nemesis square off once again:

> She had her back to me and her hood up so it covered her hair, so I didn't recognize her right off . . . . I saw that she was the big, peroxide blonde I'd run into on the third deck earlier; and I knew the instant I recognized her that she was going to perform then – we would both perform. (27)

Needless to say, the story-length performance that follows, together with whole-cast enactment, obeys its scripted instructions to the letter. Madge says the magic words expressly countermanding the Torah injunction against murder (even when such homicide is "ethical" or "merely" discursive): "'I ain't gonna work with no nigger!' she said in a harsh, flat voice."

The novel's deliberately, extravagant, p(l)ot boils over as Jones is eventually arrested for a non-rape he and Madge "perform" through anticipatory scenes. (As Fanon, an admirer of the novel, puts it in *Black Skin, White Masks*, "So it is with the character in *If He Hollers Let Him Go* – who does precisely what he did not want to do."[40]) Institutionality, finally, plays its part in the denouement. Bob Jones gets "escorted" from dockside labor to Armed Service in a more sinister sense of being "let go," this last development already hinted by the text at its beginning when Jones, reflecting on the recent internment of Japanese-Americans, says,

> It was taking a man up by the roots and locking him up without a chance. Without a trial. Without a charge. Without even giving him a chance to say one word. It was thinking about if they ever did that to me, Robert Jones, Mrs. Jones's dark son, that started to get me scared. (3)

And thus even the novel's narrative thrust knowingly *performs* itself, telegraphing, predicting, and driving towards its inevitable ending. Written on the heels of *Native Son* (Bob Jones even refers to Wright's novel in the text), *If He Hollers Let Him Go* flaunts a whole repertoire of signifyin(g), sending itself up as it sends its lead character down. No wonder, then, that each of the text's five units of actions begins with dreaming, the rest of the plot in the service of the narrator's *dreamwork*, the hard realities of racial prejudice literaturized, fictioned from within and from the start. The programmatic link between the talk of race on the one hand, and the performance of "race" on the other is also isolated by Bellow.

"Good acting is what is exactly human," says a character in *The Victim* in a classic Bellovian moment of casual profundity.[41] Later, Leventhal reapplies this maxim to the exigencies of his own situation: "he liked to think 'human' meant accountable in spite of many weaknesses – at the last moment, tough enough to hold." (That the stage for the nostrum above is a diner in which are gathered for the only time in the text, a "roundtable" of Jewish personalities, may suggest a measure of ironic distance. But the seriousness of inquiry here, however conversational, and however it entangles the topics of acting and antisemitism, is not meant to be taken lightly.)

Indeed, Bellow's novel trades just as often as Himes's does on recurrent metaphors of acting and performance. (A plot development involves Leventhal's attempt to get Allbee hired by a talent scout, an ensemble discussion of acting takes place at the text's dead-center, and the story ends with a recognition-scene in a theater, where Leventhal re-encounters Allbee on the arm of a "famous actress.") And much like the coupled pair in *If He Hollers*, Leventhal and Allbee subtend degrees of facing with angles of masking – all of it intensely physical.

> . . . Leventhal remarked to himself that there was an element of performance in all that [Allbee] was doing. But suddenly he had a strange, close consciousness of Allbee, of his face and body, a feeling of intimate nearness . . . he could nearly feel the weight of his body and the contact of his clothes. Even more, the actuality of his face, loose in the cheeks, firm in the forehead and jaws, struck him, the distinctness of it; and the look of recognition Allbee bent on him duplicated the look in his own. (Bellow, 144)

The dream-sequence shortly thereafter underscores this: "He had an unclear dream in which he held himself off like an unwilling spectator; yet it was he who did everything." (150)

As to how performativity plays out for each text, one might make the following provisional distinction. Where *The Victim* seems to leaven its quotient of acting with a margin of Bellow's characteristic humanist-realism, *If He Hollers Let Him Go* seems almost entirely circumscribed within its reflexive and contrived "theater" of race-relations. Plot, structure, and discourse in Himes all fan out from the defining matrix of a Racial Imaginary. Conversely, alongside all the talk of actors and the various performing duets in Bellow, a stabilizing arena of action, will, and choice seems to identify itself on the horizon: what the text calls variously, the meeting of payments, a being accountable (139), a being required in one's own non-exchangeable selfhood (172), and if not a running of things (255) then a minimal ability to manage, bear, and perhaps repair or even redeem them. There can be located the novel's investment in a moral talk above any talk of race – "acting" as human action.

Such pronouncements usually take the shape of Leventhal's inner thought, but also appear in scenes of dialogue. In either case, Bellow seems to intend the memorable conceits and formulations found there to be noted, underlined, and presumably cited as the text's detachable, epigrammatic, and thus self-sustaining feature. By comparison, what should we make of the following abstracted moment in *If He Hollers Let Him Go*, when Bob Jones's girlfriend, like some Bellow character in a "serious" moment, holds forth?

> And there are many other values that you are not taking into consideration – spiritual values, intrinsic values, which are also fundamental components of our lives. Honesty, decency, respectability. Courage – it takes courage to live as a Negro must. Virtue is our own, to nurture or destroy. After all, darling these are the important things in life. These things that are within us that make us what we are. And we can control them. (169)

This *sounds* like the language of a set piece, like some of Bellow's "wisdom literature," and yet it falls completely flat. A few pages later, when Jones, rejuvenated in the drive to strive, repossessed of the calmness to be simply the neutral, colorless entity suggested by his ever-so-average name, says "Big tough world, but I got you beat now, I thought exultantly. *Peace, Father, it is truly wonderful*," (172) we don't hear so much a resemblance to Leventhal's "tough enough to hold," as a kind of hollow echo of it. These are burlesques of the vocabulary of Will or Moral Decision or Equanimity, something meant to be subsumed by theatrics, not "get away" from it. Himes's refuses the consolation Bellow's finds in *drama* of an earnest, high-minded sort. His face-to-face world inscribes itself wholly within a world of *social acting*, a world of *personae* – Levinas's self-doubled or allegorical selves. Bellow's, conversely, makes acting a greater good, a model for humanity.[42]

The face-to-face, pace Levinas, is not solely an ethical relation. However differing in tropes of performance, Himes's and Bellow's novels can both be pushed toward a common thematic of recognition calling for an ethical-cum-political analysis as well. Faces – and most especially those faces distinguished in some way, by, say, racial or religious characteristics – to the degree that they are "presented," *perform* rather than simply *manifest* themselves. Supplying a pragmatic deficit in Levinas's social phenomenology, Erving Goffman's frame analysis, for example, would isolate here precisely those particularized features of human encounter Levinas takes pains to bracket: the agoraphobic, "anti-ethical," devices of self masking that cushion or keep at bay the neighbor's *proximity*, his *approach*. Performance, in short, may bleed into a politics (ethics hovering above) after all.

"A being is that which reveals itself in its truth, and, at the same time, resembles itself, is its own image,"[43] writes Levinas, speaking of the shadow that continually haunts personal identity. An external film of semblance (that is, both resemblance and dissembling) laminates the baseline level of signification – selfhood that is answerable, *prima facie* in itself, to others. This is the wardrobe clothing the "nudity" of the face. In a companion essay, Levinas writes,

> The absolute nakedness of a face, the absolutely defenseless face, without covering, clothing, or mask, is what opposes my power over it, my violence, and opposes it in an absolute way, with an opposition which is opposition in itself. The being that expresses itself, that faces me, says *no* to me by his very expression . . . . The face is the fact that a being affects us not in the indicative, but in the imperative, and is thus outside all categories.[44]

All of Levinas's philosophy is devoted to the ethical epiphany of un-masking, of showing forth, of facing. If *exposure* defines contact with the Other, then, conversely, a sort of *double-exposure* describes the ambiguous nature of identity left to its own devices. And yet here, too, we encounter the faces in Himes and Bellow as the political object lesson for ethical transcendence in human relations. For in *The Victim* and *If He Hollers Let Him Go*, to be seen or addressed or pursued as a "jew" or a "nigger" is to be ineluctably double-exposed.

The ethics of imperative intersubjectivity do not always (perhaps never fully) transcend the specificity of this or that person "culturally" singled-out, the person who has no choice but to speak in the indicative of "an Asiatic" cast or a "flat-nosed, thick-lipped" mien. By being "Black" or "Jewish" faces, in other words, Bob Jones's and Asa Leventhal's are *thematized*, allegorized from within. Double-exposure, double-talk, double consciousness: these represent the shadow-graphs limning a politics of recognition, where James

Weldon Johnson's famous phrase, "the freemasonry of race," under-scores the masque or performance aspect that (in Levinas's sense) turns the ethnic or racial subject into an allegory of itself, into its own image, into the "remainder of selfhood." Differently put (paraphrasing *The Victim*), for the literature of ethnic entrapment, *acting – good or bad, willed or forced – is what is exactly Black or Jewish*. Both novels invite witness of ethno-racial identity and ethno-racial consciousness as inevitably scripted matters for rehearsal and acting out. Bellow's does so implicitly through its contrastive and on-going sub-plot involving the death of Leventhal's nephew, etching hard-edged catastrophe and responsibility, [45] Himes's by never "letting it go" for a moment.

Brooches

In his analysis of contemporary French Jewish identity, *The Imaginary Jew*, Alain Finkielkraut says that for a certain segment of "Jewish romantics these days . . . the word 'Jew' is worn like a brooch on a dark gray suit,"[46] a wonderful turn on identity as adornment that sharply resonates with the bric-a-brac of face and recognition cram-ming the texts of *The Victim* and *If He Hollers Let Him Go* like so much make-up overapplied – like so much allegory. Finkielkraut's Imagin-ary resonates well with the pathological (or at least exaggeratedly psychological) feature of each novel. In Himes's text, Bob Jones suf-fers as much as a prisoner of his own bad dreams and a penchant for almost intestinal self-ulceration, as of institutionalized race prejudice, and in Bellow's, Leventhal keeps seeing the specter of his dead mother's "insanity" wherever he looks. Imagination – quintessential private property blends inescapably into various Imaginaries – pub-lic, ethical-politicized space. Thus, the following *made-up faces*:

> [Leventhal] was on a boardwalk . . . . On his left, there was an amusement park with ticket booths . . . . He entered a place that resembled a hotel . . . but proved to be a department store. He was here to buy some rouge for Mary. The salesgirl demon-strated various shades on her own face, wiping each off in turn with a soiled hand towel and bending to the round mirror on the counter to draw a new spot. There was a great, empty glitter of glass and metal around them. What could this possibly be about? Leventhal wondered. (245)

Or, as rendered by Himes in the climactic rape-masquerade:

> *"Help! Help! My God, help me! Some white man, help me! I'm being raped."* I saw the stretch and pop of her lips, the tautening of her

throat muscles, the distortion and constriction of her face . . . as if her face were ten feet high . . . . My [own] eyes felt as if they were five times their natural size; as if they were bursting in their sockets, popping out of my head. *"Stop, nigger! Don't, nigger. Nigger, don't. Oh, please don't kill me, nigger."* (183)

Like a brooch on a dark gray suit.

At the end of Bellow's novel, Leventhal is redescribed: " . . . his obstinately unrevealing expression had softened. His face was paler and there were some gray hairs in his hair, in spite of which he looked years younger," the same chapter where the assignment of place in life is called a "promise" that is either a "conviction or illusion." The text continues,

> In thinking of this promise, Leventhal compared it to a ticket, a theater ticket. And with his ticket, a man entitled to an average seat might feel too shabby for the dress circle or sit in it defiantly or arrogantly; another, entitled to the best in the house, might cry in rage to the usher who led him to the third balcony. And how many more stood disconsolately in the rain and snow, in the long line of those who could only expect to be turned away? But no, this was incorrect. The reality was different. For why should tickets, mere tickets, be promised if promises were being made – tickets to desirable and undesirable places? There were more important things to be promised. (249)[47]

I take the liberty of inflecting this metaphor – already grounded in the theatrical – towards the Levinasian. Tickets produce the "illusion" that inescapably accompanies "conviction." They present the evidence-checkpoint of objectified surface that interrupts otherwise unimpeded passage. They force therefore a kind of occlusion of depth. They signify "a glass darkly" anterior to any promise of "face-to-face." Pop-eyes, thick lips, and big nose – "mere feature" – act as sentries before the "absolute nakedness of a face without covering, clothing, or mask." And as in Kafka, further entry is denied where some faces are concerned.

For Levinas, the face speaks, and says "NO." But it more typically says "jew me, sue me, kick me, kike me"[48] or "catch a nigger by the toe" or "You Jews" or "Nigger!," and "even Negroes" (from Kazin) or "scrubbing 'Goldberg's' floor" (from Claude Brown). Even language can fail the test of transparency, carrying with it the places it has been.

Recognition in Bellow's and Himes's novels shows how and where the ostensibly transcendent encounter between two human faces trips over particularity – the particularity of group identity as well as the particularity of ritualized social behavior. That *If He Hollers Let Him Go* acts out its rituals of recognition in the shadow of the Homefront during World War Two, and Bellow's against the backdrop of the Holocaust also emphasizes the particularity of cultural moments, of historical revelations. In Levinas's terms, while the ethnic or racial face may indeed affect us in the imperative, it does so *within*, not outside of, categories, categories often as linguistic as they are visual, and constrained by history at the very moment they challenge such constraint. Hence, finally, the paradox of transcendent visage "sealed in blackness" (Fanon's phrase) that receives its logical extension at the end of *If He Hollers Let Him Go*, where *hollering* means precisely to be *caught*, and both transpire in real, historical time.

> "Wait, I'll let you in," I shouted above the din. "Wait, this woman is crazy!" . . . A guy leaned over the hole and swung at my head with a ballpeen hammer . . . I saw the guy's face, not particularly malevolent, just disfigured, a white man hitting at a nigger running by. I hadn't even tried to rape her. I'd been trying to get away from her . . . She'd kept me there, cornered me, hadn't let me go. I'd wanted to go but she hadn't let me. (184)

In the next chapter, we *face* head on being caught in and by historical time, and the seam or crack thereby opened up between history and fiction.

3

"Words generally spoil things" and "Giving a man final say": facing history in David Bradley and Philip Roth

> He wonders also about himself – that he cannot learn to forget, but hangs on to the past: however far or fast he runs, that chain runs with him. It is a matter for wonder: the moment that is here and gone, that was nothing before and nothing after, returns like a specter to trouble the quiet of a later moment.
> Friedrich Nietzsche, *The Use and Abuse of History*

> Submitting history as a whole to judgment, exterior to the very wars that mark its end restores to each instant its full signification in that very instant; all causes are ready to be heard. It is not the last judgment that is decisive, but the judgment of all the instants in time, when the living are judged.　　　　　　Emmanuel Levinas, *Totality and Infinity*

Question: when does an "incident" coincide with an "operation?" Answer: when a free and unreconstructed event in human experience gets smuggled and/or indentured into plot. Differently put, History entails Reconstruction, as Reconstruction, in some part at least, requires Fabulation.

Late in his narrative – after having previously defined "incident" as fact simply stated, "apparently free of any cause" (223) – the narrator-cum-historian-protagonist of David Bradley's *The Chaneysville Incident* appeals to Newtonian principles of causality to frame such apparent freedom in new perspective:

> ... every event has a preceding cause and a proceeding effect. To that assumption there are two major corollaries. First, that every event was discrete: separate and, given sufficient accuracy of measuring instruments, separately visible from both cause and effect. (In historical terms, this means that it occurs at a specific point in time, that it can be dated – that it is, in other words, an

incident.) Second, that while cause and effect might appear to be broad, vague, and diffuse entities, they are, in face, vectors: the sum total (in terms of both magnitude and direction) of a very large number (possibly an infinite number) of events – or incidents. (264)[1]

Near the end of his account, "Philip Roth,"[2] the narrator-cum-novelist-protagonist of *Operation Shylock*, pinpoints the fictionalizing impulse that underwrites plotting in art and in life, setting each in uncomfortable proximity to the other:

> [Y]ou begin to speculate, and to speculate with any scope requires a principled disregard for the confining conventions: a gambler's taste for running a risk, a daring to tamper with the taboo . . . You make mistakes. You overdo and underdo and doggedly follow an imaginative line that yields nothing. Then something creeps in, an arguably stupid detail, a ridiculous gag, an embarrassingly bald ploy, and this opens out into the significant action that makes the mess an *operation*, rounded, pointed, structured, yet projecting the illusion of having been as spontaneously generated, as coincidental, untidy, and improbably probable as life . . . [3]

Roth's work is subtitled "a confession"; Bradley (no less ambiguously), calls his "a novel." The former ends with a note to the reader disclaiming any veracity:

> " . . . names, characters, places, and incidents either are products of the author's imagination or are used fictitiously. Any resemblance to actual events or locales or persons, living or dead, is entirely coincidental. This confession is false." (298).

Chaneysville begins with a similar disclaimer, referring to itself as a "work of historical reconstruction," whose characters "are products of the author's imagination . . . any resemblance to persons living or dead [being] purely coincidental."

Otherwise markedly different enterprises, both novels run closely parallel, even perhaps intersect, at the level of the non-coincidental – or, of the cooperational – inasmuch as each is haunted throughout by the defining presence of cultural tragedy, the European *Shoah* for Roth, and American slavery for Bradley. Both, accordingly, take their bearings from History as a magnetic north of the Real, coordinating their own plots under the shadow of pre-existing, even institutionalized masterplots.

Chimes can be rung, as I have said, between the unlikeliest of textual antiphones, and it would not be difficult to do so with *Oper-*

ation Shylock and *The Chaneysville Incident*. But, taking my cue from Bradley, if we think of facile congruences as governed by a certain workmanlike logic, and "faced texts" as betokening something more nuanced, more thaumaturgic (since "the difference between logical cause and effect and magic is only a matter of which premises are chosen" [Bradley, 204]), then this chapter elects the more imaginative option, factoring its two texts into a sum different from, if not greater than, its parts.

That sum uses the following multipliers: (1) the allegorical quality of fiction when it smuggles history into its plots; (2) the resulting mimetic echo-effect when narrators undergo authorial trials of ordeal; (3) the multiple levels of reflexivity these two textual conditions seem to incite; and finally, (4) the diverse stakes for recognition that ensue. The reading of one text *through* the other produces a composite, bifold story of recognition that neither novel separately on its own fully tells.

Where these texts are concerned, my book's recurrent focus on recognition specifies the ancillary principle to the theory of selfhood ventured by *Operation Shylock*: that "a self should contain contending subselves, and that these subselves should themselves be constructed of subselves." (152) Yet selves just as inescapably open onto macro-selves, the engirdling constellations of group identity and cultural lineage. In both novels the authorial self is doubled, allegorized by like- and anti-selves, father and brother figures who bestow the mixed blessings of cultural legacy. John Washington and "Philip Roth" suffer, in Friedrich Nietzsche's phrase, from "an excess of history"; each in his own way lacks what the philosopher calls "the veil of the unhistorical."[4]

Think of this dilemma of superaddition as a certain *tax* on representation, representation in its twin sense of rendered image and collective identity. What Roth's and Bradley's novels teach is the legislative force of the no-representation-without-taxation rule for fiction: to tell, to retell, to invoke, to depict, to trace, to impersonate, to typify, to represent, all cause the solitary self to orbit *around* itself. Thrust outward, that self becomes vulnerable to history, and operated on by the gravity of kinship. As Roth has said of the polyvalent tax which is circumcision, "There is no way around it: you enter history through my history and me."[5]

"My history" for African America signifies the three-hundred year history of slave trade and slavery, and its aftermath of continuing legal and social inequity. For most American Jews, "my history" opens out onto the two-thousand year narrative of dispersion onto foreign lands culminating in the extermination of a third of the world's Jewish population and the founding of the Israeli state. When measured objectively and comprehensively from a distance, my history becomes History as datum. Represented otherwise – experientially, memorially, ritually – it becomes History as a consolidating narrative.

Yet communal traditions do not, of a surety, provide a redoubt for personal identity, as I intimated earlier in my Introduction; they do not, as *The Chaneysville Incident* puts it, have "final say." The self, particularly the writing or narrating self, if only deceptively, floats free, which is why I yoke historiography and storification together above to parallel the way incidents, sufficiently accreted, seem to promise operations. It also explains the brief detour in my analysis from one bifold to another – Toni Morrison's *Beloved* and Cynthia Ozick's *The Shawl* – for insight into the problem of literary fiction's relationship to history. The pivot point between these coupled pairs will be a small one, a minor character drawn from Roth's novel. For the loom and limits of recognition, however, that character's allegorical status looms large, and assigns limits of its own. In order to show what incidents and operations mean concretely, however, and to prepare the ground for allegory's positive face as the axis of fiction and history, I turn to this chapter's primary texts, beginning with Philip Roth.

The loom of recognition

1. Roth

Embedded at the core of *Operation Shylock* is a hardened irritant (or pearl) of facticity, a current event (incident) that refers back to historical operations from the past, and conjures them. The exchanges in chapter 9 from the 1988 trial in Jerusalem of John Demjanjuk for "crimes against humanity" in the Treblinka death camp in 1942 to 1943, consist of verbatim transcripts from that very trial. The Holocaust does not merely inform Roth's novel; it speaks in its own voice from inside it.[6]

But *Operation Shylock* does not pretend to fictionalized history; rather, it is "confession," arguably the most involuted entry in Roth's long-standing novelistic project of reflexivity. In this book, that reflexivity means, on the one hand, the peril of "Me-itis. Microcosmosis.

Drowning in the tiny tub of yourself," (55) and, on the other, the threat of "being extricated from one implausible plot of someone else's devising to be intimidated into being an actor in yet another." (345) Even these dangers of impersonation had already been pre-qualified by Roth's 1988 "novelist's autobiography," *The Facts*, where his own authorial alter-ego Nathan Zuckerman tells him,

> Your gift is not to personalize your experience but to personify it, to embody it in the representation of a person who is not yourself. You are not an autobiographer, you're a personifica-tor.[7]

As the labile writing self, so his lubricious fiction: "this unremitting ... conversion of the facts into something else," (232) in terms drawn from *The Counterlife*. Philip Roth is not Aharon Appelfeld, and accordingly, modern Jewish history does not figure for him as a topic in its own right, but rather as backdrop for the vicissitudes of selfhood and fiction-making, those "worlds where everything is words," (149) and "everything is allegory." (215)[8]

Roth might thus stand incriminated in his own work of reducing even history – terrible, tragic history – to the tiny tub of the self, laving it with "*Pipikism*, the antitragic force that inconsequentializes everything, trivializes everything, superficializes everything, our suffering as Jews not excluded," (389) diluting it with the "storification of everyday life." (231) In a novel with so many weeping men, and so many sons overshadowed by their fathers, with penile implants and fellatio as occasional comic relief, are we really that far from *Portnoy*?

But consider the following chapter-headings: "A Life Not My Own," "The Uncontrollability of Real Things," "Forgery, Paranoia, Disinformation, Lies," "Words Generally Spoil Things." We are in the realm of the irritant here. Loss or surrender of control begin and end this novel's plot; talk remains tyrannical throughout. "Roth" speaks of succumbing to the instinct for impersonation and stepping outside responsibility to be appropriated the unforeseen. (358) But the novel keeps circling back to Demjanjuk, to history (one thinks of the cautionary fate in *Invisible Man* of "plunging outside history"[9]), and to a different kind of appropriation altogether.

For example, the Palestinian trial scene in Ramallah that doubles for the Demjanjuk trial in Jerusalem in chapter 5 is one of the novel's seemingly endless series of reflexive tableaus. "Roth" finds himself confronted here with the agitprop analogy of Nazis and the Israeli military, and responds accordingly: "Nazis didn't break hands. They engaged in industrial annihilation of human beings. They made a manufacturing process of death." (142) "Please," he admonishes, "no metaphors where there is recorded history!" The "representative" Roth momentarily stepping away from the "representing" Roth? A rebuke to the limits of fiction, even his own?

What these examples suggest for me – in conjunction with Bradley's text – is that the dangers of mimesis Roth's novel displays do not confine themselves predictably to text. They summon history as well. If "Roth" is overwritten or himself "plotted" in this novel, modern Jewish history has as much a role to play as the now de rigueur Rothian gift for self-transformation, "the slipping irresponsibly in and out of 'I'." (*The Counterlife*, 210) In *The Counterlife*, to the thesis of the Diaspora as Jewish abnormality, Roth posed the antithesis of quotidian American Jewish normalcy: that by "that flourishing mundanely in the civility and security of South Orange," one makes "Jewish history no less astonishing" than the early Zionists'. (146)

In *Operation Shylock*, he offers instead "the ideology of Diasporism," the dialectical double of Herzl's plan for a Jewish state, this time in reverse, a resettlement of Ashkenazi Israelis in their original countries of origin, averting a "second Holocaust" engineered by Arabs, and repatriating Jews to "ancestral Jewish Europe" in the bargain.

> . . . it's *not* a revolution I'm proposing, it's a *retroversion*, a turning back, the very thing Zionism itself once was. You go back to the crossing point and cross back the other way . . . Zionism went back to the crossing point of the dispersion – Diasporism goes back to the crossing point of *Zionism*. (158)

The utopian reaction-formation to utopian reaction-formation. *The Counterlife*'s "construction of a counterlife that is one's own antimyth" doubled back on itself, yet driven by exactly the same impulse, "a species of fabulous utopianism, a manifesto for human transformation."[10] Levinsky postmodernized, as evinced by the following, which deposits Irving Berlin farther outside the cultural "pale" than Abraham Cahan could ever have imagined at *his* novel's conclusion:

> The radio was playing "Easter Parade," and I thought, But this is Jewish genius on a par with the Ten Commandments. God gave Moses the Ten Commandments and then He gave to Irving Berlin "Easter Parade" and "White Christmas." Easter he turns into a fashion show and Christmas into a holiday about snow. *He turns their religion into schlock* . . . Bing Crosby replaces Jesus as the beloved Son of God, and the Jews, the *Jews*, go around

whistling about Easter. And is that so disgraceful a means of defusing the enmity of centuries?(157).[11]

The problem with all this fabulous utopianism, of course, as *Operation Shylock* incisively demonstrates, is that "this is not even literature, let alone politics, this is a fable and a fairy tale." For all "Roth's" half-serious protestations to the contrary, neither a Jewish Americanism nor a Diasporism ever gets safely past *Shylockism*, the checkpoint after the crossing point where Jew meets antisemite, which in this novel marks the site of the Holocaust and goes by the countername "Demjanjuk." But I will use this nexus as a crossing point instead to David Bradley, and *The Chaneysville Incident*.

2. Bradley

Incidents, sufficiently massed, border on the realm of operations, a potentially malignant source of espionage which John Washington, the narrator of Bradley's novel holds in doubt if not contempt. For in his view, "[t]ruly efficient societies conceal the true natures of the operations, motivations, and goals of all but the most minor institutions . . . " (6) Operation or operationality, in this sense, merely expands the contours, and broadens the value it assumes in Roth's novel, a still largely covert structuration of facts and actions, rounded, pointed, but also, like life's "natural course," improbably probable.

Ironically or not, what John Washington does professionally has an oddly symbiotic relation to the very target of his critique. As historian, he plays the role of operative to culture's clandestine institutionality, "trying to find out where the lies are" in the making (and collateral unmaking) of history. "I specialize in the study of atrocities." . . . History is one long string of atrocities . . . "You could say history is atrocious. The best way to find out what they did is to find out where they hid the bodies." (186)

And in imaginatively reconstructing his father's passing at a gravesite of ancestral fugitive-slaves at novel's end, he makes good on his word. As the criminal requires his detective, so history conjures the historiographer, each maneuvered in identically double-tracked fashion. Each is possessed by "excess"; each undergoes a transference. Indeed, tracking supplies both the text's methodology and its topic, a process of self-doubling and reiteration that constitute the Newtonian analogue to *The Counterlife*'s relativist "nightmare about the return of a usurping self." (Roth, 29)

In what follows, Washington implicitly collocates woodcraft and his own brand of historiography as parallel exercises of sense and sensibility:

> . . . to bring my own breathing under control; to be methodical; to accept my limitations and compensate. I could not move quietly, but I could stand quietly and watch and listen, and when he came back for me, as he always did, I could sense him. I learned to reconstruct the man from the subtle whisper of cloth on cloth, the tiny clink of a buckle. (44)[12]

In *The Chaneysville Incident*, unlike Roth's text, the returning self is generational, his usurpation a species of patrimony, his return being the assumption of history as personal responsibility. I will have more to say about the crucial role played by tracking in *The Chaneysville Incident* but first, I treat with John Washington and "Philip Roth" as seriously as they would wish – not just as a historian and a novelist, but as theorists of history.

3. Foucault and Nietzsche

Fleshed out by Bradley, Washington comes across as more than learned enough to have digested recent meta-history on the order of Michel Foucault's *L'Archeologie du Savoir* or Nietzsche's *The Use and Abuse of History*, let alone Hayden White. But in any event, he epitomizes the task facing Foucault's archaeologist of knowledge in the traditional sense:

> to "memorize" the *monuments* of the past, transform them into *documents*, and lend speech to those traces which, in themselves, are often not verbal, or which say in silence something other than what they actually say . . . [13]

The world of documentation is coterminous and complicit with the world of operationality, and can be as mercantile in its disposition of monumental history, as operations, the sentimentalized atrocity kind as well as the "Shylock" kind, can be with incidents. Friedrich Nietzsche, whom Foucault has certainly read, regards both as species of historical "abuse": a failure to *forget*, to live *unhistorically*, to turn the past to the uses of the present.

Whereas Foucault distinguishes between silent markers of the past (monuments) and inert commentary on them (documents), "the raw stuff of history: handwritten autobiography, drafts, day-by-day journals", (222) *The Chaneysville Incident* suggests that history can itself be *monumentalized*, and just as fetishistically displaced through a mass of historicizing documentation. Where Nietzsche will ascribe to the "historical sense" a capacity to "overgrow and work harm," as opposed to a culture's or individual's "plastic power [to] assimilate the digest the past, however foreign, and turn it into sap," (Nietzsche, 7) Bradley's novel culminates in a fire-ceremony of historical record-as-burnt offering.[14] Either way, the discrete and frequently atrocious incidents of history seem to have rematerialized within a totalizing machinery of operations.

In John Washington's terms now, even if "the truth is usually in the footnotes, not in the headlines," (345) even if the end of the trail consists of a routine notation followed by a period – "and sometimes you don't even get periods" (367) – even if events can be painstakingly tracked, mapped, and trapped: even if all of this applies, unless historical reconstruction involves a living into, and a being *lived by* the incidents themselves, it fails signally as history. For it fails as storytelling.

> And then I began to think about what a man's dying really means: his story is lost. Bits and pieces of it remain, but they are all secondhand tales and hearsay, or cold official records that preserve the facts and spoil the truth . . . Funeral eulogies become laudatory biography, which becomes critical biography, which becomes history, which means everyone will know the facts even if no one knows the truth. But the gaps in the stories of the unknown are never filled, never can be filled, for they are larger than deduction, larger than induction. Sometimes an attempt is made to fill them: some poor unimaginative fool, calling himself a historian but really only a frustrated novelist, comes along and tries to put it all together. And fails. (48)

To turn once again to Foucault, at the end of his careful introduction to *The Archaeology of Knowledge*, he does a peculiar thing. He abandons academic discourse and speaks like a frustrated novelist, in his "own" voice, rehearsing the standard philippics against Foucault the mystagogue only to neutralize those very accusations through the following apologia (in quotation marks in the original):

> "What, do you imagine that I would take so much trouble and so much pleasure in writing, do you think that I would keep so persistently to my task, if I were not preparing – with a rather shaky hand – a labyrinth into which I can venture, in which I can move my discourse, opening up underground passages, forcing it to go far from itself, finding overhangs that reduce and deform

its itinerary, in which I can lose myself and appear at last to eyes that I will never have to meet again. I am no doubt not the only one who writes in order to have no face. Do not ask who I am and do not ask me to remain the same: leave it to our bureaucrats and our police to see that our papers are in order. At least spare us their morality when we write." (17)

The provocative image of facelessness arrests all by itself. But more potently, Foucault's authorial puissance here, at once assertive and covert, is key because it stands as a summary statement to a theory of history, because of its declaration of autonomy from conventional morality, and not least because it resembles the respective personae of novelist-writer "Roth" and historian-writer Washington.

Each writer (or speaker) in each text prepares labyrinths and opens up underground passages, has his itinerary deformed, loses himself from time to time. Neither, however, unlike the far more safely ensconced Foucault, is spared morality, his own let alone that of others. In *The Chaneysville Incident*, the voice Foucault diffidently waves away belongs to Washington's lover, duly distanced in the text by being assigned to the wrong race (white) and, for the narrator, dubious gender:

> "I realized that you hide things, [John]. Not just some things; everything. You don't even think; you just hide them. You've got a big lead vault in your head and you put things in it. If there's anything you haven't figured down to the last quarter inch, anything you haven't torn to pieces a hundred times, you keep it there. And if there's something you never understand in there, it will stay; nobody else will ever see it." (260)

Insofar as *The Chaneysville Incident* consists of first-person narration, however, little if anything would appear to be hidden from readers.

In *Operation Shylock*, that voice held at a distance is more general, but still close to home:

> Jews who found me guilty of the crime of "informing" had been calling me to be "responsible" from the time I began publishing in my middle twenties . . . I hadn't chosen to be a writer, I announced, only to be told by others what was permissible to write. The writer redefined the permissible. *That* was the responsibility. Nothing need hide itself in fiction. (377)

"Roth" finds that his text itself forces him up against such redefinition and the selective responsibility that motivates it. Fiction, that is, creates facings even when it seeks to avoid them. And even if *lived* history and story become transitive, enlivening, warming acts for both men – for "if you cannot imagine, you can discover only cold facts, and more cold facts" (Bradley, 146) – novelist and historian discover accidental answerabilities, the kind only not having a face succeeds in evading. Each of the two authors, too, pits his writing against not simply interrogative and interrogating voices – the judgment of easy and often self-deceived transparency – but also the everyday world as one already overwritten by history and fiction, a world beckoning re-narration, a world where everything can be words, everything allegory.

In both writer-protagonist's cases, what this kind of tension between concealment and revelation is *not* is Nietzschean "forgetfulness," "unhistory," the rebellion against the "tyranny of the actual." (Nietzsche, 54) After American slavery and the Holocaust, it becomes too late to transcend history (the "superhistorical" modality) or forget it by "drawing a limited horizon round oneself" (the "unhistorical" modality). Indeed, both novels trump Nietzsche and Foucault as theories about history in their pained awareness that "oneself" is simply a luxury, and even worse, bad fiction.

"Only strong personalities can endure history; the weak are extinguished by it" (32) trumpets Nietzsche. As a species of *anti-genealogy*, this necessitates the refusal not just of "morality" or "history" as dictated by the past, but of kinship, of the self othered from without *and* within. Neither "Roth" nor Washington can afford such loneliness. Historical consciousness for them, however ironic or artful, means the cumulative debris like Benjamin's angel faces, propelled *backward* into the future, looking "toward the obscurity ahead."[15] What elevates the historical sense in *Operation Shylock* and the *Chaneysville Incident* alike, is their twin allegiance to allegory, and to the burden of material things.[16]

Hence, the burden of narration in each novel, what Bradley's calls *story*, and Roth's, *storification*, a nonNietzschean, nonFoucaultian alternative to the use and abuse of history and a choice between monuments or documents. In Bradley's case, that burden assumes the shape of orally and generationally transmitted tales, history as a passing-on which transcends that other category of passing-on which is mortality. (The one meaning of "passed" *The Chaneysville Incident* purposefully eschews – incidentally – is that of "overwith," for *history* means something which, as the novel puts it, still discomfitingly perdures, something which continually "goes on" in and around us, something we can't "plunge outside of" since we are already immersed in it.)[17]

In *Operation Shylock*, on the other hand, storytelling means *harangue*, one narrated diatribe after another, an ultimately dizzying and fatiguing exercise in *loshon hora*, that category of evil speech or report enjoined by Jewish religious tradition.

> "Our poor Chofetz Chaim! [the nineteenth-century Hasidic formulator of the laws of *loshon hora*, or "evil speech"] He prayed to God, 'Grant me that I should say nothing that is unnecessary and that all my speech should be for the sake of Heaven,' and meanwhile his Jews were speaking everywhere simply for the sake of *speaking*. All the time! Couldn't stop! Why? Because inside each Jew were *so many speakers*. Shut up one and the other talks. Shut him up and there is a third, a fourth, a fifth Jew with something more to say." (335)

The last of the novel's seemingly interminable speakers (including "Roth" himself) thus lays bare the very logic of the text, and provides the author in turn with the opportunity for one more reflective pro/denunciation:

> Assaulted and battered by yet another tyrannical talker whose weapon of revenge is his unloosed mouth, somebody whose purposes lurk hidden, ready to spring, behind the foliage of tens of thousands of words – another unbridled performer . . . (338)

Hidden-ness – again, the author-speaker as simultaneously informer and spy. For the narrators of both novels, to speak, to write amounts to a form of possession, an overspeaking, an underwriting.[18] And although speaking in Bradley's novel is figured as a far more careful and premeditated exercise, instructive, didactic, meticulous – in a word, *skillful* – than its counterpart in *Operation Shylock*, the two texts converge in their mutual understanding of storification (both self- and other-) as sometimes a tyranny and usurpation. Both novels possess a Bakhtinian sense of language as territory: pre-occupied and contested, a borderline.

4. *The historian as proper self/the novelist as selves*

By unifying the novels so seamlessly, I want to refine their differences especially as regards this central question of transmission. In Roth's and Bradley's novels, storytelling bears on that question as distinctly recognitive inasmuch as it forces awareness of connectivities between speakers and hearers, and of the claims made on them both by history and peoplehood.

"If you would bend a man," writes *Chaneysville*'s narrator, "not just influence him or sway him or even convince him but *bend* him, do it with ritual."

> And so, when the meal was finished and the dishes washed, when the fire was stoked and the mugs warmed and sweetened whiskey were in our hands, he did not hesitate; he did not even ask. He just said: "You want a story." (77)[19]

Storial and historical narration, like objects and objectified traditions passed-on, become consecrating vehicles in their own right for inheritance, for legacy and heritage (the same dynamic serving as a governing motif for Toni Morrison's *Beloved* and Cynthia Ozick's *The Shawl*).

> But somewhere along the line it had occurred to me that the stories were not just stories. They were something else: clues. The stories had changed then, it seemed. And Moses Washington, a decade dead by that time, had changed. And I had changed. And none of the changes had been for the better. (45)

Moses Washington, John's father, tracks his immediate predecessor's history in the mimetically identical fashion to John himself. The "changes" of which John speaks are the allegorical marks of history on personal narrative. In Benjamin's pithy observation, "allegories are, in the realm of thoughts, what ruins are in the realm of things."[20] Not only does the narrating self become doubled, or more precisely, *narrated*, by a counter-self; it becomes peopled by a cultural history of damage and ruin, *living into* that history, allegorically, as a consequence.

It is vital, then to John Washington's fullness as literary character, as well as plot-agent for the novel's forward and backward movement into culture and history, that he be acknowledged not merely as historian but as "Black historian," an instance of "Black intellectual." And it is in terms such as these that I think his character and "Roth" – together with Bradley's and Philip Roth's authorial ethos for their novels – must be sharply distinguished. Without venturing into another blackjewish quagmire[21], I want simply to point to Cornel West's typology of four "models for black intellectual activity: (1) black intellectual as humanist, (2) black intellectual as revolutionary, (3) black intellectual as postmodern skeptic, and (4) black intellectual as organic catalyst, in order to underscore John Washington's resemblance to the last, the insurgency model, as surpassing the limits of the other three.[22] At his best, Washington is a walking example of what West calls a "critical self-inventory" of positional loyalties. But above all, he is self-identical. Or so he thinks.

"Roth," on the other hand – no Gramscian insurgent – begins with multiplicity as a founding fact, as the primordial sponge-material for the permeability of historical event, incident and operation alike, discerned first and foremost solipsistically, "within the individual Jew."

> Why couldn't the Jews be one people? Why must Jews be in conflict with one another? Why must they be in conflict with themselves? Because the divisiveness is not just between Jew and Jew – it is within the individual Jew. Is there a more manifold personality in all the world? I don't say divided. Divided is nothing. Even the goyim are divided. But inside every Jew is a *mob* of Jews. The good Jew, the bad Jew. The new Jew, the old Jew. The lover of Jews, the hater of Jews . . . The Jewish Jew, the de-Jewed Jew. Shall I go on? Do I have to expound upon the Jew as a three-thousand-year amassment of mirrored fragments to one [Roth] who has made his fortune as a leading Jewologist of international literature? Is it any wonder that the Jew is always disputing. He *is* a dispute, incarnate! (334)

And if "Roth's" Jew is a dispute, then his book is a rant. When "Roth" commences his narrative, he doesn't, like Washington, approach it upright and with deliberateness, he knocks knees in a Halcion-induced breakdown and weeps words. And while the same "tyrannical talker" quoted above adjudges the novel from the inside to be a book "about someone who recovers . . . a comedy in the classic sense," (394) "Roth" will sustain the histrionic mode to the end. *Operation Shylock* goes Mikhail Bakhtin one better in making a bid beyond the polyphonic novel to the novel of *cacophony* instead.

Such torrent and tumult of language cannot be what *Chaneysville* has in mind when it proclaims, "Everything a man does that makes any kinda sense, anyways, is on accounta he wants some say."

> That's why he builds a fence round his land, an' digs in the ground an' plants in rows: so every time he looks at that piece a ground he'll know, maybe he didn't make it, but he had some say. (41)

Washington's dying friend, his closest link to his deceased father, goes on to explain that standing in time and history in hard actuality establishes at best only a temporary redoubt. Earth, wind, water insist on having a reciprocal "say" of their own. But not fire. For fire "gives a man *final* say."

94

It lets him destroy. Lets him destroy anything . . . . You can get things right down to where they was to start with, down to the ground an' air an' water an' sun. Now, that ain't much say, an it ain't the best kinda say, but it's better than havin' no say at all. Because a man with no say is an animal. So a man has to be able to make a fire, has to know how to make it in the wind an' the rain' an' the dark. When he can do that, he can have some say. (42)

As we discover by reading him, Washington demonstrates most of these varieties of "say" in the text itself: an expert's say over natural resources and craft, a proprietary say over inherited land, the "final" say of destruction at the end of his narrative when he burns the complex file system of cards with which he has tracked his forbears' history, and perhaps the better kind of say which is the preceding 400–odd pages of talk – by turns angry, condescending, self-righteous – much of it instigated by the light of a fire.

Yet, other, more hidden and more dangerous kinds of say make their voices heard in *The Chaneysville Incident*. Part of the novel's plot involves the reading of Washington's father's will. Moses Washington, a self taught black man, a generation removed from slavery, established his say over a small part of Western Pennsylvania, dubbed "the Town and the County," by keeping meticulous records of all transactions between himself and the white purchasers of the moonshine he brewed and sold.

> He did what every white businessman would do with his business: he kept records. And yet there wasn't a white man who expected him to. Because it didn't make any sense to treat the bootleg whiskey business just like it was a dry goods business. But he did . . . He had us all by then, back in the days when it was a dry county, and there wasn't a one of us could have stood up to the scandal. (199)

The more literal "say" of the ledger containing those records enables the more abstract economic say of bargaining power whose most tangible result, not surprisingly, becomes the purchase of property. "You're telling me," exclaims John Washington to the scion of the town's foremost white family, "that . . . Moses Washington owned the Hill." And as the land forms part of Moses Washington's effects, so it becomes John's and his deceased brother Bill's by inheritance.

> "He had held an option on it for some years. He could have sold that option for a lot of money. He took the land."
> "Great," I said. "He made Bill the biggest slumlord this side of Pittsburgh and he turned me into a moonshiner." (191)

But the say of Moses's folio is an ultimately ironic say. In fact, as his son discovers upon unlocking its secrets, it corresponds to what Lacan called the "object small *a*," a surplus of pure seeming for human desire, a piece of elusive make-believe masking as a piece of the real.[23] The ledger is empty (another figure for writing's sometime insufficiency). It "says" nothing, although it may hold enormous sway: "Your legacy, John," says the town's brahmin, "if you acknowledge that you have come to call for it." (197) More importantly for Washington, its meaning lies in its ritual possibility: not what it may contain, but how it effects a transfer between his father and himself, between the burden of the past and its reconstruction in the present.

> Things look different in lamplight. That is a small fact, the kind of datum that escapes the notice of the average historian . . . Edges are softer. The beginnings and ends of things seem to merge . . . And the light flickers, so that anything seen is seen not only dimly, but elusively, inconstantly. And it is possible – for almost anything is possible, and the difference between logical cause and effect and magic is only a matter of which premises are chosen – that thoughts are different, too, in the soft light of a lamp . . . Moses Washington had chosen not to wire his attic simply because there was no place for electricity. He had sealed his folio with candle wax; he had most likely written whatever was inside by the light of a lamp, or a lantern, or perhaps a glowing campfire. And I would open it by a similar glow. (204–205)

Possession, legacy: they signify not manumission but indenture. Thus, when John is told that he can now "take possession" (190) of his rightful property, his intuitive reaction (more magical than logical), is the precisely right one: He *made me* the biggest slumlord/he *turned me into* a moonshiner.[24] In other words: I have been begotten once again by my father.

> And when I, armed with a flashlight, mounted the steep, folded-down stairway and emerged into the upper darkness, I was almost going back in time, and when I thumbed the switch on the flashlight and sent a cone of weak light on a homemade chair and a large, roughly carpentered table on which sat an open book and a kerosene lamp, I was looking at a perfect memory; dusty, but perfect. It was almost as if the chair, the table, the book, the lamp, the empty fireplace were items under glass; they were keys to a man's mind, laid bare to me, clues to a mystery . . . the chair was like a print of his body; each part that pressed against my body was an expression of his. (141)

Patrimony, or history in a larger sense, strike a precarious balance in Bradley's novel between a confident, easeful detection of the past, and having to feel its odd, discomforting shape against, on top of, or within one.

And it is in that same spirit of discomfort that *Operation Shylock* begins and for the most part remains. Recovering from the horrors of his recent descent into "Halcion madness," "Roth" reserves judgment, or final say,

> half-convinced that I owed my transformation – my *deformation* – not to any pharmaceutical agent but to something concealed, obscured, masked, suppressed, or maybe simply uncreated in me until I was fifty-four but as much me and mine as my prose style, my childhood, my intestines. (27)

"Roth" relates this little anecdote as a *gloss* on the novel's primary motivation and point of departure: the existence of another Philip Roth, an exact double, who has been sighted in Gdansk talking with Lech Walesa about Diasporism, and in Jerusalem as a courtroom spectator at the trial of John "Ivan the Terrible" Demjanjuk.

> The link between Halcion nightmare and Halcyon fictivity is speedily drawn: It's Zuckerman, I thought, whimsically, stupidly, escapistly, it's Kepish, it's Tarnapol and Portnoy – it's all of them in one, broken free of print and mockingly reconstituted as a single satirical facsimile of me. In other words, if it's not Halcion and it's no dream, then it's got to be literature – as though there cannot be a life-without ten thousand times more unimaginable than the life-within. (34)

But Aharon Appelfeld has already located that life for "Roth" and for us in Europe in the 1940s, where the "reality of the Holocaust surpassed any imagination." For "reality . . . is always stronger than the human imagination. Not only that, reality can permit itself to be unbelievable, inexplicable, and out of all proportion." (86)[25] The hardened irritant of facticity in the story is thus anything but an *objet petit a*, relentlessly remanifesting itself in the midst of "Roth's" adventure in postmodern doubling or self-allegory. But as facticity, the grounded story of the Holocaust takes a more personalized shape in *Operation Shylock* than the transcripts from the Demjanjuk trial would seem to promise.

Sandwiched between "Roth's" introduction of the alter-ego whom he later dubs Pipik, and the story of his own breakdown is such an atom, the minor but not unimportant figure of his cousin Apter, twice removed on his mother's side, "an unborn adult, a fifty-four year old ["Roth's" exact age] who has evolved into manhood without evolving." (18) What explains his "terrifyingly blank" mien, his dollish look, the fact that there is imprinted on his face "nothing of the mayhem of Jewish life in the twentieth century?" That very mayhem. Sold by a German officer to a male brothel at the age of nine, "He remains chained to his childishness to this day . . . someone whose whole life lies in the hands of the past."

His "chronically imploring" eyes weep often, and "his hunger is unappeasable for those who are not here." (18) Literature – particularly prose fiction – should recognize Apter as a familiar allegorical type: ruins like Dickens's Miss Havisham, or Rosa Coldfield and Reverend Hightower in Faulkner's fiction (the latter described by Faulkner as having "grow[n] up among phantoms and side-by-side with a ghost.")[26] Such characters defy the presentness of the present by giving themselves over, transfixing themselves, to the pastness of the past. They are what Nietzsche names "the weak," "extinguished" by history, in the material free fall shared by all emblems in decay.

I introduce them in order, first, to recall the obvious fact about literary narrative that it reserves a place in advance for persons damaged by time, owing perhaps to its signal property – as narrative discourse – of bending and reshaping temporality at will. Like Lazarus in the gospel text, so cousin Apter. And second, I want to intercept any speculation that I am trying to "rescue" Roth's text from its own literaturized tub of the self, its self-referential confines. Instances of the Real do not correct for excesses of the imagination. They may, however, leave marks. That is the function I assign cousin Apter in Roth's text.

Thirdly, as literary fiction lacks any Archimedean fulcrum with which to lever it soundly into the Real, *other fictions* will often provide us temporary anchorage, or at the very least, a point of comparison. Consider such a reference point from Primo Levi's novel, *The Periodic Table*. There Levi depicts the notion of a reality-kernel even more elemental, in the form of a carbon-atom whose "story" he narrates at the end of the novel. Having traced an imaginative thousand-million-year history in a few paragraphs, he finally deposits his carbon atom in the human bloodstream on the way to the brain, ingested in a glass of milk:

... and the cell in question, and within it, the atom in question, is in charge of my writing, in a gigantic minuscule game which nobody has yet described. It is that which at this instant, issuing out of a labrynthine tangle of yeses and nos, makes my hand run along a certain path on the paper, mark it with these volutes that are signs: a double snap, up and down, between two levels of energy, guides the hand of mine to impress on the paper this dot, here, this one.[27]

How subtly, yet how *factitiously*, the Real can insert itself into the imagination is the ulterior point of Levi's story. Atoms deposit themselves everywhere and if they happen to be made of carbon they have enormous staying power – not unlike Jewish memory, even if in the form of an atom which is pure lack and vacancy, and which, to paraphrase Levi, is in charge of nothing because it remains damaged beyond reclamation. Such is the figure of cousin Apter. Despite our having entered a seemingly vertiginous fictive abyss before the second page of *Operation Shylock* is turned, *abandon all hope of reference ye who enter here* is not the novel's arresting signpost. That space is reserved for the "dot" of cousin Apter.

Certainly, I make more of that figure than I think Roth wants us to, but then this chapter treats Bradley's and Roth's texts as a bifold, a sum different from its parts, and thus positions them differently in public space. Against that final limit and loom of public space, the minor figure of cousin Apter represents an allegorical one, a kind of fallen – or worse, damaged – Angel of History. He compresses into his very person the dialectic of allegory Benjamin analyzes – the preempting of adult personhood and thus its ruin, but also a kind of redemption in the way he remains chained to his childishness. He is faced forward, in other words, but pulled back, and thus as an allegorical figure and further, a figure *for* history-as-allegory, he turns a death's head into an angel's face.

A large claim for such a dollish dot, especially within the context of a satirical work of fiction. *Operation Shylock* is not German *Trauerspiel*. I stake the claim, however, in the service of teasing out the enormous problem of fiction's relation to history, standing over or at the heart of Roth's text and Bradley's alike. To call it, say, *the loom and limits of recognition*, would dignify it certainly, but that formulation already conflates two others: "the loom of history" and "the limits of representation."[28] Even one of these lies beyond the present chapter's scope. More relevantly, any attempt to address them here as the loom of the Holocaust or the loom of slavery, the representational limits of

Black American or of Jewish American culture would make for too wildly swinging a pendulum.

I will confine myself, therefore, to the domain of fiction – a large enough "tub" in its own right – in its relation to history, and cultural disasters, in the light of two other works of fiction by Black and Jew: Toni Morrison's *Beloved* and Cynthia Ozick's *The Shawl*. Both texts ask, How do you tell tragedy and trauma on a cultural scale? In addition to their own status as uncannily facing texts (of all the constructed dialogues in this book, this one singularly generates *its own* call and response[29]), Ozick's and Morrison's novels let us think about Bradley's and Roth's in a different light. They double, by imagining otherwise. And in doing so they lead us back to cousin Apter.

Khurbns[30]/havens – an excursus on atrocity

If *Shylock* and *Chaneysville* invoke history as repetition, as mimesis, *Beloved* and *The Shawl* conjure it as metempyschosis, the province of ghosts. Both mothers in the respective plots have lost their daughters – Sethe by her own hands, Rosa by Nazi extermination – and both daughters haunt their mothers after death, ghosts, *idees fixes*, idols. The past's hold on the present in these texts is a necessary idolatry, the atavistic antechamber or haunting to a redemptive home-as-found. In both stories, the women ultimately choose recovery over the self as grave-site or head-stone. Sethe and Rosa allow themselves to be weaned away, loosing the snuffed-out but still clamoring lives to which they once gave suck, so that they, too, might come back to life. That is, they escape the fate of cousin Apter.

Just as history, the living, the telling, and the retelling of it, means patrimony for Roth and Bradley, so it betokens maternity in *Beloved* and *The Shawl*, an umbilical chord as opposed to a legal will, a doubling through birth instead of through the track or trail, a matter of voice, not documentary record. Milk and blood as opposed to chronicle and diary compose the "raw stuff" of history (Bradley's phrase) in these stories, as such "stuff" constitutes the third possibility to documents and monuments both, a term bridging the personal or communal realm of *memory* and the more totalizing province of objective history.

But another kind of raw stuff resides in Morrison's and Ozick's texts, something more analogous to the proceedings of the Demjanjuk trial in *Operation Shylock* through fictive, hardened irritants of facticity that irritate and carbonize just as painfully: a newspaper clipping in *Beloved* reporting without interpreting Sethe's crime of infanticide, a similar such item in *The Shawl* together with a letter from a clinician soliciting from Rosa additional data for a study in the "social pathology" of survivors, the very remnant which is her life about whose ruined state Rosa repeatedly laments, "Thieves took it."

Where storytelling takes on a life of its own in *Shylock* and *Chaneysville*, a rocketing effect, Ozick and Morrison bestow on it a gravity, compelling and legislating resistance. "It was not a story to pass on," the narrator of *Beloved* reminds us three times. "My Warsaw isn't your Warsaw," Rosa chides her would-be suitor in *The Shawl*. "To those who don't deserve the truth, don't give it."[31] (Both texts figure narrative closure or openness in terms of closed or open *things* – "tobacco tin" hearts, letters, washing machines, pockets, rooms, and architectural structures in general.)

And yet stories do take shape, contractually, across the crevasse of loss and need. "You see," the suitor tells Rosa, "I unloaded on you, now you got to unload on me." (27) In *Beloved*, Sethe and Paul D approach narrative carefully, medicinally, ministering to one another as follows:

> He wants to tell me, she thought. He wants me to ask him about what it was like for him – about how offended the tongue is, held down by iron, how the need to spit is so deep you cry for it .
> . . . Sethe looked up into Paul D's eyes to see if there was any trace left in them. He sat down beside her. Sethe looked at him. In that unlit daylight his face, bronzed and reduced to its bones, smoothed her heart down.
> "You want to tell me about it?" (71)

At the end of *The Chaneysville Incident*, as John Washington imaginatively conjures his family history, he pictures his great-grandfather assuming responsibility for a group of slave runaways.

> He went to them, speaking to each of them in tones so low that none of the others could hear, getting their names, gently touching them, asking about their pains, their fears, gently eliciting their stories, reminding them of why they had run in the first place. (Bradley, 414)

Morrison's narrator exhibits an even greater scrupulosity. In *Beloved*, tellers resist telling:

Silent, except for social courtesies, when they met one another they neither described nor asked about the sorrow that drove them on. The whites didn't bear speaking on. Everybody knew. (Morrison, 53)

Or, in the comparable case of Rosa's in *The Shawl*, "Whatever I would say, you would be deaf." (27) And when it does come, "the tale" is less reflexively metonymic in Ozick and Morrison. Stories, even when they drive towards some climax or point, do not so much track outward as in *Chaneysville*, or spiral inward as in *Shylock*, but *hover* above their own descriptive formalism.

Formally and stylistically, then, *Beloved* and *The Shawl* exchange Roth's postmodern vertigo and Bradley's hard-boiled historicism/ realism for an object-soaked modernism, a very different modernism and a very different sense of object from Henry Roth's or Ralph Ellison's.

Stella was ravenous. Her knees were tumors on sticks, her elbows chicken bones. (Ozick, 3)

How [Sethe's feet] were so swollen she could not see her arch or feel her ankles. Her leg shaft ended in a loaf of flesh scalloped by five toenails.... And those [Amy's] cane-stalk arms, as it turned out, were as strong as iron. (Morrison, 30, 32)

Both [teats] were cracked, not a sniff of milk. The duct-crevice extinct, a dead volcano, blind eye, chill hole, so Magda took the corner of the shawl and milked it instead. (Ozick, 4)

Amy unfastened the back of [Sethe's] dress and said, "Come here, Jesus," when she saw . . . "It's a tree, Lu. A chokecherry tree. See here's the trunk – it's red and split wide open, full of sap, and this here's the parting of the branches. You got a mighty lot of branches. Leaves, too, look like, and dern if these ain't blossoms. Tiny little cherry blossoms just as white. Your back got a whole tree on it. In bloom. (Morrison, 79) (Compare the "Tree" in the form of clinician in Ozick.)

The neat grip of the tiny gums. One mite of a tooth tip sticking up in the bottom gum, how shining, an elfin tombstone of white marble gleaming there. (Ozick, 4)

I see her face which is mine . . . I follow her we are in the diamonds which are her earrings now . . . her smiling face is the place for me. (Morrison, 213)

What a curiosity it was to hold a pen – nothing but a small pointed stick, after all, oozing its hieroglyphic puddles: a pen that speaks, miraculously, Polish. A lock removed from the tongue. Otherwise the tongue is chained to the teeth and the palate. An immersion into the living language: all at once this cleanliness, this capacity, this power to make a history, to tell, to explain. To retrieve, to reprieve! To lie. (Ozick, 44) (Compare the image of a bit in Paul D's mouth.)

A shawl (debased in the form of underpants), a piece of velvet, a tombstone, a tooth-as-tombstone, a swaddled telephone-god, a bit in the mouth, a tobacco tin in the chest, the word "Tree," scraps of color, buttons, flowers, saliva, chamomile sap, blood, milk, names. Together, *Beloved* and *The Shawl* narrate an intaglio of metaphor whose cumulative effect becomes metonymized through the massing of incident. In counterpoint, Roth's and Bradley's texts start with metonymy only to end in allegory: the doubling and substitution of the narrating self by Plot, History, Operation.

If "memory" supplies the more poetic correlate to "history," then Ozick's and Morrison's stories offset the prose-dominated trials-by-ordeal of "Roth" and John Washington with a defining and self-legitimating lyricism. They de-monument and de-document the genealogies of Slavery and the Holocaust by poeticizing them. They narrate imagistically and lyrically, *not*, even if in the best sense, prosaically. Early in the novel, Sethe's daughter Denver asks the returning Paul D how long he intends to stay. Paul D turns to Sethe, and asks, "Is there history to her question?" "History? What do you mean?" (44) Although the pressing concern here is whether other men have occupied Paul D's present position in the house before him, the troubled value assigned to the meaning of "history" stands over the entire text. The Middle Passage, for example, defies narrative coherence, and can only be *represented* by disconnected phrase or image.

If history, in Levinas's sense, always exacts its own cost (there can *only* be historical excess), a compensatory service – or, better, ritual – is performed by memory, the act of integrative storytelling which *Beloved* calls *rememory*.

> Disremembered and unaccounted for, [Beloved] cannot be lost because no one is looking for her, and even if they were, how can they call her if they don't know her name? Although she has claim, she is not claimed. In the place where long grass opens, the girl who waited to be loved, and cry shame erupts into her separate parts, to make it easy for the chewing laughter to swallow her all away. (274)

Rememory, the over-going of History by language and the ineffable, takes account of the unaccounted.[32]

And yet, together with the places it has been, language in Ozick's and Morrison's texts also carries with it its own special perils of dislocation. Here is the pivot back to cousin Apter, and through him, to Bradley and Roth, the intuition Levinas voices about art letting go of the prey for the shadow. In *Beloved*, especially, narrative lyricism offers itself almost as an alternative to History.[33] But, because even word-choice and cadence are subject to a kind of indenture, language never really does float free, something Roth's and Bradley's novels show through narrating characters who are not haunted by word or image so much as they are driven by plot and the politics of language.[34]

Ozick's Rosa makes a similar point herself about the hard kernel of facticity that language can sometimes obscure and even violate:

> Consider also the special word they used: *survivor*. Something new. As long as they didn't have to say *human being*. It used to be *refugee*, but by now there was no such creature, no more refugees, only survivors. A name like a number – counted apart from the ordinary swarm. Blue digits on the arm, what difference? They don't call you a woman anyhow. *Survivor*. Even when your bones get melted into the grains of the earth, still they'll forget *human being*. Survivor and survivor and survivor; always and always. Who made up these words, parasites on the throat of suffering! (36)

Her irony here makes her almost proximate to both John Washington and "Roth." Perhaps in this respect, *The Shawl* gestures one critical step beyond *Beloved* in seeming at its close to renounce or cancel its own idolatry of figuration. Where Morrison redraws the line between re-presentation and Re-construction, Ozick's seems to cut the cord.[35]

More important for a hinge between Morrison's and Ozick's novels on one side, and Roth's and Bradley's on the other is the way in which the Real – as historical incident, as storifying operation, as rememory, as a humble telephone conversation – keeps interrupting, countering not only the impersonal judgment of history, but the personal decision to flee from facticity or repress. The "humble telephone conversation" is what interrupts and effectively terminates Rosa's narrative at the end of Ozick's story. Rosa has wrapped her dead daughter's shawl around the telephone receiver, communing with it/her in rhapsodic crescendo, until a banal, functional, and two-way communication cuts short the luxury of monologue:

> Pure Magda, head as bright as a lantern. The shawled telephone, little grimy silent god, so long comatose – now, like Magda,

animated at will, ardent with its cry. Rosa let it clamor once or twice and then heard the Cuban girl announce – oh, "announce"! – Mr. Persky: should he come up or would she come down? . . . "He's used to crazy women, so let him come up," Rosa told the Cuban. She took the shawl off the phone. Magda was not there. Shy, she ran from Persky. Magda was away. (69–70)

Even the authority of narrative, *The Shawl* seems to suggest, can end up replacing one idol worship with another, and may ironically, call for another idol-smashing – the end of story, the materiality of another's voice. *Beloved* arrives at a similar place through its commitment to a more communitarian spirit than Sethe's private dialogue with her daughter's ghost. It surmounts a "speaking to" with a "speaking for" in the way Beloved herself becomes disremembered by Sethe and Sethe's immediate community, as *community* itself and the *passing on* of story take center stage. Stories, after all, as Washington and "Roth" take pains to discover, constitute a property all their own, "passed on" through multiple conduits. That they need to end is undeniable. That they need to be grounded somehow, or that they *will* be grounded despite themselves, all four texts in different ways ensure.

The irritant of the real, of facticity, of history, keeps depositing itself. That is the significance, to recall him now, of Cousin Apter for Roth's novel and by extension for Bradley's as well. A not-so-distant cousin to Rosa inasmuch as the Holocaust has left him derelict, Apter has weeps more than he speaks in *Operation Shylock*; indeed, he really has no story to tell. Capsized in every sense, he is not even narratively marooned, and to that degree, he fails to establish even the toe-hold claimed by those human fragments who at least get to narrate themselves. Smashed by history, we could say.

In the terms Levinas uses in *Totality and Infinity*, decisively silencing Nietzsche's philosophy of history, redeeming persons from the tyranny of history means that "all stories are waiting to be heard." (298) Apter's, like so many, however, may wait indefinitely; he cannot seem to pronounce it himself. So in a very real way, his personal, incidental story yields to the operational mechanics of history, without Sethe or Rosa's power of resistance and will, without "Roth's" and Washington's narrative drive and imagination.

When Rosa smashes her store at the beginning of the story, she may seem to echo Nietzsche's "breaking up the past" in seeming to "digest" her own. But if that act is repetition, conscious or not, it can also be seen as a reinscription: of history restaged as allegory, perhaps of *Kristalnacht*, the Night of Broken Glass that begins the National Socialist nightmare in Europe. "The power to smash her own. A kind of suicide. She had murdered her store with her own hands." (Ozick, 46) Smashed by history, but in a second sense. Sethe, too, repeats as well as "beats back" the past, attesting perhaps to a force greater than simply individual pathology or "repressed animation" (in the clinician's phrase from *The Shawl*). The empirical comes back to usurp the idolatrous in all four texts, as either the return of history repressed, or some small, stubborn kernel of fact that will not go away.

Short of being handed over to history for final judgment, the stubborn kernel of Apter meets instead his cousin "Roth" the novelist. He finds his author, his "personificator," and is in a manner of speaking thereby appeased. As likewise are C. K. and Moses Washington in finding their historian in John, their cultural and familial heir. None of them *knows* he has been appeased, of course. But they have been reclaimed anyway. If Sethe and Rosa are in a certain capacity authors who have taken charge of a story and created a character for themselves, cousin Apter, C. K. Washington, and his son Moses, albeit in radically different ways, need a writer if they are, in Bradley's words, "to bend a man" or mark a story.

Their stories wait on someone else's telling, not entirely unlike the co-creative intimacy shared by Sethe and Paul D, Sethe and her daughter Denver, Rosa and her daughter Magda, Rosa and, at last, Persky. Just as narrators are forced up against the Real in any reckoning with history, so facts or persons find a certain redemption through willing or unwitting storytellers. And it is that encompassing bifold – between fiction and history mediated by allegory – that becomes more clearly manifest when two texts illustrative of it are themselves folded together. Unlike Benjamin's angel of history who faces catastrophe, in eternal recession, Black-and-Jewish fiction and Black-and-Jewish history mediated by Black-and-Jewish allegory are an imaginative consequence of a facing that only comes about reciprocally. Thus also is history turned towards (and we towards it), rather than having it slip away.

The limits of recognition

Why has "Roth's" cousin Apter been asked to bear so great a burden as to act as pivot point for a recursive meditation on Allegory and History, profounder by far than the one sketched in my introductory chapter? Is he not too frail, too childish, too unappeasably hungry for those no longer there to be so weighted down? These questions merely restate the one which begins this chapter: when does an "incident" coincide with an "operation?" And the answer remains the same: when a free and unreconstructed event in human experience gets smuggled and/or indentured into plot, when an "arguably stupid detail," as "Roth" calls it, opens out into significant action, the only difference between logical cause and effect and allegoresis being a matter, in John Washington's words, of which premises are chosen.

A simplistic dichotomy between a factual core of truth and a derivative level of interpretive reconstruction (the historiographic parallel to narratology's division between story/discourse) ignores the meaningfulness *already inscribed* in events. As Martin Jay has written, one needs to "acknowledge the formed content in the narrations that historical actors or victims have themselves produced."

> What distinguishes the events and facts that later historians reconstruct is precisely their being often already inflected with narrative meaning for those who initiate or suffer them in their own lives . . . There is virtually no historical content that is linguistically unmediated and utterly bereft of meaning, waiting around for the later historian to emplot it in arbitrary ways.[36]

One may wish to ask the same of the novelist, as well. The novelist of *Operation Shylock* emplots its historical content in all sorts of seemingly arbitrary ways, according to a whole roster of devices: ideological parody (diasporism), ideological critique (Shylockism), literary uncanniness (pipikism), and authorial reflexivity (Rothism). To that roster I have suggested adding another dimension, of carbonized historical meaning already inscribed in person and event neither waiting for meaning nor promising solution, but there to interrupt and complicate an ongoing or encompassing narration. *Apterism.*

At one point in the story, "Roth" pauses to consider the wealth of embedded writing, the literary analogue to "subselves," leaked into his account so far: notes passed by Demjanjuk to his lawyer, the supposed diaries of Leon Klinghoffer, a transcript of Pipik's *Anti-Semites Anonymous* tape, letters, interviews, etc.

> All this writing by nonwriters, I thought, all these diaries, memoirs, and notes written clumsily with the most minimal skill, employing one one-thousandth of the resources of a written language, and yet the testimony they bear is no less persuasive for that, is in fact that much more searing precisely because the expressive powers are so blunt and primitive. (298)

But such words, to paraphrase "Roth" himself, do not in fact spoil things; they do duty for things. Like Apter's incessant weeping, they constitute a formed content of their own as more or less historical narrations.

The Chaneysville Incident, too, contains its share of such "minor literature," not least the encoded writings of John Washington's father and great-grandfather and the self-canceling folio. On an affective but banal level, the mass of sub- or counter-literatures provides some respite, perhaps, from the archness and asperity of "Roth" and Washington as narrators. Theirs are both nervewracking texts to read. But more subtly, they offer rival modes of *storification*, intrinsically self-recognizing – because "so blunt and primitive" – consequently, maybe even redemptive. As species of Apterism, they have *say*.

My aim here is not to absolve Roth's postmodernism or heroicize Bradley's critical-realism, or (to recall Primo Levi's metaphor), to perform this literary–chemical analysis for the purposes of distilling a few atoms of carbon. Cousin Apter doesn't "solve" *Operation Shylock* anymore than a "figure" can be plugged into Henry James's "Figure in the Carpet." I merely point out the *marks* of allegory on history, and history, in turn, on fiction. Levi's story of the insistent atom of the Real is an allegory too, after all.

To conclude with a Rothian-cum-Bradleyan coda about conclusions: at the end of *The Chaneysville Incident*, Washington indulges in a tour-de-force of historical reconstruction. Having already tracked to the limit the clues his father has left him to explain why *he* tracked his own grandfather, "put[ing] himself into the game and head[ing] off after it," the historian configures with meticulous detail the last, sacrificial, and legatory chapter in that ancestor's life. He fabulates, in other words, "the Chaneysville incident." Spatially, he stands in the identical place where his father committed suicide and where his great-grandfather killed *himself* along with a party of runaway-slaves to avoid recapture.

But the linguistically nuanced Washington, much like Ozick's Rosa refusing the flattening terminology of *survivor*, rejects the notion of his father's "suicide," for the more nuanced belief in a "ghost-chaser" on a hunting trip into the beyond. But even that description doesn't quite capture it (as we recall from Ralph Ellison):

> "No," I said. "Ghost isn't the right word. Ghost is a word invented by people who didn't believe, like the names the Spaniards gave the Aztec gods. Ancestors is a better term . . . I guess maybe that's what insanity is, somebody believing in

something that doesn't have any kind of reality for you. Napoleon's dead; anyone who thinks he's Napoleon is crazy. The
thing is, if you accept his premises, everything he did was
perfectly logical. He wanted to understand dying, to look before
he leaped, so he went to war. He was a hero, because he wanted
to take chances, get closer to dying. He loved a woman because
[his grandfather] C. K. had loved a woman, maybe two, and
Moses Washington needed to understand that. He had a son
because C. K. Washington had a son . . . " (388)

"Roth" states the opposite case, logically speaking, but arrives at a
not dissimilar perspective (an uncanny echo itself of *Invisible Man's*
"stepping outside history", when he writes,

To do something *without* clarity, an inexplicable act, something
unknowable even to oneself, to step outside responsibility and
gave way fully to a very great curiosity, to be appropriated
throughout by the strangeness, by the dislocation of the unforeseen. (Roth, 358)

What he does is lend himself to the "operation" of the title, a maneuver for the Israeli Secret Service which requires that he impersonate
the double who impersonated him, and necessitates therefore that he
subtract the chapter entitled "Operation Shylock" detailing his "step
outside responsibility," and add the closing disclaimer, "This confession is false." An air-tight hermeneutic circle, a tiny tub of postmodern reflexivity.

Perhaps not so ironically – given the artifice imposed by the facing
of the two novels – "Roth" allows himself one last and condign fictive
fling before stepping back inside responsibility to let himself be
"edited" by his Mossad handler. (Instead of the latter's preference for
"A Fable" as the subtitle for *"Operation Shylock,"* the author, we
know, chooses "A Confession.") Like his counterpart, the historian,
"Roth" the novelist fabulates: he invents the closing chapter in the life
of *his* double, the impostor Philip Roth.

No, John Washington and "Roth" do not mirror each other at the
end of their respective narratives – as though, paraphrasing Joyce,
Novelist/Historian is Historian/Novelist. Extremes meet. But for Black
historian and Jewish novelist alike, one man's someone "who thinks
he is Napoleon" is another man's *author* – the difference a matter of
which premises are chosen, the common burden (and advantage)
being an excess of both history and identity.

The lesson that discursive field called blackjewishrelations unwittingly allegorized by fiction might learn from the facing here is this:

will it overwrite "the interplay of ritual and recital in the service of memory"[37] as something narratively open or closed? Will it allow those enmeshed in such interplay to shuttle between the demands of history and the open possibilities of transhistory? Can they recuperate their past "without pretending for long that they can recoup its plenitude?"[38] What roles shall they choose for themselves as they take up positions in nonliterary public space. Napoleons? Apters? Or – a third possibility – siblings of "Roth" and Washington, Roth and Bradley: *authors*? The next chapter proposes a fresh set of possible answers.

4

Literaturized Blacks and Jews; or, golems and Tar babies: reality and its shadows in John Edgar Wideman and Bernard Malamud

> Rava created a man and sent him to Rabbi Zera. Rabbi Zera spoke to him and he did not answer. Then he said: You must have been made by [talmudist or pietist] sorcerers; return to your dust.
> Tractate *Sanhedrin 65b*

> [A continuation:] And what would have enabled the man to answer? His soul. But has man a soul that he might transmit? Yes, for it is written in Genesis 2:7: "He blew into his nostrils the breath of life" – thus man has a soul of life [the ability to speak].
> *Sefer Bahir*

> De same ebenin eh mak Tar baby, an eh gone an set um right in de middle er de trail wuh lead to de spring. So Buh Rabbit come along to git some water. Wen he ketch de spring, he see Tar Baby duh tan dist een front er de spring. Eh stonish. Eh stop. Eh come close. Eh look at um. Eh wait fur em fuh mobe. De Tar baby yent notice him. Eh yent wink eh yeye. Eh yent say nuttne. Eh yent mobe. Bu Rabbit say, "Hey titter, enty you guine tan one side an lemme git some water?" De Tar Baby no answer. Rabbit said, "H'llo, old man, what you doin here?" De Tar Baby didn't answer. "Don't you heah me talkin' to you?" De Tar Baby ain't said nothin'. De Tar Baby stan day. Buh Rabbit haul off an slap um side de head. "Turn me loose, turn me loose, or I'll hit you with the other paw!" De Tar Baby hole um fas. Eh yent say one wud. "Tar Baby," from *Negro Myths*

This chapter is about "making up people."[1] Its proof-texts consist primarily of short fiction, perhaps not as capacious a space as the Novel for literary characters to walk around in and stretch their legs, but well lit, nonetheless. But due to the cramped space of the minor literature[2] in this case, my readings proceed with dispatch. The short stories by John Edgar Wideman and Bernard Malamud assembled here all converge in a common *imagining* of otherness: Black faces

111

given voice by Jew, Jewish faces made sonant by Black. And inasmuch as literary representation suspends personhood uneasily between character and caricature, this chapter again faces allegory head on.

But instead of tracking African American and American Jewish "image-repertoires" (as the Black–Jewish relationship is typically re-situated for literary study) I want to explore what Bakhtin called the relationship between author and hero (the second-person in the text)[3]. In the case of Malamud's and Wideman's stories, that means, (1) a necessary asymmetry between Black and Jew, and 2) the way in which literary invention either mimes or else critiques a real-life "making up" of people. In this chapter I am thus more interested in when American Black and Jewish authors actually lend voice to "the other" than in touristic scene-painting or the occasional ethnic snapshot – the infamous portrait, for example, of the black pickpocket in Saul Bellow's *Mr. Sammler's Planet*:

> [Sammler] was directed, silently, to look downward. The black man had opened his fly and taken out his penis. It was displayed to Sammler with great oval testicles, a large tan-and-purple uncircumcised thing – a tube, a snake; metallic hairs bristled at the thick base and the tip curled beyond the supporting, demonstrating hand, suggesting the fleshly mobility of an elephant's trunk, though the skin was somewhat iridescent rather than thick or rough. Over the forearm and fist that held him Sammler was required to gaze at this organ. No compulsion would have been necessary. He would in any case have looked.[4]

Sadly, readers don't have a choice, either. It would have to be a *black* penis. And uncircumcised. And mesmerizing. And perhaps more telling than anything else, of course the description would begin, *"He was never to hear the black man's voice."*

An *organ* in place of the organ of speech. A mute golem, or visually adhesive tarbaby, for literary personhood. Unvarnished specularity for some profounder *anagnorisis*. It is here – in the fiction – not on the plane of mis-communicated observations about Zulus and Tolstoy, that Bellow's uncritical ethnic chauvinism . . . makes one want to holler.[5] Moments like this dot the landscape of Black and Jewish fiction alike, literary Blacks and Jews sporting so many tragic masks of humanity as emblem pure and simple. In keeping with previous chapters, that landscape begs to be surveyed *otherwise*, generating more compelling, and critically conscientious maps for it.

The stories I discuss in this chapter are Malamud's "The Jewbird,"

"Angel Levine," and "Black Is My Favorite Color," and Wideman's "Valaida," "Fever," and "Hostages." A running gloss is provided by Cynthia Ozick's essay, "Literary Blacks and Jews," which in analyzing the uncanny doubling between the plane of textual "Blacks" and "Jews," and the real-world level of blackjewishrelations, unleashes its own, *behind the back, as it were* (Ozick's own phrase), in a review of Cornel West by Leon Wieseltier. Mentioned separately in my introduction, the latter texts are entangled, or entangle themselves, here.

As to the chapter's epigraphs, they suggest an allegory of literary creation, generally; but obviously, my purposes are more specific. How does an author "realize" a certain kind of otherness? What is special about "racialized/ethnicized discourse" when it is lent voice, and bidden to speak?[6] What legitimates, incriminates, redeems it? In the Talmudic anecdote of the golem-like creature,[7] an echo of the creation story (specifically Genesis 1:1 and 2:7), is heard in the service of an inquiry about idol-worship. The surrounding discussion in the Talmud affirms the significance of human language in cases when suppressed or artificial in the case of idols and surrogate creations.[8]

The God of Genesis, in his capacity as *Tzur* or purposive artist, forms man, having acted on the rest of mere matter (golem-like shapelessness) through a more generalized creative process known as *briah*). Through *nishmat chayim*, divine in-spiriting (Genesis 2:7), man becomes a *nefesh chaya*, the customary translation being "a living soul." Onkelos, second-century translator of the Pentateuch Targum into Aramaic, interprets this phrase as betokening "a speaking spirit" – a communicative soul, human by dint of intelligent speech.[9] Levinas, in an essay about a Hasidic treatise titled with that same Biblical phrase, extends its reach further:

> In spite of his humility as a creature, man is in the process of damaging [the worlds of spiritual collectivities, people and structures] or protecting them. For all that, by existing he *is*. This is a fundamental non-narcissism.[10]

By contrast, the golem is a simulacrum of a human, and like its vernacular American counterpart Tar Baby, lacks speech. Its very aglossia *communicates* its artificiality. At the very least, not answering brings one up short, as Rabbi Zera's impatience attests, closing the subjective self onto itself. In Brother Rabbit's case, even worse, it can get one stuck. In Bellow, most culpably, it sanctions an act of literary idolatry.

The questions put to the short stories in the readings to follow are therefore: will the imagined Blacks and Jews who people them be, as in Genesis, speaking spirits, answering for both themselves and their author-creators who, in turn, assume an answerability for them? Or will they be so many golems and Tar Babies, dead souls in Gogol's sense, "shadowy creatures" as Sartre conjures the colonized in *Wretched of the Earth*? Will they be heard to demand, as does a character in Ozick's novella, *Envy*, "Breathe in me! Animate me! Without you I'm a clay pot!"?[11] Or will they manifest the "faceless faces and soundless voices" Ellison describes in *Invisible Man*?

How does the sympathetic imagination fare when it comes up against ethno-racial Imaginaries? When do literary "Blacks" and "Jews" exceed being merely Imaginary Blacks and Jews, and when, conversely, does literature compensate for literaturization?[12] Such questions may in fact deflect any easy answers, for unlike homiletic anecdote or folktale, the distinctions in literary fiction are not so easily drawn.

Were I to face the following stories according to a strict correspondence between Black and Jew, the resultant pairings would take the shape, for example, of Malamud's "Black is My Favorite Color"/Wideman's "Valaida". But because the texts are all so short, and because my critical strategy designs a progressive sequence for them, the story-treatments themselves will follow the logic of *tableaux* – a set of variations on the same theme. I begin briskly, with Malamud's three Black secret sharers to the Jew – collectively, that rare instance in a body of short fiction that can bare comparison with Hawthorne's, when the author's demotic good sense fails him, when *chiaroscuro* and the *half-life* become aesthetic loop-holes instead of epiphanies, the grace of moments in the face-to-face.

Bernard Malamud's Jewblacks

1. "The Jewbird"

A talking, black bird named "Schwartz" visits a Manhattan apartment through an open window, seeking respite from persecution, running from "Anti-Semeets." The father of the Jewish family whose life he briefly disturbs, accuses him of being a dybbuk or a devil, at the very least a "foxy bastard," but the bird insists on both its avian-ness and its Jewishness. Cracking Jewish jokes, speaking Yiddish phrases, praying Jewish prayers, the bird states unequivocally at

114

one point, "Mr. Cohen, on this rest assured. A bird is a bird."[13] At story's end, after a final fracas with Mr. Cohen, the Jewbird is chased away, found dead several months later it seems, his eyes plucked out – probably by the same crows he mentions early in the story as a species of "Anti-Semeet," who, we are asked to consider finally, can also be Jews. "Who did it to you, Mr. Schwartz?" says Maurice the son. "Anti-Semeets," answers his mother, in the story's final sentence. (154) "What kind of anti-Semites bother a bird?" Cohen had asked early on. "Any kind" (145) is the answer.

Black and a "Schwartz," the Jewbird is not yet one of Malamud's Jewblacks, but merely a birdJew; Jewishness is a transportable metaphor (presumably, that's why he flies). The story works as a bit of Jewish conjuring, a bite-size piece of ethnic semiosis, ideal for an anthology. One wants to send the story flying just a little higher, however, and say more. Maybe the text is saying something interesting about Jewish identity, as a difference *between*, as a well as a difference *within*. The Jewbird is part bird and part Jew, each identity demanding its due. The Cohens, as Jews, fail to negotiate the other Jewishness (or Jewish otherness) of Schwartz, their fellow Jew. Jewish "difference" attracts (precipitates) Jew-hatred. Antisemeet-and-Jew.

One thinks of Philip Roth's early story "Eli, the Fanatic" (roughly contemporary with Malamud's) about a culture clash between white Jews and black Jews, suburbans and Hasidim, what *Operation Shylock* characterizes as "the Jew's hatred for his fellow Jew." (334) Perhaps the story is asking Roth's question (less postmodernly), "Why couldn't the Jews be one people?" Roth's answer is that "inside every Jew there is a *mob* of Jews," upping Malamud's simpler ante that differences *between* compound (an original?) difference *within*.

The story could also be expressing its own sense of diasporism, a tension between *going and resting* emblematized by the text's introductory *mise-en-scene* at a window: "That's how it goes. It's open you're in. Closed, you're out and that's your fate." (144) Or, in tracking the Jewbird's flight arrivals and departures, as well as the more vertical moral dimension he poses for his host-family, we could note alternatively, an oscillation between *aliyah* and *yeridah*, periods of going up and going down – another kind of barometer for Jewish identity, as doubled (and still self-divided) host/guest.[14]

Finally, but perhaps most obviously, the Jewbird allegorizes almost every possibility of Jew from the fraternal pairs in Genesis or the division of Biblical Israel into Northern and Southern Kingdoms on down: a composite entity, a being-Jewish together with a being something else. This dual identity – the Jewbirdness of Jews – and its potential for dual loyalties, of course, itself divides in two: internally, in the form of Jewish self-understanding, and externally, contingent on (mis)recognitions from without. Thus, if Art Spiegelman's *Maus* takes the animal-logic of Malamud's story to its inevitable and dark extreme, "The Jewbird" has already introduced the proximity, if not the outright tie, between composite identity and allegory.

Now, obviously, apart from Malamud's own artistic dictates and the thrust of his fictional project in general, such elaborate interpretive paradigms as these suggest themselves because of the very *nature of the text*: a modernist update of Aesopian fable, a species of *aggadah*, folktale-apologue. When, in his important introduction to *The Malamud Reader*, Philip Rahv circumvents narrative structure in order to locate Malamud's "poetics" in his characters' *speech*, dialogue-as-humanism, the necessary and proper vehicle for "speaking spirits," we discern in shadow the important role played by form in Malamud's short fiction.

Does "The Jewbird" even justify an opinion like Rahv's? Or does its beast-fable character, unlike, say, the multi-layered structure of *Maus* (a different animal tale entirely), flatten instead? Discretion shall leave the Jewbird to its fate, certainly unfortunate on the level of plot, perhaps not less so in terms of potentially more complex recognitive dynamics. The Talmud's Rabbi Zera would probably have remained unimpressed.

2. *"Angel Levine"*

"Angel Levine" introduces us to another flying Jew, without feathers, this time simply black, a magical black man, Alexander Levine, by name, but by narrational locution, "the Negro." His visitation to the story's protagonist, Manischevitz (no first name given), features a familiar Malamudian patter, and includes the following set up and punch line: "'So tell me,' Manischevitz said triumphantly, 'how did you get here?' 'I was translated.'" Levine's reply is in keeping with a certain stilted, straight-man tonality the story assigns him during its first half.

Let us hear such an answer at least one punning register higher. Where *does* such a magical black man come from? From Hollywood? Burlesque? Folklore? From what text of culture has he been *translated*? And in speaking his part, has he accidentally betrayed the story's embarrassing secret? "Angel Levine" leaves Cynthia Ozick with other concerns in mind. In "Literary Blacks and Jews," an essay first published in 1972 that treats, in layered symmetry, Malamud's *The Tenants*, essays by Irving Howe and Ralph Ellison, and contemporary Black–Jewish relations, Ozick concludes her brief discussion of Malamud's text with a different question from mine:

> A distinction must be made. Is it the arrival of a divine messenger that we are to marvel at, or is it the notion of a black Jew? If this is a story with a miracle in it, then the only miracle it proposes is that a Jew can be found among the redemptive angels. And if we are meant to be "morally" surprised, it is that – for once – belief in the supernatural is rewarded by a supernatural act of mercy. But the narrative is altogether offhand about the question of the angel's identity: Levine is perfectly matter-of-fact about it, there is nothing at all miraculous in the idea that a black man can be a Jew. In a tale about the supernatural, this is what emerges as the "natural" element – as natural-feeling as Manischevitz's misfortunes and his poverty. Black misfortune and poverty have a different resonance – Manischevitz's wanderings through Harlem explain the differences – but, like the Jews' lot, the blacks' has an everyday closeness, for Manischevitz the smell of a familar fate. To him – and to Malamud at the end of the fifties – that black and Jew are one is no miracle.[15]

The commentary is apposite, but it functions as a point of departure for Ozick's argument about Black/Jewish discord, not for any more elaborate or careful a reading. I pick up on such discord, and Ozick's own possible complicity in it, later in this chapter, and simply let my question stand.

Later in the story, the angel's discourse changes dramatically from one kind of mock-formal – "It was given me to understand that both your wife and you require assistance of a salubrious nature" (281) – to another, that is, antic Black English Vernacular: "Speak, Ah is a private pusson . . . Kindly state the pu'pose of yo communication with yo's truly . . . Anythin else yo got to say?" (288) Angel-speak and Black-speak, but, as yet, no Jew-speak. The "translated," that is, borrowed, second-hand quality of the speech in both halves of the story gets doubled tropologically in the strange scene of the Harlem synagogue – the space itself doubled when it abruptly translates into a "honkytonk."

> Around the table, as if frozen to it and the scroll which they all touched with their fingers sat four Negroes wearing skullcaps . . . . "Neshoma. No waht dat mean?" "That's the word that means soul," said the boy . . . . "Souls is immaterial substance.

That's all. The soul is derived in that manner. The immateriality is derived from the substance, and they both, causally an' otherwise, derived from the soul. There can be no higher." . . . "Now how do all dat happen? Make it sound simple." "It de speerit," said the old man. "On de face of de water moved de speerit. An' dat was good. It says so in de Book, From de speerit ariz de man." . . . "But has dis spirit got some kind of shade or color?" . . . "Man, of course not. A spirit is a spirit." "Then how come we is colored?" . . . "Aint got nothing to do wid dat." (286–287)

Uncannily or not, the focus of the lesson here is the same source in Genesis describing the *nefesh chaya* (the soul of man) and *nishmat chayim* (God's breath of life mentioned above), but in a hybrid Thomistic/Black Preacher manner all its own. The proposition that "a spirit is a spirit" may hover at least a level above that of "a bird is a bird," but it remains just as sheepishly *grounded* in tautology – rhetorically, aerodynamically inert.

Has the story merely stacked its deck with stock device: a black curio, Black dialect, Jewish dialect, effigy synagogue, and effigy bar? Does Angel Levine – last described by the text as "a dark figure borne aloft on a pair of strong black wings," (289) – come off as one more Jewish literary golem, somewhere between a talking crow (Malamud) and a mute blackamoor (Bellow)? And perhaps more pertinently, if "Jews are everywhere!" ("Jew" being an all-purpose slot for "goodness") why does Levine's Jewishness seem the least substantial element in the text? Why is "half-drunk Negro angel" (288) its preferred mode of categorization?

When Ozick underscores the natural as opposed to the supernatural element of the story (the descriptions of Manischevitz's lonely and run-down circumstances), as resonating differently than the comparable descriptions of Black shabbiness, what she really means is that those portions of the text about the Jewish quotidian show Malamud at his best: humanizing, solicitous, sensitively literary in ear and eye. Those that ventriloquize the black everyday, on the other hand, translate it into the *Black Fantastic*, whether in synagogue or honky-tonk, the story's "blackness" spoken by and through "Jewishness."

At one point, Manischevitz tells Levine, "'If you are a Jew, say the blessing for bread.' Levine recited it in sonorous Hebrew." (281) Malamud consigns the story's sole moment of genuine Black sonority (in Roland Barthes's sense of acoustic richness between selves, of really *hearing* the other[16]) to description, not representation; we don't see, hear the recitation, but are simply told about it (obviously one doesn't expect literary fiction to work like a phonograph, but there are ample devices of representation available that a mere assertion abruptly cancels). Moreover, besides his name, this stands as the only other indication of his Jewishness, left similarly occluded and un-pronounced. For the story's composite visitor, in other words, there is still no "Jew-speak," the ethnic province solely of Manischevitz. As he himself correlates a statement about identity with a demonstration of ethnic authenticity, "Is here Manischevitz."

At the beginning of his essay, "Author and Hero in Aesthetic Activity" (in *Art and Arrivelability*), Mikhail Bakhtin writes,

> In order to see the true and integral countenance of someone close to us, someone we apparently know very well – think how many masking layers must first be removed from his face, layers that were sedimented upon his face by our own fortuitous reactions and attitudes and by fortuitous life situations. (6)

Bakhtin speaks of an "aesthetic objectivity" here (a relationship to his text or protagonist somewhat analogous to the Levinasian desider-atum of ethical care), that emphasizes authorial *position*: "his loving removal of himself from the field of the hero's life, his clearing of the whole field of the hero and his existence," (16) the coefficient of an entirely exterior aesthetic compassion.

The author–hero relationship consists then of two "noncoinciding consciousnesses," two horizons meeting at a point where value is creatively "bestowed" onto an otherness that keeps its integrity *as other*, but needs, in Bakhtin's phrase, a consummating enframement. Aesthetic realization, in other words, depends on a simultaneous involvement and detachment, an empathy respectful of boundary limits. Bakhtin's bias throughout this essay is visual, but in the terms I have introduced so far, the relationship he addresses just as palpably "speaks to" aurality. Heroes, then, can be said to possess only a latency or potency for speech. Authors bear the responsibility of breathing expression into them: through the mouth (or defectively – as the Talmud puts it – through the armpit), or, finally, in Tar Baby's case (and that of Mr. Sammler's pickpocket), not at all.

For "Angel Levine," it seems, we would have to connect author-Malamud with Job-like hero Manishevitz, making "the Negro," the story's bit of surplus blackness axiologically *de trop*. Now, as with "The Jewbird," such a decision may be critical deliberateness on Malamud's part; the turns of plot retain their mystery for the story's Jew precisely because the story's Black – angel or not – could only present a refractory mystery and opacity *in himself*. Recognition misfires in the face of white obtuseness, even if ethnically inflected. Indeed, what Manischevitz sees and hears – dialect, shuls translated into bars – may very well depend on, derive from, the state of his "belief." After all, his very name bespeaks comic cliché, an overly sweet, almost comic name-brand Jewish "product," the Jew as textual commodity and Malamud's wink perhaps at his own work. To paraphrase *The Tenants*, here one stereotype feels the *manufacturing* possibilities of the other.

Manischevitz and Levine, the priestly and the commercial, may thus be made to coincide on the linguistically lay level of denomination (the "Jewish name") and the thematically bargain-level of cartoon-stereotype. But otherwise they offer each other non-coinciding consciousnesses in a very different sense than Bakhtin's. Real-world affinities – political, social, economic – cannot develop between a frayed-at-the-edges Jew and a frayed-at-the-edges Black, hence the supernatural solution: "*Angel* Levine," as opposed to, say, "*Black*" or "*Negro* Levine."

It is only after Manishevitz is rewarded for his belief, that he asserts, "*Believe me*, Jews are everywhere" (italics mine). What about the Black Jews in the synagogue, one wonders? Didn't they count? Were they not supernatural enough to overwrite blackness with Jewishness? The point Ozick elides in her précis (ironic, given the contrast she means the story to present to the non-magical realities of Black/Jewish incommensurability), is that the narrative is not at all offhand about its refashioning of Blacks *as* Jews; a "miracle" is precisely what is needed if literary Black and Jew have anything of substance to say to each other.

One could pursue this same allegorical vein, invoking various models of Jewish identity or hybridity to tease out the story's cross- and inter-ethnic subtleties. But the story stays grounded. By its own terms, the fiction inhibits high-flying maneuvers of interpretation, and grounds through inarguable mundanity, a not-seeing or not-hearing in place of what Bakhtin calls "the excess of seeing," the "recognition that descends upon one like a gift." (49) The story reads out its own lumpish idolatry *because of* the kind of Blacks it imagines and gives voice to.

In an odd and polemical essay, "America: Towards Yavneh," Ozick inveighs against the current state of literary practice that she labels a form of idol-worship. By stark contrast, the nineteenth-century novel in its reach beyond device to History and Idea was nothing if not "a Judaized novel."

George Eliot and Dickens and Tolstoy were all touched by the Jewish covenant; they wrote of conduct and the consequences of conduct; they were a society concerned with will and command-ment. At bottom it is not the old novel as "form" that is being rejected, but the novel as a Jewish force. (24)[17]

The new novel, the Gentile novel, conduces to neither Idea nor History but "poem" – pure aesthesis, and therefore, *idol*. New Jewish fiction especially, Ozick maintains, must seize the day and speak to and out of a "liturgical" Jewishness, "a choral voice, a communal voice, the echo of the voice of the Lord of History." (28) Otherwise, it cedes the day on two fronts: to a literary gentile-paganism, art nar-rowly conceived, and to a literary-Diasporism which blows into the wide (wrong) end of the shofar, (35) muting the authentically Jewish voice in the service of universalism's background hum.

I cite the essay to note Ozick's own concern with voice and its proper projection. Grant her point about literature-as-liturgy, and let us wonder about a Jewish writer, Malamud, less in need of a ram's horn than an ear trumpet when it comes to amplifying the sound of otherness. In his case, a problem of form *combines* with a problematic of ethnically particular "force," bestowing (a mixed blessing, to be sure) on its titular character not the special condition of "Angel" Levine, but "Idol" Levine, instead, with the story's other Jew, Manis-chevitz, faring little better himself.

3. *"Black Is My Favorite Color"*

What of entirely earthbound and thus presumably ordinary black-ness in Malamud's short fiction? Mrs. Ornita Harris in "Black Is My Favorite Color" holds out as the only candidate left. Neither a bird nor an angel, and a woman to boot, she would seem at first sight to bear little resemblance to her closest Malamudian kin (though *sight* in the story does not play a minor role). Venturing outside of Malamud's ouevre for close literary relations, although the remotest of kin, Stein's "Melanctha" does suggest a parallel between a "pale yellow negress" from the country who functions almost entirely as a vehicle for prose style and this story's "cleaning woman from Father Divine." Charity Quietness also recalls the character of Zulena, the "mahogany-colored maid" in Nella Larsen's 1929 novel *Passing*, who is disregarded even by the text. (See the section on Larson in my "Incognito Ergn Sum.") Like her, a bit of minor local color, Charity's plot function requires that she sit "in the toilet eating her two hard-boiled eggs," (73) so her Jewish employer can muse about his "fate with colored people." (74) But if Charity recalls Melanctha and Zulena in her textual serviceability, she also represents flattened counterpart to the more rounded Ornita, the story's black "heroine." Of all Malamud's stories about "Blacks" and "Jews," "Black Is My Favorite Color" finally warrants critical reckoning entirely on its own terms.

The narrating voice in this first-person text belongs to Nat Lime, the name not so ethnically decisive, the person very much a Jew (although the kind, the story tells us, who eats ham sandwiches) – self described as "forty-four, a bachelor with a daily growing bald spot on the back of my head . . . who enjoys company so long as he has it," (73) and whose "favorite color" is . . . not green, but black. With Charity sequestered by the text until the end of the story – "That's how it is. I give my heart and they kick me in the teeth. 'Charity Quietness – you hear me – come out of that god-damn toilet!'" (84) – Nat Lime explains his affinity for Negro people: he's "drawn to them." He has "an eye for color." He "appreciate[s]," (74) perhaps from negrophilia or merely from fellow-feeling conditioned by proximity (he owns a liquor store in Harlem). Either way, he tells us, it is not reciprocated except during "short quantities" of luck.

> At this time of my life I should have one or two good colored friends, but the fault isn't necessarily mine. If they knew what was in my heart toward them, but how can you tell that to anybody nowadays? I've tried more than once but the language of the heart either is a dead language or else nobody understands the way you speak it. Very few. What I'm saying is, personally for me there's only one human color and that's the color of blood. (74)

Two qualifications, however: (1) As his address to Charity in the toilet suggests, the "language of the heart" can be numbered among several others he speaks; (2) the black persons who "draw" him tend to be "shes," not "hes." But independent of readers' processing such details, perhaps Malamud means to alert us to the structural paradox of first-person narration flaunted by his story: that confessing can also mean withholding, or to put it into terms that better capture the paradox, telling frequently doubles as (inadvertent) showing.

Lime narrates other anecdotes, including the almost obligatory one of young Jewish boy befriends disadvantaged black peer[18] – "a one-way proposition" (77) that includes invitations and gifts which only precipitate an antisemitic outburst:

One day when I wasn't expecting it he hit me in the teeth. I felt like crying but not because of the pain. I spit blood and said, "What did you hit me for? What did I do to you?"

"Because you are a Jew bastard. Take your Jew movies and your Jew candy, and shove them up your Jew ass." And he ran away. I thought to myself how was I to know he didn't like the movies. When I was a man I thought, you can't force it. (77)

To repeat Ozick's metaphor, maybe Nat's problem is that he speaks through the wrong end of the shofar, although by the text's logic at either end it would still have to be a "Jew shofar." Indeed, a page earlier in the story's set-up, Nat wonders, "Why did I pick him out for a friend?" (75) when rebuff was more or less imminent; he says "I like his type," which seems to refer to the boy's solitary habits, but must at some level betray Lime's (fitting) "eye for color."

In the early pages of the story, then, Black violence, allure, standoffishness, and unaccountability line up on one side, Jewish earnestness, desire, projection, and (paternalist) solicitude on the other. Jews approach; Blacks demur. " 'Why don't you wait for me, Buster? We're both going in the same direction.' But he was walking ahead and didn't hear me. Any way he didn't answer." (77) At least one can say Blacks and Jews talk alike here. Refusing to answer bespeaks choice or will, not incapacity and muzzling (though Charity Quietness *does* sit in the toilet eating eggs for the duration of the story's narration).

Nat recounts his courting of Ornita, occasioned by a discount at the liquor store, which leads to an awkward date, and later a romance with possibility. The date yields the following cautionary ruth:

We went in like strangers and we came out like strangers. I wondered what was in her mind and I thought to myself, whatever is in there, it's not a certain white man I know. All night long we went together like we were chained. (79)

In other words, Nat's narrating consciousness remains defining and exclusive (his rhetorical tic throughout is "I'm the kind of man who . . . "). Black minds remain off limits unless their owners speak them.

In preparing for the clash that predictably follows, wrecking Nat's and Ornita's chances for Black–Jewish relations, the text sequences two versions of the latter and implicitly links them. The first consists of a description of clothes stripped off before lovemaking, tellingly focused through Nat's eye for color: "[S]he wore a purple dress and I thought to myself, my God, what colors. Who paints that picture paints a masterpiece."

Under her purple dress she wore a black slip, and when she took that off she had white underwear. When she took off the white underwear she was black again. But I know where the next white was, if you want to call it white. (80)

As if in response to that last indiscretion, in the next paragraph (in story-time, "that same week"), the narrator's store gets held up by two black men with revolvers. In the story's climax, black street violence once again intervenes in the form of the couple's being accosted on the street, a brutish, sexualized, recognition scene of verbal and bodily assault: "Shut your mouth, Jewboy. No more black pussy for you." (83) Ornita gets slapped, and so does Nat – significantly or not – on the mouth. Black (female) and Jew (male and more broken-hearted) cease relations.

The story's final anecdote features Nat's abortive attempt to escort a blind man. "I figured we were going in the same direction so I took his arm. 'I can tell you're white,' he said." (84) A black woman intervenes; violence of a sort ensues: "She pushed me with her shoulder and I hurt my leg on the fire hydrant." Nat emphasizes the role differential: Jew gives heart (spills gratuitously); Black kicks teeth (plugs up the hole).

4. "Literary blacksandjews"

In the afterword to "Literary Blacks and Jews," Ozick repeats almost the same phrase she used in reference to "Angel Levine," this time to assess the Crown Heights conflict of 1991, for her the uncanny coming-to-life of Black/Jewish apocalypse predicted by Malamud's *The Tenants*: "But distinctions are called for." (70) Or in Nat Lime's terms, Blacks and Jews face different directions. Or rather, "Blood-suckin Jew Niggerhater" and "Anti-Semitic Ape" – Malamud's valediction to a world of nongoyish Blacks and nonwhite Jews – face each other only to kill each other.

But distinctions are exactly what Crown Heights revealed, according to Ozick, in a way that authorial equity in its assignment of mutual culpability at the end of *The Tenants* did not. There, Jew and Black kill each other off. Throughout the novel, Lesser (like Lime), is awarded the privilege of focalization, but on the last page, the narrator allows the two characters (writers both) to inflict corresponding anguish with reciprocal barbarity – "Each, thought the writer, feels the anguish of the other,"[19] – for *each* is "the writer."

Ozick begins her essay with "Angel Levine" as Malamud's late

1950s exercise in moral radiance in order to highlight the societal shift behind the re-evaluation that his late 1960s "parable of political anxiety" (66) evidently demonstrates. In one, we find the "truth of aspiration"; in the other, the "truth that matches real events." (44) But the stories suggest political implications of their own (even if "politics" does a good impression of an angel or bird who has flown south). And in the same way, a logic of distinction (though not in Ozick's sense) underlies each of them.

Thus, since they evidently *are* called for from somewhere, distinctions get dutifully made, to different degrees, in "The Jewbird," "Angel Levine," and "Black Is My Favorite Color," unifying themselves along two clearly distinct parallels. In this instance, however, parallel does not signify facing. Either we see the stories collectively as gentle satire on Jewish identity, meant to laugh Jews, along with everybody else, out of their all too human vices. Or we see them less sympathetically as perhaps well-meaning but still culpable *instrumentalizations* of Black identity. In the first case, we get souls, however flawed, everyman Jews whose misfortune redemptively hinges them to others. In the second we get so many Black golems, a distinctively false note in an oeuvre so resolute about the everyday – the rumpled raincoats of "ethnicity" or "culture" worn by personhood as always a size too large or too small.

True, "Black Is My Favorite Color" does hold itself at some distance. Nat Lime deserves whatever skepticism readers want to give him, or whatever sympathy they prefer to withhold. No doubt, in that light, the story "reads out" its own critique. Yet even so, "Black" functions little more than *color* in a notably sentimental and depoliticized – or under-ethicized – sense: another instance of ethical-politics as mere *assistant* in Malamud's work. It remains unclear whether such sentimentality should be limited exclusively to its narrator-protagonist; in three stories of belabored blackness in *The Magic Barrel* ("Angel Levine" placed last in Malamud's order) real ethno-racial sensitivity remains the elusive literary property, obscured by its literaturized surrogate.

John Edgar Wideman: the ethics of exteriority

> Odd that it took him years to realize how small she was . . . . No one had asked him so he'd never needed to describe his cleaning woman. Took no notice of her height. Her name was Clara Jackson and when she arrived he was overwhelmed by the busyness of her presence. (167)

The kapos hesitated, astounded by what she dared. Was this black one a madwoman, a witch? They tore me from her grasp, pushed me down and I crumpled there in the stinking mud of the compound. One more kick, a numbing, blind smash that took my breath away. Blood flooded my eyes. I lost consciousness. Last I saw of her she was still fighting, slim. beautiful legs kicking at them as they dragged and punched across the yard.
-You said she was colored?
-Yes. Yes. A dark angel who fell from the sky and saved me.
-Always thought it was just you people over there doing those terrible things to each other. (174)

He thinks of Clara Jackson in the midst of her family .... He tries to picture them, eating and drinking, huge people crammed into a tiny, shabby room. Unimaginable, really. The faces of her relatives became his. Everyone's hair is thick and straight and black. (175)[20]

Once again, the narrator, a death camp survivor, is Jewish. The author, however, is counterfigure – the African American novelist, John Edgar Wideman. The passages above appear in his short story, "Valaida" from the 1989 collection *Fever*. If, against the background of the texts so far, the selections above suggest an amalgam of Malamud's "Angel Levine" and "Black Is My Favorite Color," and in voice, something far subtler than either, it is doubtless because Wideman's story subsumes them both in complexity and daring. The sequencing of this chapter's texts does not therefore exclusively follow the dictates of chronology, but answers instead to a crescendo, from stories of the stillborn to those with the breath of life.[21]

It is here, consequently, that the recurrent thread of Ozick's essay about blacksandjews runs into deepest trouble, given its differential estimation of novelistic characters, critic-novelists, and populations-at-large. In Malamud's novel, the black writer Willie Spearmint is made totemic, "an object, an artifact, a *form* representing an entire people," (59) Tar Baby, in other words, who, accordingly, cannot get beyond seeing Lesser as objectified "Jew," while Lesser himself, until the end, appears as both less self-fabricated and more humane.

In the world of literary criticism, according to Ozick, Irving Howe and Ralph Ellison cut parallel figures.

> What happened between Ellison and Howe (behind the back, as it were of literature) was bound to be seized on by the larger metaphor of the novel. In my own case I have not found it possible to think about *The Tenants* without first turning Howe-Ellison round and round; together they make a bemusing arti-

fact in reverse archaeology. Dig them up and discover, in gen-
teel form, the savage future. (55)

What Ozick finds is the otherwise fluid and capaciously imaginative
Ralph Ellison unable to credit Jews – or representatively, Howe –
with a specifically Jewish willingness to "identify" with black realities. Rather, their guilt in Ellison's words, "lies in their facile, perhaps
unconscious, but certainly unrealistic, identification with what is
called the 'power structure.'" (52) When they're not therefore passing
for white, and in asserting the phenomenological priority of Black
plight and protest, they don blackface. In this chapter's terms, Jews
approach; Blacks demur.

In the ontologically prior "real world," both in 1974 when Ozick
wrote her essay or in 1993 when she appended an afterword, Jews
hold their hands out while Blacks return the favor by holding them
up. "If Jewish identification with black causes," she wrote originally,
"was after all not intended to be traitorous, then it was destined by
Jewish success to become so . . . Lack of sympathy is an obvious
offense; sympathy turns out to be more so." (48)

As for totemism: it remains a black malady. Blacks "made" Willie
Spearmint, at the expense of Jewish compassion, a sad contrast to
the authenticity of Jewish self-critique (and perhaps Jewish anti-
idolatry). For contemporary Black/Jewish relations (worse than
Malamud's fictive apocalypse of joint culpability), as reflected in the
"race war" of Crown Heights, "only one side did the stabbing." (69)
The fictive totemism of Malamud's Blacks echoes the lapse into
totemism of Ellison's criticism, just as it fore-echoes the lived totemism of contemporary Black Jew-baiting.

And so the essay goes, warily tracking its way into the present.
Although Ozick confesses to being "radically uneasy" (72) when she
writes "the blacks," "the Jews," the essay and afterword do not flinch
from deploying terms like "role," "a Jew/a black," or "collectivity"
as stable terms of definition, in addition to a whole set of selective
noun-complements like "Jewish commitment," "Jewish concern,"
"resentful blacks," "black militancy" "black suffering," and so on.
Moreover, collectivity *for Jews* implies one thing, collectivity *for Blacks*
means something else, the latter it seems always a political threat.

The essay, that is, does not *itself* entirely step out of the vicious
circle of totemicization, fabrication, or the drift of identification it
assigns to novel, critical exchange, and current event. And further,

Ozick has (not ingenuously) stacked *her* deck, with select examples and attributions in such a way that the matrix she describes of necessity spirals in on itself, the claustrophobia of Malamud's novel replaying itself concentrically on every concomitant level.

What Wideman's stories do so brilliantly, by contrast (only the Caribbean writer, Caryl Phillips, has as gifted a feel for such alterity) is to subtend the circle, not orbit it inside or out. They alter the terms Ozick takes for granted by imaginatively re-creating them – terms like "identification" or "representation," and especially – within a created literary world recognizably answerable for its creation – "Black" and "Jew." In "Valaida," a complex layering of spaces gives shape to the facing and conjunction – the and – of "Black and Jew": two spaces asymmetrically and tentatively inhabited by a survivor and the two black women on different peripheries of his life, and the overlapping or "virtual" space shared by them forty years apart, each the custodian, buffer, housing, counterskin, for a Jew who has lost the shelter of others. Encompassing these three persons and spaces, the text constructs its most subtle tangencies: of coming and going, of look and proximity, of other ever-so-lightly touching other. I invoke Ozick's essay again at the end of this chapter, but concern myself now with the richness of Wideman's *nishmat chayim* and the faces – eyes, ears, and voices – it so conscientiously animates.[22]

1. *"Valaida"*

The title name belongs to a jazz-trumpeter, singer and dancer (c. 1900–1956) who found herself interned along with Jews, Gypsies, "even Germans who were not Jews" (172) in a concentration camp, saving the life of the narrator by shielding him from being beaten to death.[23] Her voice is the first to greet us, a spectral monologue by a black ghost – somebody's Beloved, but one who never came back to life, except through the text's introductory contrivance and the memory of its primary narrator, Cohen. Across the story's grain, or perpendicular to it, both characters share the same "literary" fate, the only difference being that one has been conjured *from* life, the other, it seems, *wholly* imagined.

Valaida's version:

> *They beat me, and fucked me in every hole I had. I was their whore. Their maid. A stool they stood on when they wanted to reach a little higher. But I never sang in their cage, Bobby. Not one note. Cost me a tooth once, but not a note . . . And yes. There was a pitiful little*

stomped-down white boy in the camp I tried to keep the guards from
killing, but if he lived or died I never knew. Then or now. (166)

Cohen's version:

> A woman like you. Many years ago. A lifetime ago. Young then
> as you would have been. And beautiful. As I believe you must
> have been, Mrs. Clara. Yes. Before America entered the war.
> Already camps had begun devouring people. All kinds of
> people. Yet she was rare. Only woman like her I ever saw until I
> came here, to this country, this city. And she saved my life. I was
> just a boy. Thirteen years old. The guards were beating me. I did
> not know why. Why? They didn't need a why. They just beat . . .
> Then a woman's voice in a language I did not comprehend
> reached me. A woman angry, screeching. I heard her before I
> saw her. She must have been screaming at them to stop. She
> must have decided it was better to risk dying than watch the
> guards pound a boy to death. First I heard her voice, then she
> rushed in fell on me, wrapped herself around me . . . (173)

We, too, hear her voice first, speaking to her friend Bobby, telling
him to tell of her, of "fabled Valaida Snow who traveled in an
orchid-colored Mercedes-Benz, dressed in an orchid suit, her pet
monkey rigged out in an orchid jacket and cap, with the chauffeur in
orchid as well." (165)[24] Her anecdote of Cohen's rescue drifts from the
rest of her speech, untethered to what she wants or expects to be told
about her, a fragment of her own memory that suddenly asserts itself
in consciousness, and just as quickly subsides. The monologue ends
trailing off into reverie, "*figure and ground, ground and figure,*" conceivably a figure itself for the story's own rhythm.

Cohen's reverie faces outward, too, addressed to his black maid,
Clara Jackson, in evidently the first such "conversation" they have
shared in the many years she has worked for him. The story thus
revises its counterpart in Malamud (as it suggests an alternative to the
mute, discursively foreshortened fate of cousin Apter in *Operation
Shylock*). Clara's talking is limited to a mere handful of responses. To
Cohen's initial mention of Valaida's saving his life, she says, "No
Mistah Cohen. That's one thing I definitely did not know." (169)
Asked to sit at the table with him, she replies, "Mistah Cohen, I'm
feeling kinda poorly today. If you don mind I'ma work straight
through and gwan home early. Got all my Christmas to do and I'm
tired." (171) "Poor thing" (173) she says when Cohen pauses in his
story, though it is ambiguous whether she means him or Valaida.
"You say she was colored?" (174) she asks after he finishes. "Always

thought it was just you people over there doing those terrible things to each other." (174)

Except for a couple of italicized (formulaic) expostulations – *Yes, Lord. Save me, Jesus. Thank you Father* – those five short utterances constitute the extent of Clara's voice. After Valaida's monologue, the text speaks alternately through Cohen's direct speech and through a mixture of free indirect style, anonymous narration, and focalized thought.[25] Unlike Nat Lime's purchase on Charity Quietness, Cohen's awareness of Clara remains blunted and also engrossed, mediated: fuzzy but at the same time intense.

The story's thematics can be forced into a syntax of looks or utterance, but they sit more comfortably in subtler ones Wideman overtly manipulates: space, proximity, distance.

> She'd burst in his door and he'd felt crowded. Retreated, let her stake out the space she required. She didn't bully him but demanded in the language of her brisk, efficient movements that he accustom himself to certain accommodations. They developed an etiquette that spelled out precisely how close, how distant the two of them could be once a week while she cleaned his apartment. (167)

Later, this modulates toward touch when Cohen contemplates Clara's hair:

> Under the webbings were clumps of hair, defined by furrows exposing her bare scalp. A ribbed yarmulke of hair pressed down on top of her head. Hair he'd never imagined . . . . So different from what grew on his head . . . so different that he could not truly consider it hair, but some ersatz substitute used the evening of creation when hair ran out . . . He'd been tempted countless times to touch it. Poke his finger through the netting into one of the mounds. He'd wondered if she freed it from the veil when she went to bed. If it relaxed and spread against her pillow or if she slept all night like a soldier in a helmet. (168)

The prose vibrates with an almost accidental embodiedness, somehow getting inside the head, the skin, behind the attentive eye, of its narrating "other."

In "Black Is My Favorite Color," Nat Lime prides himself on an "eye for color," an untrustworthy calibrator for all kinds of inventoried material, be it his merchandise or other people. His paternalism reflects his propensity for self-aggrandizement: "his" bed, "his" place of business, "his" heart: all safely bounded spaces as opposed to, say, Ornita's neighborhood, or the side of the street Buster crosses over to. Nat gives to get, and not surprisingly, receives a negative return leveled right where he speaks – "they kick me in the teeth" – his mouth, a dispenser for communicative currency, being as suspect as his eye.

Cohen's not fully conscious imaginativeness, conversely, proposes another kind of dispensation – what Bakhtin called the gift-giving capacity of "aesthetic love," the active "production" of another's embodied form, a coming-to-meet it from outside its bounds. True perhaps, Clara's defamiliarized presence may threaten to cross the discursive threshold into the stubborn othering that is ethnic chauvinism, or worse. Finding a strand of her hair in the bathtub, "he'd pinched it up in a wad of toilet paper, flushed it away. Cohen imagines her family "brown and large, with lips like spoons for serving the sugary babble of their speech," the same family whose Negroid hair is re-envisioned in the last sentence of the story to be like his, "thick and straight and black." (175)

And the text describes the same strand of Clara's hair as "curled like a question mark at the end of the sentence he was always asking himself," (168) intimating Cohen's impoverishment of plot and storyline at the level of the "I" – despite the story always hanging over his life – and, again, the barely articulated sense that though he may be in himself the condition of possibility for his own life, he is not its valuable hero.[26] Valaida is. Or perhaps, at such moments, Clara is.

Thus, the same seemingly "racialized discourse" is no less merciless about describing Cohen, or his own self-perception in contrast to Clara: "The female abundance, her thickness, her bulk reassuring as his hams shrink, his fingers become claws, the chicken neck frets away inside those razor-edged collars she scrubs and irons." (170) Their two bodies weighed as if in a counterbalance, Clara has substance, extension, "flesh on her bones was not excess, a gift"; Cohen, conversely, renders, in a double sense, his physical state in language that pares and defleshes: "Oh you scarecrow. Death's-head stuck on a stick. Another stick lashed crossways for arms." (170) Remembering his humiliation once liberated at having to be seen by others, he thinks, "Who in God's name would steal a boy's face and leave this thing?" (171)

Cohen seems to grant Clara her diffidence when he first makes conversation with her. Perhaps, one thinks, it has to do with the word "colored" he uses. He interprets it as taking offence to something "unseemly, ungentlemanly, some insult," (169) she has probably imputed to him (though we recall the unmistakably erotic component in his observations of her), some cruel trespass that deserves an answering look of non-recognition, that "you do not exist." Yet he persists, asking her to sit and offering to make her coffee while he drinks his tea.

Part of the story's genius lies in its capturing how blackness on the most material level stays alien, distanced, unhomely to the Jewish mind that at the same time communes with it, with the wakefulness of the stranger. And, indeed, because "time weighs more on him," (172) he sleeps less, nights seeming to bring with them the encroachment of his own absence, the space he used to occupy. Jew and Black, employer and servant, do avoid each other, or eye each other warily, no room being "large enough to contain them and the distance they needed." (168) The text may replicate Jewish approach and black demurral, Cohen's curiosity and the one-track "busyness of [Clara's] presence." (167) But in its unequal distribution of represented thought and speech, the story appears to renegotiate the simple *space* of relatedness as first shared by Valaida and Cohen half-a-century before.

In place of family relations or thwarted desire, Wideman's story substitutes adjacency and tentatively shared space, somewhere between what Ozick in her essay calls "grasping" and "turning away."[27] As to the uses of blackjewishrelations, "Valaida" illustrates one meaning of "use" and the deepest import, I have argued, of "relations": a *narrative* linking of Black and Jew through the telling/ listening that ever so briefly bonds selves on the plane of story. Certainly, that bond seems to say more about Cohen than Clara, not only because "telling" defines his role as opposed to hers in their relational asymmetry, but because he and another black maid in the dim past co-tenanted first inside the space of voice. "I heard her before I saw her," he says of Valaida. Clara, on the other hand – at least from within Cohen's perspective – keeps her distance:

> He closes the china cupboard. Her back is turned. She mutters something at the metal vacuum tubes she's unclamping. He realizes he's finished the story anyway. Doesn't know how to say the rest. She's humming, folding rags, stacking them on the bottom pantry shelf. Lost in the cloud of her own noise. Much more to his story, but she's not waiting around to hear it. (174)

The sound of clicking cupboards will have to simulate, or suffice as, response, to "punctuate the silence, reassure him," and keep Cohen company after Clara leaves. Yet Clara does, if only virtually, "touch"

Valaida, and thus by extension, Cohen himself. As Valaida shielded, so do the shirts Clara assiduously cleans and irons. The stamped numbers on their collars dimly trace those embossed on Cohen's arm. Two black supporting players: one offers herself as a protective wall, the other, precisely within or superseding the framing social asymmetry of domestic servant and employer, fills out slightly the *horror vacui*, briefly taking up its slack.

But in "Valaida," any space of recognition shears less within or across the text than above it in Wideman's own ethnically marked configuration of "author and hero." We are not the heroes of our own lives, Bakhtin says, since story, as aesthetic communion and consummation, belongs in the "category of the other." [28] It is, finally, as an architectonic of impinging spaces, authorial, textual and literary person-al, that Wideman's story faces Blacks and Jews, taking Ozick's essay at its (last, and best) word, to create a "breathing space." (75) A space of proximity, a third term beside the feast of brotherhood and the famine of otherhood, an improvisatory, limited, and short-lived coffee-and-tea. Just one other poses a hard enough ethical challenge for selfhood; a whole people allegorized as secret sharer seems positively indiscreet.

2. *"Fever"*

"Fever," the final story in Wideman's collection (and the third in which Jewish voices narrate), rehearses a by-now familiar surface level of difficulty in the author's poetics. Readers must sort through a set of voices left undifferentiated in conventional ways. In Wideman's fiction, a new voice will pick up where another has left off, with only a paragraph break to mark the difference. For "Fever" and "Hostages," such structural idiosyncrasy fairly invites an ethical or political reading: when it comes to discursive space, Wideman may be telling us, dialogism and hybridity rule, rebuking the jealously guarded boundaries of a certain pinched and constricted ethnic life, where breathing space is consequently held at a premium.

"The primary narrator of "Fever" is a black nurse and undertaker, assigned to tend the dying and bury the dead at the Bush Hill clinic during an outbreak of yellow fever in eighteenth-century Philadelphia. The story oscillates between a first-person account (based on the 1797 *Narrative* of Richard Allen and Absalom Jones) and third-person narration that monitors Allen's fluctuating consciousness, as he narrates a progress through the city.[29] Several pages in, not set off in any way except through the nurse's initially cryptic deixis, the text reads, "he watched him bring the scalding liquid to his lips and thought to myself that's where his color comes from," (248) it not being immediately clear who "he" is. A first person interrupts:

> Despair was in my heart. The fiction of our immunity had been exposed for the vicious lie it was, a not so subtle device for wresting us from our homes, our loved ones, the afflicted among us, and sending us to aid strangers . . . My fellow countrymen searching everywhere but in their own hearts, the foulness upon which this city is erected, to lay blame on other for killing fever, pointed their fingers at foreigners and called it Palatine fever, a pestilence imported from those low countries in Europe where, I have been told, war for control of the sea-lanes, the human cargoes transported thereupon, has raged for a hundred years. (249)

The name comes later, offered by the speaker himself in a later anecdote – "Master Abraham," father to a son "clubbed to death when they razed the ghetto of Antwerp" (259) – but it becomes gradually apparent that he is a Jew, probably Sephardic, his services commanded during the epidemic as nurse and undertaker, but now dying of the fever himself. He speaks of a "dark skin . . . seen not only as a badge of shame for its wearer [but] evil incarnate, the mask of long agony and violent death." (249) He voices the untenable double-bind of first, pariah, then forced laborer, "how the knife was plunged in our hearts, then cruelly twisted." (249)

Late in the text Abraham says to Allen (echoing Levinas, echoing Bakhtin, echoing Sartre's *Wretched*), "The circumstances are similar, my brother. My shadow. My dirty face." (259) But even if such commonality between the social conditions of a certain set of prototypical American Jews (merchants) and those of a certain set of prototypical African Americans (indentured servants or slaves) two hundred years in the past were not being overtly signaled, Wideman ensures a shared public space and proximity between them on the level of plot.

> If an ordinance forbidding ringing of bells to mourn the dead had not been passed, that awful tolling would have marked our days, the watches of our night in the African American community, as it did in those environs of the city we were forbidden to inhabit . . . When my duties among the whites were concluded, how many nights did I return and struggle till dawn with victims here, my friends, wandering sons of Africa whose faces I could not look upon without seeing my own. (250)

Nor is Wideman above placing in Abraham's mouth even more deplorable "racialized discourse" than that he inserts in Cohen's head in "Valaida." In order to shake Allen out of what he regards as a kind of immoral "busyness," a slaveship "immobility" that takes the form of an "endless round of duty and obligation" (261) to a charlatan physician who evidently kills more patients than he saves, Abraham lashes him with language. "You are a fool, you black son of Ham. You slack-witted, Nubian ape. You progeny of Peeping Toms and orangutans." (257)

But again, as in "Valaida," if Abraham permits himself the invective of "mindless, spineless black puddle of slime with no will of its own," (258) the text counterbalances an answering discourse of sorts, Allen's own Black rendering of Jewish Abraham:

> His finger a gaunt, swollen-jointed, cracked-bone, chewed thing. Like the nose on his face. The nose I'd thought looked more like finger than nose . . . Finger wagging, then the cackle. The barnyard braying. Berserk chickens cackling in his skinny, goiter-knobbed throat. (257)

Where Willie Spearmint's and Lesser's parting verbal assaults in *The Tenants* may give shape to Ozick's deepest-seated fears about Black–Jewish discord, Wideman's story, by contrast, does not hurl gratuitous epithet so much as it heterogenizes and historicizes two voices already dialogically linked.

Abraham and Allen's heteronomy tracks a common narrative about family athwart ethno-racial difference and repetition. Abraham explains that in being commandeered by municipal order for the "general task of saving the city," he was forced not only "to leave this neighborhood where my skills were sorely needed," but to leave his family: "I nursed those who hated me, deserted the ones I loved, who loved me." (250) And so in their mirroring or doubling, he offers himself as object-lesson, admonishing Allen for mistaken loyalties, for serving abstract authority, and deserting kin.

> Once, ten thousand years ago I had a wife and children. I was like you, Allen, proud, innocent, forward-looking, well-spoken, well-mannered, a beacon and steadfast. I began to believe the whispered promise that I could have more. More of what I didn't ask. Didn't know, but I took my eyes off what I loved in order to obtain this more. Left my wife and children and when I returned they were gone. Forever lost to me. The details are insignificant. Suffice to say the circumstances of my leaving were very like yours. Very much like yours, Allen. And I lost

everything. Became a wanderer among men. Bad news people see coming from miles away. A Pariah. A joke. I'm not black like you, Allen, but I will be soon. Sooner than you'll be white. And if you're ever white, you'll be as dead as I'll be when I'm black. (258–259)

In this, its embedded story, "Fever" sustains a supplementary discourse, an "inside narrative," a cautionary tale about metaphysical freedom and political bondage, its local differences unified *sub specie aeternis* by what Abraham calls G–d's "one book – the text of suffering." (260) Inside or over the racial provocations, Wideman back-projects a Fanon-like existentialism, for as the black man "join[s his] brother, the Jew in suffering" in *Black Skin/White Masks*, so out of Abraham's mouth, Allen hears an emancipatory summons:

> Can you imagine yourself, Allen, as other than you are? A free man with no charlatan Rush to blame. The weight of your life in your hands. You've told me tales of citizens paralyzed by fear, of slaves on shipboard who turn to stone in their chains, their eyes boiled in the sun . . . . Your life man. Tell me what sacred destiny, what nigger errand keeps you standing here at my filthy pallet? Fly, fly, fly away home. Your house is on fire, your children burning. (261)

In such passages we discern one more inside narrative, a meta-story about storytellers and hearers as legatees of a common fate of recognition. Allen first introduces us to Abraham, as we now more clearly realize, as partners in conversation, the Jew's part a "soliloquy," the Black's that of "listener, a witness learning his story, a story buried so deeply he couldn't recall it, but dreamed pieces . . . a reverie with the power to sink us both into unreality." (249) And although Allen perceives it as "a ceaseless play of voices only [Abraham] heard," driven by a "summoning," "possessing" quality which "enables him to speak, to be," such a description applies as well to Allen's "authorship" of Abraham as "hero," and to the text's overall capacity to breathe otherness into life.[30]

Wideman's story, finally, attests to a claim advanced by both Bakhtin and Benjamin that an author realizes a narrative's breathing space most successfully in the shadow of a character's (and a text's) death, when last breaths are drawn – ironic, perhaps, since, in Bakhtin's words, "aesthetic memory is *productive* – it gives birth, for the first time, to the *outward* . . . on a new plane of being." [31] That is how golems and Tar Babies, literaturized blacks and Jews, may finally have something to tell us through a "*living* space that has the character of an aesthetic *event*."[32]

By death, Bakhtin means the *terminus a quo* from which a life can be perceived as an integral whole. But for fiction where author and hero diverge along ethnic or racial lines, wholeness can also be a function of a consciousness and body of experience or tradition sufficiently foreign that its apartness bestows upon something analogous to the *removed* character Bakhtin takes pains to emphasize as aesthetically optimal.

> Within itself, a lived life can express itself in the form of an action, a confession-as-penitence, an outcry; absolution and grace descend upon it from the Author. An ultimate issue out of itself is not *immanent* to a lived life; it descends upon a life-lived-from-within as a gift from the self-activity of another – from a self-activity that *comes to meet* my life *outside* its bounds.[33]

Against the immediate background of Wideman's fiction, such labor of exteriority applies both to authorial obligation *and* to the kind of criticism that performs correlative acts of answering approach when it imagines texts in beckoning call and consummating response – two domains of public space. And indeed one could extend this dialogue between amplifying outsideness (in the double sense of acoustics and measure) and the boundaries of self to ethnic and racial identity generally.

3. "Hostages"

"Form is a boundary," says Bakhtin. Aesthetic activity – especially when politicized by the ramifications of group identity – faces outward, toward the sphere of *another's* self-activity. (85) In "Hostages," Wideman, true to his name, takes his widest stretch. The double-voiced narration is shared between an African American man and an Israeli woman. Again, the text possesses a refractory, paradoxically alienating quality as readers must puzzle out the precise borders between one self-activity and the sphere of another; the story needs several readings in order to stabilize its play of voices.

The theme of "hostages," not surprisingly, unifies much of the discourse, intermittent radio or television reports of a "hostage crisis" (never specifically located anywhere, but presumably involving Arabs and Jews), occasional analytic excursuses on the phenomenology of "being a hostage," and the implications to be culled from each narrator's story as respective "hostage" – to culture, class privilege, marital asymmetries, motherhood, skin color, historical event – for example Auschwitz.

Wideman's story (and a passage spoken by Abraham in "Fever," as well) invokes the Talmudic legend of the *lamed vov*, the righteous thirty-six who at any given time give succor to the rest of humanity – in Wideman's words, "sponges drawing mankind's suffering into themselves." (185)[34] Perhaps the story does thus faintly echo the hostage-trope in Levinas's later philosophy, which could be pushed in the direction of the purely textual field of author-hero-reader relations. [35]

But Wideman's penchant for the hostage notion, in addition to its plain real-world implications of anti-ethical behavior in the extreme, concentrates on the economic dimensions of its use and exchange value. Hostages are people held for ransom, the text will tell us; some kind of payment is required. (179) "Value," "fraction" and "calculation" are spoken of. "Is it possible to bank hostages against future needs? A stockpile available for potential renegotiations . . . Can the body be turned in for credit?" (186)

Certainly for the woman narrator, the question of payment revolves around what she has relinquished for the sake of class-comfort and family security – not merely her own freedom, but, one suspects, a bartered ethnicity: a life in Israel (she has emigrated to America), a first husband who was an Egyptian Jew ("darker than I am," (176) says the black narrator), a life lived among darker skin and dark voices. Evidently, erotic possibility for the story's two narrators has come and gone, although an affinity at skin-level remains: "She said she could tell me everything because I was black. Because I was black, I would understand."

And yet a cryptic moment in the story suggests something more ambiguous:

> . . . she lifts the covers, and cool, merciful air infiltrates the clamminess beneath the blankets she steeples with her knees. A slab of icy hip beside her. Someone naked and dead in her bed. She is afraid to move. She know's it's her body lying next to her and the thought of touching it again paralyzes her. She's soaked in her own sweat. Thick as blood or paint. She can't see it's color but knows it's dark. The color of her lover, a man whose sweat turns her to a tar baby too, wet and black and sticky. (184)

Is "her lover" a dream version of her first husband, the Sephardi? Or is it her black friend, the other narrator? Or, straightforwardly, merely an anonymous dark man? In any case, she seems to configure color itself as an element in a hostage-relation, something that, as with Brother Rabbit's Tar Baby, gets her stuck, makes her adhere. As

George Eliot's Silas Marner remarks of the deficiencies of rational understanding vs. the surplus of adhesion between embodied (and internalized) selves, "It isn't the meaning, it's the glue."[36]

Intermittently throughout the story, the Israeli contemplates the servant-women in the well-to-do houses proximate to hers, "black girls [,] Jamaican, Haitian, Puerto Rican . . . Emigrants like her." (182) The text insistently reminds us that she does not speak or commune with them in any way, but rather *spies* on them from above, from within her house. They remain merely exterior, superficially so ("aesthetically spurious products" Bakhtin might call them), that signify a racialized yearning for a life of forfeit color.

The story's final sentences impress color on readers one last time. Fantasizing about the possibility of her husband being hijacked and held for ransom (she imagines a snapshot of him taken as a child, the same year that her mother was surviving in Auschwitz) the woman thinks, "An exchange is being sacrificed. She wonders how many dark lives must be sacrificed." (188) Once again in a story by Wideman, rival kinships of family, ethno-racial identity, and Black/Jewish proximity crisscross and complicate each other. Such crosshatching, finally, would seem to defy the easy oppositions and dichotomies Ozick rehearses in "Literary Blacks and Jews." Perhaps that is because Wideman succeeds in insulating his black and Jewish narrators from facile literaturization. Since there must be hostages, after all, why not let recognition descend upon them like a gift (Bakhtin), a plangency and roundedness of voice in exchange for the boundaries of literature?

Tenants

I return, one last time, to city streets, and to Ozick's blacksandjews. Alphabetically perhaps, it is but a small distance from Wideman to Wieseltier and West. Sadly, in other respects the gap yawns . . . wide. "A face is a face: it changes as it faces," wrote Malamud in *The Tenants*. (11) If one maintains with Levinas that faces locate and express ethical answerability, then it makes a perverse sense that at the end of Malamud's novel the Jewish intellectual Lesser takes an ax to the Black writer's head: what better site to commit murder than the very part of the person that expresses the interdict against murder.

In a recent article, Leon Wieseltier purports to review the oeuvre of Cornel West, but comes out another Lesser; a fair description of the piece would call it a hatchet job.[37] Unlike the denouement of

Malamud's novel, it is the Jew who goes for the head here, a character-assassination out of proportion to any deficits in West's work to date[38] – which, to grant the substance if not the tone of Wieseltier's reservations, are not impervious to critique. More distressing than the lapse itself, however, is the missed opportunity for genuine response and mediation between the tradition of public Jewish intellectuals and its African American counterpart. It could be fairly said, then, that both figures lose face, and for that reason alone life once again returns the favor by duplicating art, with both parties now ending up the lesser.

That would leave Wieseltier's very public animus toward West far more gratuitous in its own way than either Willie and Lesser's bloodletting in *The Tenants*, or Irving Howe and Ralph Ellison's belletristic disagreement four decades earlier, or even Cynthia Ozick's tessellated musings on them both (lofty but still positioned well within the fray), if, for no other reason, than for pure belatedness. And if Ozick is right about the way literary fiction "reads" critical debate, then I leave it with one last overdetermined grudge match between Black and Jewish Intellectuals to referee.

Wieseltier takes on Cornel West's entire intellectual project only to take it apart. Worse, Wieseltier impugns West's credentials *as* an intellectual, as though what were at stake was not a match between equals, but rather defending the honor of the ring itself – discursive public space – against a pretender or worse, no contender at all. As the very stuff of blackjewishrelations, Wieseltier's ad hominem attacks fold analysis inside immoderate contempt. And if West ends up Tar Baby by default, Wieseltier, as the critic who cuts too unkindly, risks being sent back to the magicians of the Talmudic Academy.

Michael Henchard has criticized the recent spate of "Black Public Intellectual" discourse as imagining an analogous relationship between scholars like West, Henry Louis Gates, Jr., bell hooks, on one side, and New York Jewish intellectuals like Rahv, Howe, and Trilling on the other, more correctly perceived as a *tension*.[39] If so, then Howe and Ellison, and Malamud's fictive tenants, Lesser and Spear, merely adumbrate Wieseltier and West, except for the crucial fact that the last instance is, in Nat Lime's phrase "a one-way proposition," and to that degree, stands apart. West has no literary facsimile in Willie, unless, from Wieseltier's side, one views the affair on an entirely grosser level of competitiveness, with the former "trying to steal [the] manhood" of the latter. In any event, Lesser's question from Malamud's novel can be applied to Wieseltier and West both:

"Who's hiring Cornel West (or Leon Wieseltier) to be my dybbuk?" (149)

Though Malamud's novel ends with Black and Jew "feel[ing] the anguish of the other," (211) earlier in the story, Lesser articulates another principle: "each proclaims consideration of the other." (13) As Ozick herself points out in her reading of the novel, the word mercy is repeated one hundred and fifteen times at the end, and once in Hebrew. Unlike those characters earlier in their story, one does not expect intellectual embrace from two contemporary intellectuals who, if they do occupy different partisan spheres, still co-tenant within public space (not to mention the same place in the alphabet should one need to look them up). Nor does one expect intellectual contempt when it takes the form of one-sided contumely.

What then? A fairer symmetry? A less pointed asymmetry? I step back and allow literary fiction to pass a final, answering judgment of its own: "they were both writers living and working in the same place and faced with the same problems – differing in degree because they differed in experience."[40] That such differences erupt as irritants or provocations, should not mystify since they leave the strictly literary realms for the more unmediated one of blackjewishrelations. My book finally pays a call on that realm in its concluding full chapter, where a bout between Leon Wieseltier and Cornel West appears a mere warmup in the light of more reckless contests.

5

Black–Jewish inflations: face(off) in David Mamet's *Homicide* and the O. J. Simpson trial

> I know
> you don't love us
> We are not like the others
> We have swum through too many streams
> people who rest and people who wander
> Have a totally different face.
> I know you don't love us
> But let us come to rest
> Then we shall have the same face.
> Georg Mannheimer, "Lieder Eines Jude"

> I've got to keep on moving,
> blues falling down like hail.
> and the day keeps worrying me,
> there's a hellhound on my trail.
> Robert Johnson, "Hellhound on my Trail"

The preceding chapters' asymmetries all function as variations on a central theme. In this last full chapter, I exchange literary Blacks and Jews for two other kinds: cinematic ones, and the entities enmeshed in the accidental allegory called blackjewishrelations. As a medium of symbolic exchange rather than a natural state of affairs, perhaps the latter is no more than the literaturizing component of human relations writ large on the plane of cultural identity; or perhaps it is what is meant by cultural identity itself, the transpersonalization and enlargement of the self, back-lit by the postmodern. But given the kathartic pressure commonly brought to bear on such exchange, together with the outsized dimensions it must bear in cinema and "real life" – precisely *not* the novel – the resulting ghostly coefficient seems all the more apposite at the seam where Life itself conjures Art outside the strictly literary.[1]

In the following readings, therefore, I depart finally from allegory's positive face to concentrate on that phenomenon peculiar to its more negative aspect: *displacement*, in the form of David Mamet's film, *Homicide* and certain overdetermined moments in the O. J. Simpson trial. Where film may be the result of conscious decision, trial in this case proves even more unbound and aleatory – a "continual allegory" (Keats's phrase), best glossed, I believe, by a proper fiction: Ishmael Reed's *Reckless Eyeballing*. Here particularly, as Borges memorably noted, "in allegory, there is always something of the novel."[2]

Homicide: Kike on the streets or, Chicago PD Jew

I first saw David Mamet's *Homicide* at its premiere at the Jerusalem Film Festival in the summer of 1991. The film was received perplexedly, the palpable tension in the movie theater relieved only once through nervous chuckles during the few moments in the film when Hebrew was spoken unpersuasively by Israeli characters. I was no less baffled by the film than anyone else. What I *was* sure of, however, was the film's uncanniness, which was partly its topic, and partly a matter of its general affect.

Homicide goes full bore, as one might expect, at all the familiar Mamet targets: betrayal, not belonging, utterance as shout or rant. And so it did not surprise me when Mamet, present himself at the festival, spoke about the film at a special question-and-answer session a few nights later. Fielding the audience's puzzlement – this was Israel, and *Homicide*, whatever else, is a very American movie – he would explain only that its genesis had something to do with his own recent Jewish-identity crisis, during which what had previously been lost to or by him was found, re-circulated through Mametary exchange.

That was quite fitting, as the movie itself concerns finding and losing, along with hitting and missing, righting and wronging, killing and "serving and protecting"; such are the film's symbolic denominations, allegorical motifs not at all shy about their allegoresis. To take just the first motif as example, Bobby Gold, the police detective and Jew around whom the action revolves (as narrative center, but hermeneutically unmoored) keeps losing his firearm. Just after he is told by a fellow officer, "Don't forget your gun," a prisoner on his way to the holding cell wrests it from him, tearing the leather holster before he is subdued. "I wanted your gun," (19) the prisoner says, and to complete the symmetry, explains "I wanted to kill myself," chiming with Gold's own rejoinder to an earlier warning not to forget his gun, "For what? To protect myself?" (15)

Here is the full inventory: Gold leaves his revolver on his desk (21) and on the seat of his car, (25) shifts it, conspicuously, from holster to jacket pocket, (45) only to drop it shortly thereafter, (66) only to lose it again fatefully at the end of the movie, (117) just before he is shot. A floating, if never fired, signifier, Gold's piece circulates throughout the entire film, but unlike Chekhov's famous first-act gun, it never does go off (it is his fellow officers who fire the fatal shot that saves him from his assailant at movie's end).

As symbolic object, the gun functions indexically rather than iconically. It simply points, structurally equivalent to other meaningful pieces of flotsam floating in and out of the story: (1) a torn paper which reads "Grofaz" (either an acronym for Hitler – *Grosster Feldherr aller Zeiten* on a piece of antisemitic propaganda, or, rather a harmless shred of packaging copy *"Grofazt Pigeon Feeds – Nutrition, Quality, Value"*); (2) an address where the crime plot's denouement is supposed to "go down"; (3) a list of names of Zionist patriots who may have been gun-runners, an invoice for machine-guns dated 1948; (4) a flyer showing a yarmulke-wearing rat towering over the ghetto and reads *"Crime Is Caused By The Ghetto, The Ghetto Is Caused By The Jew."* Together, all of these mysterious signifiers crosshatch neo-Nazi antisemitism, African American Jew-hatred, and Jewish terrorism into a single wildly overdetermined nexus of overlapping conspiracies which may or may not be real.[3]

At the film's allegorical ground zero, Gold finds himself in a library of synoptic Judaica (itself improbable), researching the provenance and meaning of "Grofaz," when he notices a religious student, whom the screenplay calls a "Chasidic scholar", at a nearby table.

> GOLD: I'm a police officer. The revolver disturbs you. The gun disturbs you? I'm a police officer.
> SCHOLAR: The gun doesn't disturb me.
> GOLD: You were looking at me.
> SCHOLAR: The gun is nothing. The gun is a tool. We have nothing to fear from a tool. The *badge* concerns me, you see . . . the badge is a *symbol* . . . The badge, you see, is the *symbol*. Of that which constrains us. The *star* . . . you see. The star. The five-point star. The *pentagram* . . . it is identified as a star, but it is not the symbol of heaven. It is the symbol of *earth*. The Mogen David is the intersection of the opposites and can be deconstructed into heaven and earth, but the pentagram cannot be deconstructed. You see?

You're Jewish . . . ? Are you Jewish?

GOLD: . . . yes.

SCHOLAR: Well. You see? From the Book of Esther. "Esther" From "Sathar," to *conceal*. But what is concealed? What is *concealed*? In the name "Esther"? And the answer is here. Here is the answer. Do you see? [he gestures to a Hebrew *sefer*]

GOLD: . . . I can't read it.

SCHOLAR: You say you're a Jew?

GOLD: I can't read it?

SCHOLAR: You say you're a Jew and you can't read Hebrew? What *are* you then . . . ? (89–91)

Of course, like the enigmatic paper-scrap reading "Grofaz," the answer to what is concealed is never revealed, just one more of the film's *petit objet a*'s. For the duration of the film's crisis-of-identity plot (not its only one), Gold's competing personas of cop and Jew, pentagram and Mogen David, continually clash.

The gun is already irrelevant, a piece of stage business (whatever its import as a token of potency and/or emasculation). As a symbol, like "Grofaz" or the mysterious list of names or the anonymous flyer, its value remains largely inert, paling in comparison to a police badge or a Jewish star around the neck of a murdered shopkeeper, which suggest conversely defining marks of identity and affiliation.

In this same scene, the librarian cannot give Gold any information on "Grofaz" despite the detective's insistence that "this is official police business," (93) the file having already been "requested by Two Twelve." (92) "Two Twelve," as the next scene explains, is a Mossad safe house where an attempt is made to recruit Gold's services: the Israelis wish him to retrieve an incriminating piece of evidence. Gold pleads his willingness to help (also improbable, considering the lack of any immediate motivation, and the instantaneous jump from ethnic self-hatred to nationalist loyalty), but demurs at violating policy: "The list is evidence. I've logged it, into an evidence bag. I took an oath." (100)

Not surprisingly, then, Gold identifies Jewishly only in para-military terms: he might as well be a space-alien in the Jewish library, but he shifts from peace-officer to urban terrorist in the blink of an eye. At the instigation of the Israelis, he breaks into a storefront which may or may not be headquarters for a neo-Nazi organization, and sets an explosive device, though it remains perfectly plausible within the film's own paranoid logic that the storefront is merely just a *front*. That the name of the suspected organization is the "United Action

Front" in a film where "united action" and "front" function as unstable concepts to begin with, anyway seems suspicious.

"Two-Twelve"/"official police business." "I'm a police officer"/ "Are you Jewish?" "Then be a Jew"/"I am a sworn police officer." This conflict rehearses the film's underlying dichotomy, a polarity never clearer than when Gold is assigned to the case that thrusts him into the identity plot, and interrupts the case, and plot, on which he is already engaged. A Jewish storekeeper in a Black neighborhood is found shot to death, and her surviving family, "the Jewish guys downtown" with "clout," (40) want the case assigned to Gold, having blundered into it while on the way to more pressing business. "You were there," Gold's lieutenant tells him, "you're his 'people,' you're on the case." "I'm his people?" Gold responds, "I thought I was *your* people, Lou?" (40)

It is here, at the intersection of the film's two storylines, that the plot thickens, where Jewishness blurs into blackness, and police work or "community relations" fold into a version of blackjewishrelations. The film's opening scene establishes its framing narrative. The FBI unsuccessfully stages a raid, hoping to capture a black drug-dealer named Randolph who nevertheless escapes (he is called a cop-killer, but it is never made entirely clear when those murders are supposed to have taken place). Gold and his partner had been tracking Randolph, were asked to "stand down" and defer to the FBI, and are assigned to the case one more time by the mayor's office.

The black-outlaw plot is one-dimensional in its conventionality; the opening scene, with its escape onto tenement rooftops recalls the flight and capture scene of Bigger Thomas in *Native Son*, the lurid white nightmare of black criminality ever so minimally adjusted for contemporary sensibilities. "We've got a black man who the FBI is trying to lynch, and we got a lot of people yelling 'Black Panthers' and 'Government Assassination Squads . . . '" (6–7)

As if that were not gratuitous enough, Mamet follows it with two parodic portraits of belligerent black officiousness: the screenplay identifies the men as "*Deputy Assistant-Mayor Walker and his assistant, Patterson, two black men in well-cut suits,*" (6) the latter taking an immediate dislike to Gold, noticeably pricking his ears when Gold's name is mentioned:

> PATTERSON: I said do your job.
> GOLD: Mister, I'm trine' a do my job.
> PATTERSON: . . . . n'you got an answer for *everything*, smart guy, s'zat it? Mr. *Gold*, Detective Robert *Gold*, hostage negotiator

... Barracks Room Lawyer ... Is that it?
GOLD: No, uh ... Sir, Mr. Patterson, sir, it seems you're ...
PATTERSON: I'm what? I'm through with you, Mr. Gold ...
(*under his breath*) Little *kike* ...

Three very important signifiers make their first appearance here. To take the last and harshest first, "kike," like a fired shot, traces a parabola over the action of the film, reappearing at the end when cop and criminal, Jew and Black, square off against each other; Randolph shoots Gold, telling him, "One Smart Kike. Ain'tcha, Mr. Gold? All you forgot. If you want to *kill* me, you best come armed." (121) Gold and his partner Sullivan bandy the term twice among themselves (23, 85) to diffuse it, but Gold has some trouble letting it go: "he had no fucken call to get *racial* on me" (21), "motherfucker called me a 'kike' ... Job's changed. It ain't the same Job." (23)

And indeed, it is "job" – the second of the three taglines – not "kike," that serves as the linguistic leitmotif unifying the entire film.

> PATTERSON: I said do your job. (11)
> GOLD: It ain't the same job. (23)
> CAPTAIN: You caught the case. Do your job. (35)
> GOLD: It's all part of the job. (43)
> GOLD: *I'm Trine' a Do My Job.* (56)
> DR KLEIN: You're paid to do a job. *Do* your fucken job. (56)
> GOLD: I'm going to do the job . . . . I'm here to do the job. (57)

The third and last piece of symbolic language is a simple matter of *naming*, a set of sobriquets for "Detective Robert Gold": "hostage negotiator," "barracks room lawyer," "the *talkin'* man," (38) "the Mouthpiece," (39) "the Orator," (49) culminating in Gold's own self-lament late in the story:

> What can I tell you about it. They said . . . I was a *pussy* all my life. They said I was a pussy, because I was a Jew. 'Onna cops, they'd say, send a Jew, mizewell send a *broad* on the job, send a *broad* through the door . . . I was the donkey . . . I was the "clown" . . . (103)

Not by accident is Gold's signal gift as a policeman his *verbal* deftness.[4] As to "homicide," Gold himself best personifies the word, since, something of a floating signifier himself, he precipitates and multiplies so many of them – his partner's, Randolph's, the death of his own career. In *Homicide*, words have the same effect as other mobile modes of signification – detachable fragments, the junk-shop of Mamet-talk: swagger, epithet, iambic rattle.[5]

Despite its verisimilar look, its grit of speech and personality and situation, *Homicide* plunges us once again in the signature world of Mamet's anti-naturalism. It is a film by turns baffling, irritating, and portentous, the very qualities that lend it an unmistakably allegorical air – hardly surprising in a film about identity as "singularity" (L. *ipse*) and "sameness" (L. *idem*) alike. If its purposes remain finally opaque, one can still try to formalize, if not wholly clarify, its decidely uncanny effect.

Alongside the cadenced iambs of its speech, then, *Homicide* adds the syncopated pulse of displacement. Above, I called the film's racism gratuitous, but indeed, *everything* in the film appears gratuitous, a constant sliding from one thing to another. Thus, Gold metamorphoses from self-hater to freedom-fighter instantly. One moment he's saying "Not 'my' people, baby . . . *Fuck* 'em, there's so much anti-Semitism, last four thousand years, they must be doin *something* to bring it about;" (6) the next he tells the "Israeli heavy hitters," "What you're doing tonight. Let me help. Please. I'm begging you." (102)

The film can, of course, be read as no more or less than the portrait of a rootless man, homeless outside of the entirely artificial "constraining force" of his policeman's badge and the flawed and violent solidarity it posits: diasporism as unmoored solipsism. Gold would then function as merely the aggregate of signs – his name, his badge, his gun, the film's title – a torn sack, as Levinas would say, unable to contain them. Not surprisingly, the murdered shopkeeper's daughter will ask him, "Do you belong nowhere?" (63) He himself will plaintively remark to one of the Israelis, "You have your *own* home . . . . Now what can that be like?" (104) That same woman reflects his existential predicament back to him while he bemoans his status as a Jewish cop: "you were the Outsider . . . doing Other People's Work for them." (103)

But what is the logic that motivates his actions? Perhaps it is shame. Rebuked by shopkeeper's daughter, he repines, "I swear, I'll find the killer, I swear, I . . . Listen to me, please, I . . . " (63) Chided by the student in the library, he violates in the next scene the very police business which his policeman's badge has just been shown symbolically to represent. Gold's tenuous grasp on himself, his essential ad hoc manliness, gets 'made' in the following exchange with his partner, the film's crass low point on the question of divided loyalty, and its hermeneutic center:

> SULLIVAN: Bob. I want to tell you what the Old Whore said – and this is the truest thing I know – When you start coming

> with the customers, it's time to quit. What is this . . . ?
> GOLD: It's the strap the guy tore off my holster.
> SULLIVAN: Well. Go and get it fixed, will you? Go take a cooling walk, something.
> GOLD: You mad at me?
> SULLIVAN: Yeah, I'm mad at you. I'm not going to invite you to my birthday party, you dumb kike. Go get your holster fixed. (84)

Or maybe the film strikes so many allegorical chords because it *is* an allegory . . . not of ethnic identity *per se*, but rather of divided loyalty *per se*, hence the presence of Israeli operatives. What could be more paradigmatic of modern America than "police work," and more foreign than Zionist gun-running? Yet, all these character changes, together with the tiered levels of paranoia and parallel-tracked conspiracies, the recycling of words and objects, and last but not least, the collision of Jewish-identity and black-outlaw plots – all is flagrantly gratuitous.

Whether Mamet intended this I cannot be sure nor do I think it decisive to resolve; the film leaves the matter open-ended. I think a more intuitive reading of *Homicide* must center on the very riot of gratuity itself, the motor behind all the slippage. On a narrative level, the Black bureaucrat's "kike" almost seems by itself to *precipitate* Gold's stumbling into the Jewish shopkeeper's murder, shortly thereafter. Just as the word itself interrupts the smooth flow of "police work," so that very work is itself interrupted as Gold "catches" one case on the way to disposing of another.

Unsurprisingly, "kike" frames the film in the two scenes where the detective is Jew-baited by a Black man.[6] Thus it makes perfect sense that the film's sole racial slur – Gold hurls himself into the story's climax after Randolph shoots his partner, screaming "You shot my partner, you fucking *nigger* . . . I'm going to kill you" (117) – is uttered by Gold himself, as though once hate speech is loosed, displacement dictates a fugue-like transit from mouth to mouth, from Black to Jew.

The prisoner who momentarily steals Gold's gun at the beginning of the film keeps intermittently reappearing. All we know about him is that he has dispatched his wife and children with a deer rifle, and for all we know, may be the missing link to the neo-Nazi organization, to "Grofaz" and the antisemitic flyer. He remains, however, foreboding and opaque (the screenplay names him "the Grounder.") He nevertheless remains linked with Gold, pleading for his firearm – "Give me the gun, give me the gun" (17), tearing it thereafter, offering

149

to "help" him after Gold has "stood up" for him, to "repay" Gold and "make it up to" him. He briefly appears at just those moments when Gold is trying to puzzle out the meaning of "Grofaz", most dramatically in the movie's final moments when he looks at Gold and nods while being led away as an officer hands Gold a flyer (*Grofazt Pigeon Feeds – Nutrition, Quality, and Value*), and says, "We've been holding this for you." (126) Is he Gold's double? his nemesis? his fate?

In perhaps the film's most artful sleight of hand, in the early arrest scene the Grounder tells Gold, "Perhaps someday I could tell you the nature of Evil. Would you like to know how to solve the problem of evil?" to which Gold laconically responds, "No, man, because if I did, then I'd be out of a job." (20) But then, the "job" occupies the axis around which the film gyrates, story and discourse alike, so its "problem of evil," unfortunately, remains unsolved: the shopkeeper dies, Gold's partner dies, Randolph dies.

Randolph's mother is talked into providing information which eventually kills her son, as the Klein family lends itself to an enchaining trail of information which only indefinitely postpones the solution of their mother's murder. Gold cradles his partner's head as he is dying, just as he cradles the head of his partner's killer in the very next scene. The entire film bends back on itself, nothing is clarified, everything seems to recirculate and transpose.

The screenplay groups the cast according to mise-en-scene: "The Homicide Squad," "At the Police Station," "Randolph's Apartment," "At The Variety Store," and so on. In fact, the film's demographics can be broken down into an alternate set of categories: cops, criminals, Jews (or Jewishnesses), Blacks (or Blacknesses), whites (or whitenesses), which not only intersect tangentially; they interpenetrate and laminate. Bobby Gold is Jew, cop, and intermittently, criminal. "Jew" means bourgeois family, "Chasidic scholar," Israeli, deracinated cop, all overconnected in a paranoid version of Jewish kinship. "Black" means cop and outlaw and city official. The Israelis are "heroes," but also above-the-law operatives. The film groups and then regroups its characters after the fashion of a Venn diagram (with "Black," perhaps not so surprisingly given Mamet's primary agenda, remaining the least rounded of all the circles).

Either *Homicide* is postmodern reflexivity made so superfine as to be ultimately tendentious, or it is just out of control. If it seems that I am strong-arming the film towards *Facing Blacks and Jews*, it is, rather, Mamet's film itself that complicates matters by facing "Blacks" and "Jews" – obliquely, anamorphically, metonymically, as *already* the stuff of surplus allegory. For, plainly, Gold, the Jewish detective and Randolph, the black criminal, have nothing to do with one another as Jew and Black; their link along such lines *is* gratuitous in the extreme. The film's story of Jewish identity lost, then found, then lost again, and its parallel pursuit plot about a renegade black man meet tangentially by means of displacement, as only skewed parallel lines can. To recall an earlier set of terms from chapter 5, the wholly *incidental* loosing of the signifier *kike* engineers the conspiratorial, the plotted, *operational* necessity of *nigger*.

Differently put, recognition takes place entirely by accident, off the bias. No other logic requires that Blacks and Jews "face" here, as opposed to, say, the necessitarian climax of Malamud's *The Tenants*. The back-cover blurb for the screenplay to *Homicide* says the film "exposes the fear and paranoia at the heart of today's multiracial urban fabric." While that may be Mamet's own manipulative point of departure, what the film really exposes is a crisscrossing of Black and Jew, whatever the narrative and dramatic possibilities of "today's multiracial urban fabric" may portend, as, allegorically speaking, a *fait accompli*. Or to paraphrase once again from Joyce's version of the symbiotic hinge between disparate cultures: *Black/Jew is Jew/Black.* *Morphemes meet.*

Recklessnesses

Did extremes (if not morphemes) meet, at the O. J. Simpson trial? Marcia Clarke, Johnnie Cochran, Alan Dershowitz, Robert Shapiro, Christopher Darden, Barry Scheck, Perter Neufeld, the Simpson family, the Goldman family, the Jewish Defence League, the Fruit of Islam: the trial was a veritable cavalcade of blacksandjews (albeit a sideshow to the "gargantuanism"[7] of bigtop attractions like race, class, gender, or media coverage). Writing of its centerpiece – a new kind of "Black outlaw" – Stanley Crouch suggests the following about public perceptions of O. J.'s blackness:

> Twenty five years ago, no writer black or would have been allowed to impose such a limited vision of "authenticity" on a Negro. Individual freedom was then the issue, not joining a movement . . . In this era when Woody Allen was in the middle of his big mess with Mia Farrow, he wasn't asked to reinstate his foreskin because of the women he's chosen over the years. No one asks Allen to suppress his urban neurosis in favor of the elegant worldliness of Leonard Bernstein. Nor is Susan Sontag

told to emulate Fanny Brice in order to truly represent the group
. . . . The only ethnic under that pressure is the Negro, whose
unlimited variations on Americanness must now meet not the
infinite meanings of our natural humanity but some short-order
ethnic recipe written up and agreed upon by insiders and outsiders.[8]

As with what I will say about the trial itself, I am far less concerned
with defending or arguing such statements, than with the sliding
between "Black" and "Jew," the logic of displacement betraying
blackjewishrelations' own accidentally heavy hand of allegory. What
follows, then, is only a snap-shot, and does not pretend to be anything
more.

Before Crouch, then, there was Ishmael Reed. "What's the American dream? A million blacks swimming back to Africa with a Jew
under each arm,"[9] reads the epigraph to *Reckless Eyeballing*. What
both Crouch and Reed deploy, albeit for different purposes, is "Jewishness" as an always available, detachable co-referent for even critically self-aware racialized discourse. And indeed, something very
similar demonstrated itself during the Simpson trial. Whatever
Reed's intent for this epigraph to a very slippery text, if we picture
each underarm Jew as so much grease to facilitate the ocean's journey, we isolate the lubricious function of "Jew" as fossil-fuel–like
"Black," one of the word's great, ever-replenished sources of cheap,
reusable oil.

Reckless Eyeballing offers an uncanny perspective on the Simpson
trial, not least because it features a trial as one of its main events, the
inspiration for which having been drawn from a real life incident (the
Emmet Till murder) made into a play by Ian Ball, the novel's protagonist, with adjustments to please the sensibilities of militant femin-
ists. In the text's own *précis*,

> It's about the lynching of a black lad for staring at a white
> woman. Only Ball has introduced a twist. He has the woman the
> kid allegedly stared at demand that his body be exhumed so that
> the corpse can be tried. She wants to erase any doubts in the
> public's mind that she was not the cause of the eyeballing she
> got. (39–40)

Reading such a description now, after the O. J. Simpson trial, one
can almost imagine it as someone's parodic inversion of the trial's
own thematic imaginary.[10] Here, for instance, is the defense attorney's summation in Reed's novel:

"Something is wrong with Cora Mae. You see, white people can't own you anymore, so they try to own you with their eyes. They can't punch you anymore without getting harmed, so they try to punch you with their eyes. They try to control you. Nigger, what are you doing here, we don't want you here, they are saying to you with their eyes. Years ago it was the lynch rope. Now it's the rude stare. They look at you in airports, in restaurants. They stare at you like they're not used to anything." (. . . the black jury members nod their approval.) "They've been accusing the blacks and the Jews of owning the evil eye when they are the ones with the evil in their eyes." (102–103)

The text cycles the eyeballing trope with a vengeance, a trope of recognition so blatant as to warrant little comment.

Reed's novel exults in its satire, exploiting the gender and culture war battles within which it positions its plot, and just as cannily anticipating whatever fallout might be generated outside the text (indeed, feminist critics and reviewers lost no time in grieving its antifeminism, as Jewish critics and reviewers continue to express mixed feelings about its parodic antisemitism). That the play underpinning the plot shares title honors with the novel itself suggests some idea of the reflexive spirit at play here.

Two motifs, or running gags, stand out in the novel for sheer grotesqueness. The first features a nearly-literal restaging of the Leo Frank lynching in 1912, centering on Jim Minsk, a broadway director invited to Mary Phegan College in the south, as "celebrity spectator at an annual play that had been performed by the Mary Phegan drama department since 1912." (35) The play (and episode) end with Minsk gruesomely beaten to death by the crowd, which has had its eyes glued to him the whole time.

The other recurrent theme involves a feminist recuperation of Eva Braun as a figure who "epitomizes women's universal suffering," (5) "an innocent bystander in conflict between Jewish and German men," (49) in the form of a play called *Eva's Honeymoon*. But if the engine of the text gets its power from Reed's *epater la feminine*, it depends on antisemitism for lubrication, which slides all over and through it.

The Simpson trial had its own share of parody, some disingenuous and impeachable, some simply fortuitous with Reed's novel as gloss. Two moments stand out there also, not because they necessarily suggest analogy with the examples from *Reckless Eyeballing* above (although they obviously *can*), but because they depend on an equivalent machinery of allegorical reference, so well oiled that it cannot help but spill over in the form of repetition and displacement. They both feature Johnnie Cochran. (In the spirit of equity, one may wish for counter-instances featuring Marcia Clark, but aside from point-scoring for symmetry's sake merely replicating the logic of black-jewishrelations, nothing on the other side of the courtroom really compares.)

At one point during the defense's cross-examination, Cochran took a witness to task for identifying a voice as "black," calling such a remark out and out racism, and taking the opportunity to inveigh against discrimination in a color-sighted society. Of course, Cochran's charge was, to use his favorite term of dismissal, preposterous, as it denied ethnoracial particulars in the very service of an argument that *required* them if prejudice was to demonstrate its objectifying, mis-recognitive work.[11] Denying timbre, accent, or inflection of voice as markers of ethnicity logically demands absenting color as a sign of race; tonedeafness instead of color-blindness merely ensures a specious vocal uniformity.

I was reminded of the fictional defense attorney's summation in *Reckless Eyeballing* above, its recklessness of rhetoric, its substitution of *Supervisibility* for Ellison's trope of *Invisibility* and reification through false equivalence. That lawyer's summation had already been fore-echoed in Reed's novel by a character who, in the course of an antisemitic tirade, says, "they serve the white man by keeping an eye on us, monitoring us," (67) a statement recycled late in the novel by a Jewish theater critic nicknamed "Eye Spy" for his Van-Vechten-like propensities, who heaps praise on the Anti-Defamation League for "keeping an eye on people." (84) Obviously in this case as well as Cochran's, one grants the discriminatory *uses* to which eyeballing and its aural equivalent can be put as racist conduits. The point is the decontextualizing logic at work in such lay sociology which exemplifies not so much the race card as the unmoored referent card instead.

That was the card Cochran himself played during his own summation when he suggested a resemblance between Mark Fuhrman's brand of racist invective and National Socialist ideology. Despite Allan Derschowitz's defense of Cochran's defense as not being strictly an exercise in analogy, i.e., a racist police officer vis-à-vis a state-sponsored policy of mass-extermination, given the inflated nature of blackjewishrelations as an ever-present fact of the trial if rarely acknowledged as such, given the reported tensions between Shapiro and Cochran, and finally, given the angry, sensitized presence of the

Goldman family, the call paid by Cochran on the Jewish Imaginary was at the very least . . . reckless.

In his autobiography, Cochran finishes his discussion of this moment in the trial, and his denial that he intended any facile Fuhrman/ Hitler correspondence, by quoting the Talmud. As Jeffrey Rosen noted in his article on Cochran and critical race theory:

> What makes this especially grotesque was Cochran's refusal, when he brandished Hitler during the trial, to speak the word "Anti-Semitism" . . . Cochran was surrounded at this point by the Fruit of Islam, and he was loath to ruffle the sensibilities of his jurors that he told a story about Hitler that omitted the central detail of what Hitler did.[12]

But I do not want to convey the notion that it is the purported analogy itself – whether intended or (mis)inferred – that chiefly interests me. For were I Jewish *or* Black, I would still be fascinated by how language moved from Black to Jew, despite the way in which the word "Jew" and its clustered associations may have been omitted by an African American lawyer comparing American racism with National Socialist Jew-hatred.

Thus, just as Malamud's *The Tenants*, Ellison and Howe, Cynthia Ozick, and Wieseltier and West all uncannily enchain each other, the very propensity of Reed's novel to loose its motifs and metaphors of recklessness seems to find *its* echo in the way Cochran's comments spilled over into a subsequent staging. After the summation, Fred Goldman appeared with his family to denounce Johnnie Cochran in a news conference, referring to him as "one of the worst men."

But "one of the worst men" was a phrase *borrowed* from Cochran's own earlier courtroom analogy between Mark Fuhrman and Hitler; it more or less recapitulated it, carrying with it the place it had been. Yet another (go)round followed after Goldman spoke, when the Simpson family was trotted out to hold its own news conference, accusing the Goldmans of recklessly eyeballing Cochran, and by extension, his defendant. This may all just be the stuff of coincidence or casual displacement. As even the most sophisticated essays about the trial demonstrate, it *lends* itself to analogy, allusion, polymorphous narrativity. But against the background of Cochran's own choice to raise the rhetorical stakes insuperably by invoking the cultural capital of the Holocaust, the sliding from Jew to Black to Jew to Black is not just reckless but uncanny, in Freud's sense of the unfamiliar and the familiar trading places.

As the photo-negative to my prefatory facing of Benjamin and Levinas, I have assembled the details here into some loose, kinetic conjunction because in this case, novel and trial mirror each other so well in lability and drift, and show uncannily how words overtake face. Is such drift possible merely because blackjewishrelations, like Mamet's compulsively displacing film, itself traffics in overdetermination? Does it not then merely illustrate postmodernity's "social logic (albeit in gargantuan proportions)?"[13] Needless to say perhaps, the way of putting the question twice, predetermines a certain answer. Perhaps all one should note by way of conclusion is how amazingly mobile the signs "Jew" and "Black" are, how more like language than person when untethered to the grounding force of face a challenge, a rebuke, an obstacle, to recklessness of all kinds.

> We are poor passing facts,
> warned by that to give each figure in the photograph
> his living name.   (Robert Lowell)

One more epigraph to add to the three that began this book. Levinas would extend "living name" to "speaking face," thus glossing his sense of disenchanted encounter by insisting on the necessary conjunction of face and discourse: the face "denuded" or laid bare in its non-dissimulating exposure to others. The narrator in Issac Rosenfeld's *Passage From Home*, on the other hand, imagines recognition on the order of immersion, a speculative empathy left uncorrected by the rectitude of speech and the boundaries it enunciates. Darryl Pinkney, more cautiously, locates recognition in *the word*, signaling to us his care for the places it has been while he carries it. And in the final analysis, he may be the most instructive of the lot.

Throughout this book, I have used facing as a strategy that underscores the varieties and vicissitudes of recognition, intertextual, interspatial, intercultural which happen in language. Asa and Allbee trying on each other's countenance. David Schearl disintegrating his face into mirrored fragments. Philip Roth looking at "Philip Roth." Nat Lime's "eye for color" vis-à-vis Mister Cohen's. Invisible Man's ear for voice and Bob Jones's radar for lip, nose, hair, and hue. However literarily "real," all these faces and facings are the allegorical stuff of language.

Outside strictly literary bounds, Wieseltier and West totemically faced-off, and even further afield, all those faces embossed into memory during the O. J. Simpson trial can be descried by us and faced (most memorably of all, perhaps, Simpson's itself as artificially darkened in a *Times* magazine cover.[14]) But however empirically "real" such faces are, when they enter the domain of blackjewishrelations they wear the larger face – even if only the negative one – of allegory. As a composite counter-text, what that face still has in common with its literary counterpart at a bare minimum is the uncanny linkage of Black and Jew according to modalities of recognition: looming/limiting, holding forth/having say, shrinking/amplifying, and thus they provide us with another optic through which to take the measure of Black-cum-Jew. To paraphrase *Chaneysville's* John Washington, it all depends on which of allegory's two faces you choose.

Or maybe it has something to do, finally, with my own authorship, as the ghost in the critical machinery of facing. Borges, quoted at the beginning of this chapter, also wrote, "A book which does not contain its counter-book is considered incomplete."[15] Self-allegorized, perhaps this book does contain its counter-book – a very different treatment of Blacks and Jews as well as a wholly other order of literary criticism. I have tried to imagine such a counter-book, and even its counter-author. Would s/he be Black? Would it? Is mine therefore a "Jewish" book? Or does a book that propose a congeries of Jewishnesses and Blacknesses moot such questions? Without seeming to silence them, perhaps a concluding gesture should defer rather to the plurality of faces, and a necessary incompleteness. I close this chapter with a parable about face from within my own tradition.

Using the scriptural description of Moses and God speaking face-to-face, a midrash explains that since the word for face in Hebrew is itself already plural, four faces must be counted, one for Scripture, one for Mishna (its oral commentary), one for Talmud (the commentary on the commentary), one for Aggadah (homiletic story), each bearing a different countenance, a different mien. It is *text*, that is, which can be said to possess its own face, what one looks at hard looking back hard in return. If that is so, than readers of this book along with its writer have played the role of third party to the textual face-to-faces themselves, but also second person to the text itself. In that dual capacity, faced at as well as bearing witness to facing, readers and author alike discover the power of a created face.

The Post*face* that follows takes one last supplementary look at that role and at possibilities for such a face.

Post*face:* Déjà-vu all over again; or, mirrors and the face–Anna Deavere Smith after Levinas

All those forgotten faces! There hasn't been a new one added
for quite some years. Whoever enters my life no goes and
fetches a face from the pile of old ones. I help Him find one. He
is not himself, he is like someone out of the heap
Elias Canetti, *The Agonony of Flies*

If you were beside another and looking into his eyes – as I one
day looked into somebody's eyes – you might as well be a
beggar before a door never to be opened to you; for he who
does enter there will never be you, but someone unknown to
you with his own different and impenetrable world . . .
Luigi Pirandello, *Henry IV*

It is the power of allegory, and its demonic force as well, to say
something quite different from and even contrary to what
seems to be intended through it.
Jacques Derrida, *Memoires: for Paul de Man*

A tale told out of (Hebrew) school: Rabbinic tradition relates the story
of the angel Gabriel's descent to earth in order to show one man what
awaits him after death. Emissary and man enter a splendid room with
a sumptuously prepared table – the choicest delicacies, the rarest
china. Around the table's perimeter sit several souls, mesmerized by
the feast but unable to partake: strapped to wooden slats, their arms
cannot bend to feed themselves. "This is *gehinnom*" (Hell) says the
angel Gabriel. He turns, shows his charge the door, and escorts him
into an adjoining room; upon entering, the angel announces, "This is
pardes" (Paradise). It is the identical room, the identical table, the
identical display of food. The same guests sit around its perimeter,

158

the same slats pinion their arms. There is, however, one difference: they are all eating. How? By feeding each other.

A nice story, to be sure, but reversing the spin of Kafka's parable on parables, one can win in parable and still lose in reality. If conceived of as a crosscultural version of such a scene, blackjewishrelations, I have suggested, typically conforms to the circumstances found in the first of the two rooms. Defined by the redundant circularity of the table's perimeter, its roster of guests do not successfully engage the task at hand, tending to reach neither each other nor any constructive point of reference. In more than one sense, they simply fail to relate. To paraphrase from another vernacular, *their arms too short* – not in this case to box with God but to eat with each other.

Scenes of eating, of course, form a *topos* for ethnic solidarity and group identity, the classic *chez-sois* moment which frames an us at home in relation to that which is neither "us" nor "home." But in the case of the Blacks and Jews of Crown Heights in Brooklyn, NY, such a scene, whether it features the famine of otherhood or the feast of brotherhood, would be mooted if only by dietary restrictions on one side of the would-be welcome table, a certain species of indefeasible hard fact. Anna Deavere Smith's *Fires in the Mirror: Crown Heights and Other Identities* sketches a different room altogether, a middle ground, hallway, or corridor, a common space, but also a space of juxtaposition. And space, in its relationship to identity, is Smith's especial concern, identity being a kind of property, something we believe we own, but also a terrain, a house we live in.

Proximate thus to the space my own project has staked out is a language almost identical to its own – a vocabulary of points and vectors, a concomitant theory of art as the motion between self and other, a mapping of the territorial imperative that is cultural difference. All these spatial relations are, in Smith's introduction to her work, something we can "watch and document" [xxvii] through the framing space of performance and theater.[1]

Superficially at least, *Fires in the Mirror* seems to have anticipated the very logic informing *Facing Black and Jew*. The "facing" of Black and Jew; a representational grammar for the intra-ethnic dilemma of "twoness"; the double edge of identity connoting sameness as well as difference: all these describe what the foregoing chapters have attempted to tease out. As Smith puts it, she is interested in "the bridge [which] displays how two unlikely *aspects* are *related*." [xxix]

Fires in the Mirror has been acclaimed in academic and journalistic quarters alike as a primer for the complexities of identity and difference; a booklet of teaching strategies and essays by Barbara Johnson, Michael Eric Dyson and others accompanied its broadcast on PBS. But it is precisely *the contrast* between (1) the lessons it is intended to teach, (2) the logic of juxtaposition upon which it is built, and (3) the ultimate shape it assumes as "public space" on the one hand, and my own purposes on the other, that I will foreground here. In using Smith's work, I want to clarify the space it takes up, in order to justify the way I have framed that space, publicly, myself. Obviously, the disparity in genre here between a performance piece on the one hand, and prose fiction on the other moots a completely equitable comparison. Nevertheless the publication of Smith's work in book form invites treating it *as* a text, which is how I proceed.

But then I am more interested at this final juncture in the *ethos* animating Smith's exercise in face work, than any specifically textual features. Moreover, it is the conscious institutionalizing and academicizing of the work – performance-piece-as-agitprop-as-teaching-aid-as-theory – that provokes my skepticism. It should be understood that my critique depends on seeing *Fires in the Mirror* more as a foil or counterweight to the terms of *Facing Black and Jew*, than as necessarily flawed on its own terms.

I begin with the recurrent directional image Smith employs for the guiding metaphor behind her work. "This project is not about a point, it is about a route. It is *on* the road. Character lives in the linguistic road as well as the destination." (xxxii) Smith calls this interstitial perspective, "other-oriented technique," "identity in motion," a fluid, mimic "travel" between self to other that reveals identity to be more gap than place: the wandering of human relatedness.

As such, however, the aptly titled *On the Road* (Smith's larger project in which *Fires* functions autonomously) demonstrates a theory of difference based *not* on "the face" but on something closer to Erving Goffman's notion of *facework* adapted to the freeplay of postmodern ethnic identities. Identity is a mobile phenomenon, and what better way to convey such mobility than through ethnicity, itself the very marker of negotiated difference within totality?

After all, the American motto, *e pluribus unum*, makes that very point along three parallel semiotic axes: the baseline language of national identity; the *langue* of Americans, defined by their differential relation to each other *as* ethnic; and the *parole* of selfhood, never unitary but always selfdivided. If "the self," as Valéry writes, "is a dialogue," then cultural difference is a dialogue of dialogues, a pluralism of masks and roles. Although *Fires in the Mirror* is about the nonnegotiable differences of two American communities living side by side (who) "have refused to melt into the melting pot," its structure places characters side by side in such a way that they effectively *revise* each other. The whole work negotiates among its various nonnegotiable differences. While this may sound like the logic of facing, it differs significantly.

Each of the first four segments of *Fires in the Mirror*, "Identity," "Mirrors," "Hair," and "Race," plays variations on an underlying theme of diasporic personality as quintessentially American cultural property. Everyone in this country owns a small piece of portable homelessness – that is what forms the common roof over all our heads, what Frank Sinatra, in his younger, democratic days, called "the house I live in." In sequence – from "identity" through "mirrors" and "hair" to "race" (or "ethnicity") – the segments suggest that self and culture are both subject to the sort of recursive "dynamic" the ethnomethodologist Herbert Garfinkel aptly dubbed *ad hocing*.[2]

For example, in the juxtaposed monologues by Al Sharpton and Rivka Siegel in "Hair," Reverend Sharpton explains his hairstyle as a personal tribute to James Brown, an emblem of *cultural* filiation. Straightened hair may have associations with ethnic selfhatred, but that is not why he wears his hair the way he does. "It's certainly not a reaction to Whites," he says. "It's me and James' thing." (23) In this same vein of differentiation, Ms. Siegel explains the dissonance between personal authenticity and cultural constraint: . . . "now that I'm wearing the wig, you see, with my hair I can keep it very simple and I can change it all the time . . . But I feel somehow like it's fake, I feel like it's not me." (25)

Now, juxtapositionally speaking, one is prompted here to interrogate what is left openended; as Barbara Johnson and the other essayists have noted, Smith's work is to its audience as a musical score is to an instrumentalist or conductor. I used a similar metaphor myself to describe this book in its opening pages. But there, I spoke of a call-and-response, a sonority between readers and text, prior to any performance. In *Fires in the Mirror*, conversely, viewers are *made* performers along with Smith and Al Sharpton alike, a very different role.

Is an analogy being proposed between Al Sharpton's assertion of selfhood through the claims of patrimony, and Rivka Siegel's *anxiety* about a self submerged in the claims of orthodoxy and uniformity? Are an improvised, exuberantly exposed identity on the one hand,

and a disguised and therefore troubled identity on the other, being equated as structurally equivalent responses to the roleplaying dictates of American ethnic semiosis? How *should* we read this juxtaposition? If according to our performative dictates, then we will find ourselves in synch with the work's own spirit. And yet one's performance of the text in this instance will efface differences just as surely as it will discover them, producing a performance that is, finally, only *apparently* one's own since it is already programmed within the work.

Another answer to my questions may be found encoded in the first monologue in "Hair" in which an anonymous girl looks in the mirror, and grounds her blackness in a correlative act of differentiation, comparing and contrasting: "When I look at my parents, that's how I knew I was Black." (16) (The remainder of the monologue explains how Black girls "bite off" Spanish girls, imitating their looks while at the same time repudiating them.) One shapes an identity by marking a line between self and other, a line as itself a response to how deeply entangled self and other are in the first place.

The monologue by Ntozake Shange in the segment entitled "Identity" makes this a kind of overarching existential principle:

> I am part of my surroundings – and I become separate from them and it's being able to make those differentiations clearly that lets us have an identity . . . It's an important differentiation to make because you don't know what you're giving if you don't know what you have, and you don't know what you're taking if you don't know what's yours and what's somebody else's. (34)

This quasi-Bakhtinian model is another way of putting Smith's own syntax for human relations (and the spirit of performance that reproduces them): "American character lives not in one place or the other, but in the gaps between the places, and in our struggle to be together in our differences." (xli)

This yields some disturbing implications, however. Gaps can be filled with preassigned contents, or they can remain empty signifiers. Smith makes an important disclaimer when she admits that "mimicry is not character," that "[c]haracter lives in the obvious gap between the real person and my attempt to seem like them. I try to close the gap between us, but I applaud the gap between us. I am willing to display my own *unlikeness*." (xxxvii)

Yet, the performing self-hood at work recalls Isaac Bashevis Singer's *bon mot* in regard to Barbra Streisand's *Yentl*: "Streisand was not off the screen for a minute, and my Yentl was never on it." Smith makes her position unmistakable directly from the beginning of her introduction, opining, "If you say a word enough it becomes your own." (xxiii) But one's word *is already half someone else's*. Personal identity in this sense of self-possessed identity, private property, is always a fiction. As the various personae Smith dons are borrowed by her, so in turn does she "lend" them out to an audience: a function of the work's contaminating logic of mimesis. Perhaps the most troubling moment in the accompanying teaching booklet, then, is its recommendation (picked up by Johnson) that students perform the parts like so many "parts in a play." Thus does the work's ideology of performance fully play itself out.

It is a dangerous sort of semiosis that ignores the copresentness of audience and performance which can mean either complicity or accountability. As Stanley Cavell has suggested in his essay on *King Lear*, watching isn't merely accountability, it is complicity. "On the road" too easily translates into a comfortable hermeneutic circle. Something more costly, less bloodless should be demanded from an audience, namely, a genuine reckoning with the epistemologic loophole of "the gap," especially that which divides mimicry from lived experience.

Presenting oneself as "an empty vessel" for respectively different Black and Jewish personae (as Smith describes her role), serving as "a repeater" of their not randomly juxtaposed utterances can *obscure* and *dissolve* salient differences in ethnic self-understanding which, only from such a privileged, third personal vantage, conveniently "melt" into the combinatory pot of *e pluribus unum*. I cavil not because the characters in Smith's piece are "real people" ("Blacks" and "Jews" signal terms rather than entities for my own project as well), but rather because they are real people who have been wrenched free of context, at the mercy of framing juxtaposition on the one hand, and "performance" on the other. *Fires in the Mirror* takes already two-dimensionalized and symbolic types or figures, that is, "Blacks" and "Jews" (not just any Jews but the most alien-seeming of Jews, black hat orthodox), only to inflate their symbolic content all over again.

When Smith says of her work that it "*displays* how two unlikely aspects are *related*," the problem doesn't lie with relation but rather display (as for the discursive field of blackjewishrelations generally). The significance of Smith's work lies in its capacity for such relatedness through display, its performability; its consequentiality for an audience, then, would be a function of its openendedness. Smith leaves her juxtapositions ostensibly uninterpreted within the work, in order to elicit, indeed require, an audience's *responsive* work. (When performing Smith would build in such response by incorporating postplay discussions into each performance.) But this only raises other obvious and unavoidable questions. Who comprises such an audience? Should it mirror the play's own multiplicity and heterogeneity? Or does it not matter? What roles *is* the audience assigned by this piece?

To return to the examples from "Hair," Smith observes the unifying fact about Crown Heights that "everybody w[ears] their roots on their heads." (xxxiv) Now, this is true to the same degree that *at first glance*, "the overall picture of Crown Heights [is] black and white, the residents [being] for the most part, Blacks and Whites, [t]he Hasidim usually [wearing] black and white." But Crown Heights would look this way only from a point of view exterior to it, the vantage of third person universalism.

While the neighborhood may serve as a graphic display of "negotiated identity," such identities are *differentially* negotiated; the Hasidim understand themselves in relation to the neighborhood's blacks, not only as Whites, but as Jews in the company of nonJews who happen to be Black.[3] The Jews of Crown Heights could not possibly understand themselves as Jews outside of a *religious* matrix: *Jewish* in the same way that Caribbean and African Americans (nationally distinct) would both define themselves as *essentially black.*

To dramatize the similarity between Al Sharpton's hairstyle and Rivka Siegel's wigs in terms of an equivalent and punning concern with "roots" risks eliding the very nonequivalences that define the *particular* rootedness of each. It sidesteps the test of dialectical allegory, where roots mark, and don't simply mirror, each other (as in my adaptation of the Rabbinic parable above). Their juxtaposition thins the respective meanings of "identity," "hair," and "race," as it pares the connectivity between them. The logic of juxtaposition, in other words, is a very different from the asymmetry of the face-to-face. *Roots* (at least as they are at issue in "Hair") may go only scalp deep. What's missing is rootedness of *context*, of lifeworld – the blood and sinew of habit, practice, and belief[4] – what literature as text, not performance, can embody.

But *Fires in the Mirror* does not aspire to thick description; and that may be precisely its point. Certainly the section entitled "Roots," creates such a dissonant polyphony among its several monologues that the root meaning of "roots" is all but neutralized by the force of contending definitions. The last words in the section emphasizing the poverty of vocabularies that ground our discourse seem to pronounce the last word on the necessary instability of concepts like "difference," "race," "otherness," and "roots": "we have a very, very bad language," (66) says Robert Sherman. Grandiose categories of being like "identity" or "difference" can wander as far and wide as the disparate elements of personal identity, and thus be comparably "on the road."

The publisher's blurb for Smith's work calls attention to its "Rashomonlike" design, a structure like Kurosawa's film, of leveled differences, a relativity of truths. But the danger then lies in mistaking a design integral to the performance piece for an innately relativized series of facts and circumstances. "Crown Heights" does not equal *Rashomon*. To equilibrate the Blacks and Hasidic Jews of Crown Heights as "two marginalized groups," for instance, elides the salient *difference* between the comparative size of their populations, or the way in which New York's municipal structures have responded to and filtered them.

Indeed, if the accompanying workbook were to be scrupulously honest, it would detail the painful asymmetries in income and political leverage between the "Jewish" and "Black" communities of Crown Heights, since what distinguishes them involves class realities as well as race and ethnicity. In reference to each other, and not to some abstract mainstream, *each* community experiences itself as residing in margin. Each (paraphrasing Ellison) is preoccupied with creating the uncreated features of its face.

The teaching materials contain a section entitled "working definitions," of words like "cultures," "discrimination," "racism," and "antisemitism." But Robert Sherman's trenchant critique of language-as-loophole – "we have a lousy language" – may justly be leveled at the teaching materials themselves, since never are crucial words like "Lubavitcher" or "Hasidic" or "Caribbean," crucial precisely because of their dependence on a context of local meaning and discrete particularities, unpacked or explicated. Similarly "antisemitism" is made definitionally and functionally equivalent to "other forms of oppression" like "sexism, ageism, and classism." These are commensurate realities and discourses only in an abstract and theoretical sense. As exterior facts, racism and antisemitism are different matters; blurring them a prismatic, multicultural paradigm does not necessarily differ in consequence from its monocultural counterpart.[5] Totalizing and tertiary frameworks alike, mosaic and melting pot, can equally cancel the thick features of lived experience.

This is why I find the related blindness in Cornel West's remarks quoted in my introduction so insightful, after all – precisely *pre*- or *post*-face. The figures displayed in *Fires in the Mirror* are so uprooted from native ground, the faces placed in such suspended orientation *away* from each other – since they remain directed *at* us – that something very like "faceless universalism" in its troubling neutrality becomes the work's paradoxical result. The mirror effect so crucial to the work – between character and character, and characters and audience – undercuts more complex opportunities for face-to-face encounter.

"The mirrors of society do not mirror society." (xxvii) The compensatory performance ethic of *Fires in the Mirror* that challenges this fact implies that, on the contrary, one learns best about identity through the dissonance created by performance. In that way the mirror of performance can actually *do* transformative work, by reflecting the differences present at any given time in an audience. Against the grain of Smith's purposes for it, however, her nostrum can be read alternatively: that the task of aesthetic work is precisely *not* to "mirror," if mirroring – again, both character-to-character, and character-to-audience – means reducing intersubjectivity to the redundancy of *reflection*. In Levinasian parlance, performer and audience thus assume the role – and responsibility – of quasi-third parties (*le tiers*).

One may object that I am misconceiving *Fires in the Mirror* if I regard it as an exercise in face, since it is precisely *not* about conjunction, but, rather, *disjunction*. The various juxtaposed portrayals are not mirrors of one another, but as so many dissonances instead. Rivka Siegel and Al Sharpton's sense of identity, of roots, of cultural markers, are frankly, obviously incommensurate. *Difference*, not facile similitude, is what such mirroring forces us to acknowledge. The characters see as through a glass darkly, but, we, on the other hand, must see face to face.

Let us say, then, that this spirit of gap (the differences *between* ethnicities) rather than that with which my analysis begins (the difference *within* ethnicity, the fissure cracking open the stable self) animates Smith's work. Grant that the *katharsis* yielded by such implicit misfires of recognition within the piece is designed to give pause in the negotiated recognitions *outside it in the street*. Unpacked, the title would mean: (*kathartic*) fires in the mirror of dramatic performance.

But this circles back to Smith's programmatic apologia for her own work. I do not believe it is misreading either that program or that work (indeed, Smith's metacommentary points unambiguously in this direction) to see *Fires in the Mirror* as essentially a vehicle for its own theory of performance – as a vehicle for impersonation (dangerously endorsed in the accompanying booklet as a form of "ritual shamanism").

It is fair, then, to ask where a work like this takes us. Does it let us see blackjewishrelations with new eyes? Does it reconfigure our understanding: of ethnicity? of difference? of American identity? Or does it merely seem to do these things by *restaging* them? If there are fires in these mirrors, do they clarify more than they occlude, give off more light than heat? I reply skeptically, owing in part to a faulty optic catching my eye, in part to a theory of performance projecting the ethnic self as mobile and shifting – like nothing so much as an *actor* or performance artist.

The problem (and, for that matter, the model of "ethnic semiosis" it illustrates) lies in the frame of reference. Even though Smith insists on the "other-directed" thrust of her characterizations, the ambit remains decidedly what Levinas renders, "from the same to the same." Troubling the aesthetic through the aesthetic's own voice, Levinas asks "What is Hecuba to me?" and elsewhere, "Is art an activity that lends face to things?" Potentially at least, art exerts a claim not only upon our witnesssing but upon representation itself as a facing with *with* us – the way we identify with and through it. But left to its own devices art runs the risk of letting go of the prey for the shadow.

I have suggested there are more ethically demanding ways to position African American and Jewish American cultures *vis-à-vis* or *face-to-face* such that their contact with one another is genuinely a matter of enlightenment, of discovery not performance (Smith's own distinction). I have favored a literary-critical model here because I believe text yields a more reliable optic than performance for black-jewishrelations. But other possible models would still require that the role of the third party – readers, interpreters, witnesses – involve more than the luxury of synthesis, of resolving difference into sameness through the mere extension of the first person eye. *On the road* to enlightened witnessing, ever "towards the Other," we third-parties undertake a political duty that seeks to extend the ethical difference to all the Others, the infinity of third-parties. Only thus is the face-to-face intergrafted onto the public face of society as a whole, and proximity made into a tensile movement among many points, vectors, and gaps across the illimitable horizon of public space.

As the *space* of reading or interpretation, on the other hand, it is defined not by fullness, but rather by partiality, by a gap or interruption seeking not to commensurate differences but simply to expose them to each other. To return to this book's opening and governing

thematic, it is a space between full disjunction and full complementarity, an intermediate space of recognition, neither tritone nor octave
but an unexpected harmony – as between Du Boisian bright sparkles
and kabbalistic sparks, superficially improbable perhaps, but no
more or less so than the "Blacks" and "Jews" of Crown Heights.

Notes

Preface

1 Lest my use of "discursive" seem inapt, one has only to consider the journal *commonQuest: The Magazine of Black Jewish Relations*, which is fully committed not only to Black/Jewish solidarity, but to a *magazination* of it in as many ways as possible: politics, religion, humor, personal anecdote, and so on. Happily, this magazine is not wholly premised on crisis or nostalgia, suggesting that the critical practice of facing and Black Jewish relations as discourse may at a certain point intersect.

2 Alain Finkielkraut, *The Wisdom of Love*, trans. Kevin O'Neill and David Suchoff (Lincoln: University of Nebraska Press, 1997), 19. Finkielkraut continues, "Considerable progress has been made from the scorn or fear of blacks [for example,] to the formula 'Black is beautiful': but in both cases, the countenance remains chained to its manifestations, sentenced to the uninterrupted expression of an unequivocal message. Idolatry perpetuates slander." The same argument applies to Jewish triumphalism, needless to say.

3 Wishing to do justice to the ethical courage of Levinas's entire work itself as a composite and answerable whole I have confined any rapprochement between Levinasian and literary analysis to a discrete and limited *thematic* application, much as I did in my *Narrative Ethics* (Cambridge: Harvard University Press, 1995). While not a "reading" of Levinas's philosophy in any sense, both the present book and its precursor remain faithful to his liturgical sense of a text as lying in the hands of answerable readers. For a short but excellent treatment of the relation between Levinas's philosophy and his scriptural hermeneutics, see Jacob Meskin, *Critique, Tradition,* and the Religious Imagination: An Esssay on Levinas' Talmudic Readings," in *Judaism* (Winter, 98), 91–106, also the introduction to *Nine Talmudic Readings by Emmanuel Levinas*, trans. Annette Aronowicz (Bloomington: University of Indiana Press, 1990). Finally, Robert Eaglestone's *Ethical Criticism: Reading After Levinas* (Edinburgh: Edinburgh University Press, 1998) picks up where my own book leaves off, with particular attention to the

relation between art and philosophy, and the consequences for criticism of Levinas's thought.

4 Walter Benjamin, *The Origin of German Tragic Drama*, trans. John Osborne (London: *NLB*, 1977), and "Theses on the Philosophy of History", *Illuminations*, trans. Harry Zohn (New York: Schocken Books, 1969). Theresa Kelley's treatment of Benjamin in *Reinventing Allegory* (Cambridge: Cambridge University Press, 1997) and Doris Sommer's even more adventurous "(mis)reading" of him in "Allegory and Romance: A Match Made in Dialectics," *boundary 2*, 18:1 (1991) have both been invaluable to me. Susan Handleman's *fragments of Redemption: Jewish Thought and Literary Theory in Benjamin, Scholem, and Levinas* (Bloomington: Indiana University Press, 1991) treats Benjamin, Gershom Scholem, and Levinas separately; finally, Rebecca Comay's "Facies Hippocratica", in *Ethics as First Philosophy: The Significance of Emmanuel Levinas for Philosophy, Literature, and Religion*, ed. Adrian Peperzak (New York, Routledge, 1995), 223–234, couples Benjamin and Levinas, but not in the context of allegory.

5 Benjamin, *Tragic Drama*, 233.

6 I thank David Suchoff for his expertise in the Frankfurt School of cultural criticism, and for his suggestions. In addition to his own *Critical Theory and the Novel: Mass Society and Cultural Criticism in Dickens, Melville, and Kafka* (Madison: The University of Wisconsin Press, 1994), see *The Essential Frankfurt School Reader*, ed. Andrew Arato and Eike Gebhardt (New York: Continuum, 1982) and the essays by Theodor Adorno in *Aesthetic Theory*, trans. C. Lenhardt (London: Routledge, 1984), *Negative Dialectics*, trans. E. B. Ashton (New York: Continuum, 1983), *The Stars Down to Earth and Other Essays on the Irrational in Culture*, ed. Stephen Crook (New York: Routledge, 1994).

7 *Reinventing Allegory*, 260.

8 Emmanuel Levinas, *Totality and Infinity: An Essay on Exteriority*, trans. Alphonso Lingis (Pittsburgh: Duquesne University Press, 1979), 67.

9 Witold Gombrowicz, *Ferdydurke*, trans. Eric Mosbacher (New York: Grove Press, Inc., 1978), 71. Perhaps the best evocation for me of such shadow-play comes from a story by Gombrowicz's contemporary, Bruno Schulz, "The Street of Crocodiles": "Reality is as thin as paper and betrays with all its cracks its imitative character . . . The tenseness of an artificial pose, the assumed earnestness of a mask, an ironical pathos tremble on [its] façade . . . [O]ne has the impression of a monotonous, aimless wandering, of a sleepy processing of puppets . . . a row of pale paper-cut figures, fixed in an expression of anxious peering . . . We spoke of the imitative and illusory character of that area, but these words have too precise and definite a meaning to describe its half-baked and undecided reality. Let us say bluntly: the misfortune of that area is that nothing ever succeeds there, nothing can reach a definite conclusion. Gestures hang in the air, movements are prematurely exhausted and cannot overcome a certain inertia . . . a montage of illustrations cut out from last year's mouldering newspapers." *The Complete Fiction of Bruno Schulz*, trans. Celia Wieniewska (New York: Walker and Company, 1989), 67–72.

10 See Rita Copeland and Stephen Melville, "Allegory and Allegoresis, Rhetoric and Hermeneutics," *Exemplaria* 3 (1991), 159–187.
11 Theresa Kelley nicely parallels this idea as well when she speaks of allegory's redemptive possibilities as "the reverse sign of the emblematic coin" – that is, a coin with two faces.
12 The figure comes from Maurice Blanchot, *The Writing of the Disaster*, trans. Ann Smock (Lincoln: University of Nebraska Press,1986), 78.
13 "Reality and its Shadow" in Emmanuel Levinas, *Collected Phiilosophical Papers*, trans. Alphonso Lingis (The Hague: Martinus Nijhoff, 1987) 6, 9. (It may well be that Levinas is adumbrating a Biblical sense of *tzelem* and *demut*, image and likeness, from Gen 1:26, as refracted through the subsequent interdicts against idolatrous representation in Ex 20:4 and Deut 4:15–16.) For the complex relationship between Levinas's purely philosophical writings on the one hand, and his essays in Judaism and his Talmudic readings on the other, see the essays by Richard Cohen, Jonathan E. Bauer, and Ephraim Meir in *Jewish Philosophy and the Academy*, ed. Emil Fackenheim and Raphael Jospe (London: Associated University Presses, 1996), and by Robert Gibbs, Zeev Levy, Ephraim Meir, and Annete Aronowicz in *Paradigms in Jewish Philosophy*, ed. Raphael Jospe (London: Associated University Presses, 1997), and finally, the interview with François Poirié in *Emmanuel Lévinas – Qui êtes vous?* (Lyon: La Manufacture, 1987).
14 Ibid., 7.
15 While Benjamin and Levinas may be its tutelary spirits, methodologically this book probably comes closest to Theophus H. Smith's *Conjuring Culture*, which enacts the very conjuring it locates culturally. See Smith, *Conjuring Culture: Biblical Formations of Black America* (New York: Oxford, 1994).
16 What was to have been the first and chronologically earliest chapter now appears separately as "Incognito Ergo Sum: Riding the Hyphen in Cahan, Johnson, Larsen, and Yezierska," in Jarab and Melnick (eds.) *Race and the Modern Artist* (New York: Oxford University Press, 1999).
17 See William Thornton's contribution to the "Forum on actual or potential relations between cultural studies and the literary" in *PMLA* 112:12, 261–262. In its forum, *PMLA*, distributes the response-pieces into Critiques, Reworkings, and Interconnections, suggesting its own awareness that any polarity between the literary and the cultural may be a relationship more cognate and symbiotic than strictly Manichaean. But inasmuch as cultural studies, in Leslie Bary's words, "was conceived as a paradigm shift toward history and sociology," (269), it does risk a certain discursive parasitism. I defer to Rachel Bowlby's description of a "common, critical ground" where cultural studies and the literary meet, as in the work of Walter Benjamin whose "close reading of cultural texts becomes creative sociology: the reading changes the object, shows it up in a new perspective." (277)
18 Levinas, "Reality and Its Shadow," 7.

Acknowledgments

1 *Hasisdic Tales of the Holocaust*, ed. Yaffa Eliach (New York: Oxford University Press, 1982), 109–110.
2 "Preface to *Sésame et les Lys*," from *On Reading Ruskin*, trans. J. Autret, W. Burford, and P. J. Wolfe (New Haven: Yale University Press, 1987), 114–15.

Introduction

1 W. E. B. Du Bois, *The Souls of Black Folk* (New York: Penguin Books, 1989), 6.
2 Eric Sundquist, *To Wake the Nations: Race in the Making of American Literature* (Cambridge: Belknap Press of Harvard University Press, 1993), 486.
3 From "Children's Children," quoted in Sundquist, *To Wake the Nations*, 473.
4 Quoted in Harold Bloom, *Kabbalah and Criticism* (New York: Continuum, 1984), 8.
5 Ibid., 82.
6 This analysis of *kabbalah* is associated with the work of Gershom Scholem, in particular, *Major Trends in Jewish Mysticism* (New York: Schocken, 1961), and *On the Kabbalah and its Symbolism* (New York, 1969). For a more recent study which takes issue with Scholem, see Moshe Idel, *Kabbalah: New Perspectives* (New Haven: Yale University Press, 1988).
7 Sundquist notes that "bright sparkles," in recalling the African custom of decorating graves with broken glass, represent "the glint or spark of the soul that is released in death on its journey to the home world of the ancestors." *To Wake the Nations*, 510. Also see Robert Farris Thompson, *The Flash of the Spirit* (New York: Random House, 1983). Compare the African American folk tale (sadly marred by antisemitic caricature), about God's creation of the soul recounted in Zora Neale Hurston's introduction to *Mules and Men*: "It's de strongest thing Ah ever made. Don't aim to waste none thru loose cracks. And then men got to grow strong enough to stand it. De way things is now, if Ah give it out it would tear them shackly bodies to pieces . . . Way after while [people] come out of holes and corners and picked up little chips and pieces that fell back on de ground." *Novels and Stories* (New York: Library of America, 1995), 11. See also my introductory section to chapter 6.
8 From *Parashat Vayeitzei* in *Kedushat Levi*.
9 The historic exile of the Jewish people reflects the mystic exile of the *shekinah*, or divine presence, as related consequences of the *shevirat ha kelim*. See Scholem, *Major Trends* and *Kabbalah*. Moshe Idel questions Scholem's historiographic assumptions as methodologically problematic, since they "place psychology between history and theosophy, and a theory that attempts seriously to connect all three must be carefully proved, not merely stated in an eloquent manner," (265) but

allegory, especially in Benjamin's sense, is entirely foreign to Idel's purposes, which are predicated rather on the Symbol, traditionally understood.

10 Another felicitous correspondence between Benjamin and Levinas: the process of *tikkun* is initiated and controlled by structures built on those *kelim* that remained intact, substituting for the original divine emanations of *sefirot*; they function, according to Scholem, as "power centers through which the creative dynamism of the Godhead was able to function and assume form." (*Kabbalah*, 141) The term for these replacement structures is, *parzufim*: "faces" or "physiognomies," a word-choice consonant with the imagistic role played by Face, both human and divine, in Torah and liturgy.

11 "Peace and Proximity" in *Basic Philosophical Writings*, ed. Adrian Peperzak, Simon Critchley, and Robert Bernasconi (Bloomington: Indiana University Press, 1996), 168.

12 See Bloom on representation in *Kabbalah and Criticism*.

13 A fore-echo of Benjamin's own sense of allegory's ability to "spring over" (*uberspringt*) in the "Angelus Novus" passage is the Biblical story of bondage and deliverance the story, in part, of God's "springing over" – which became *the* typological text for nineteenth-century Americans of African descent. (The Jewish observance of the Passover holiday from very early on was itself a complex forging of event and symbolic memorialization. Rashi, the renowned eleventh-century commentator, for example, explains Exodus 12:11 as follows: "You must do, therefore, every act of service connected with the Passover sacrifice in honor of God [as though you were] springing and leaping over [i.e., hastily] as a reminder of its name, which is called the 'springing' offering." A whole concatenating series of event, sacrifice, sign, and name is, one could say, already *allegorically* built into the Biblical narrative.) Thus, "Israel in Egypt" supplied perhaps the most common referential image through Emancipation for the experience of Black Americans, the references far too numerous to cite. Let us just note W. E. B. Du Bois's own allegorical correctness in troping on the intrinsic mimeticism of the Biblical story when he re-imagined "Egypt land" bivalently – "a complex figuration that combined past and present, the passage into bondage and the deliverance from it." [Sunquist, *To Wake the Nations*, 507.] Notwithstanding the syncretism of Christian and African elements in Black religious life, or even the peculiarly American obsession (as Sacvan Bercovich and others have argued) with the mythos of enslavement and emancipation, there is still a special *allegorical* piquancy in the enfolding of American Black and Biblical Jew.

14 Levinas, "Peace and Proximity," 165.

15 Julia Kristeva, *Strangers to Ourselves*, trans Leon S. Roudiez (New York: Columbia University Press, 1991), 11. See also Abdelfattah Kilito's "Dog Words," in *Displacements: Cultural Identities in Question*, ed. Angelika Bammer (Bloomington: Indiana University Press, 1995), xxii–xxxi, and Rey Chow, "Where have all the Natives Gone?" *Displacements*, 125–151.

16 Leon Wieseltier, "Letting Go," in *The New Republic*, 209:14 (October 4, 1993), 27–29.

17 In a brilliant essay on *The Rise of David Levinsky*, Isaac Rosenfeld proposes that the insatiable yearning that characterizes Levinsky as quintessentially Jewish – the Diaspora Man – is more than slightly analogous to *American* bourgeois desire as such. Writes Rosenfeld, " . . . if Levinsky's career is understood in its essentially Jewish aspect, it may explain why the Jews, as an immigrant group, were among the first to achieve a virtually flawless Americanization." "David Levinsky: The Jew as American Millionaire," in *An Age of Enormity* (Cleveland: World Publishing Co., 1962). In "The Black Mask of Humanity," Ralph Ellison argues that in *its* cultural history of striving and unfulfilled promise, the African American character is American *par excellence* – *Shadow and Act* (New York: Random House, 1953), 22–44. See also Toni Morrison's analysis of the repression mechanism of a black presence in American literature in her essay, "Unspeakable Things Unspoken," *Michigan Quarterly Review*, 28:1 (Winter, 1989), 1–31.

18 C. Eric Lincoln as quoted in A. Stein and R. Weisbord, *Bittersweet Encounter: The Afro American and the American Jew* (Westport: Negro University Press, 1970), viii. See also Laurence Mordekai Thomas's *Vessels of Evil: American Slavery and the Holocaust* (Philadelphia: Temple University Press, 1993).

19 James Wolcott's comments from his review of the film in *The New Yorker*, 71:19 (July 15, 1996), 80–81, are apposite: "When Smith and Goldblum share a spacecraft on a near-suicide mission to the alien mothership they show how black and Jew can bond; they're the Cornel West and Michael Lerner of extraterrestrial *tikkun.*"

20 As Irving Howe formulated it, "If Jews have been the great obsession of Christianity, blacks have been the great obsession of Americans." (*World of Our Fathers* (New York: Harcourt, Brace, Jovanovich, 1976), 631.) I am arguing, obviously, that "America" is where those twin obsessions meet and engage in palimpsest. The literature on Blacks and Jews as emblematic or symbolic constructs is extensive. George Fredickson's *The Black Image in the White Mind* (New York: Harper and Row, 1971), provides valuable historical perspective. Leslie Fiedler's *The Jew in American Literature* and Catherine Juanita Starke's *Black Portraiture in American Fiction* (New York: Basic Books, 1971) are reliable motivic accounts. The Nation of Islam's anonymously composed *The Secret Relationship Between Blacks and Jews* (Chicago: Latimer Associates, 1991) bears reading alongside its rejoinder by Harold Brackman, *Jew On The Brain: A Public Refutation* (Los Angeles: Simon Wiesenthal Center, 1992). See also the model of "cross-ethnic analysis" developed in Adam Meyer, *Cooperation and Conflict: Cross Ethnicity in Contemporary Jewish American and Afro-American Literature* (Diss. Vanderbilt University, 1991), and Jeffrey Melnick, *A Right to Sing the Blues: The Uncanny Relationship of American Blacks and Jews* (Cambridge: Harvard University Press, 1998).

21 Tony Martin, *The Jewish Onslaught: Dispatches From the Wellesley Battle-*

front (Dover: The Majority Press, 1993), viii.

22 *Can You Hear Me? African Americans and Jews in Coalition and Conflict*, Claire Schoen and Corey Fisher, writer-producers. See in this vein, the novel *Her First American* by Lore Segal (New York: Knopf, 1985).

23 In *Terrible Honesty: Mongrel Manhattan in the 1920's* (New York: Farrar, Straus, and Giroux, 1995), Ann Douglas points out that "Aframerican" was the term of choice for writers like James Weldon Johnson, precisely to emphasize the welded status of Black America. Even more to the point, "As one Negro writer in the *New York Age* rather snobbishly put it on October 5, 1916, whatever the Negro may be, 'at least he is no hyphenate.' In his pamphlet of the early 1930s on *Negro Life* in *New York's Harlem*, Wallace Thurman dismissed the Lower East Side as the place where 'the hyphenated American groups live.'" (308)

24 K. Anthony Appiah's "The Multiculturalist Misunderstanding," in *The New York Review Of Books* xliv:15 (October 9, 1997), 30–36 is a valuable guide to the implications of social identity here.

25 Among others, see Paul Berman, *Blacks and Jews: Alliances and Arguments* (New York, Delacorte Press, 1994); Harold Brackman, "The Ebb and Flow of Conflict: A History of Black–Jewish Relations Through 1900" (UCLA, 1977): Hasia Diner, *In the Almost Promised Land: American Jews and Blacks 1915–1935* (Westport: Greenwood Press, 1977); Nat Hentoff, ed., *Black Anti-Semitism and Jewish Racism* (New York: Richard W. Baron, 1969); Jonathan Kaufman, *Broken Alliance* (New York: Charles Scribner's Sons, 1988); Michael Lerner and Cornel West, *Jews and Blacks: Let the Healing Begin* (New York: G. P. Putnam's Sons, 1995); A. Peck, *Blacks and Jews: The American Experience* (Cincinnati: The American Jewish Archives, 1988); Jack Salzman, *Bridges and Boundaries: African Americans and American Jews* (New York: George Braziller, Inc., 1992); Jack Salzman and Cornel West, *Struggles in the Promised Land: Towards a History of Black–Jewish Relations in the United States* (New York: Oxford University Press, 1997); Alfred Shankman, *Ambivalent Friends: Afro-Americans View the Immigrant* (Westport: Greenwood Press, 1982); J. R. Washington, ed. *Jews in Black Perspectives: A Dialogue* (Rutherford: Farleigh Dickinson Press, 1984); and Weisbord and Stein, *Bittersweet Encounter: The Afro-American and the American Jew* (Westport, Conn.: Negro Universities Press, 1970). The 1996 documentary, *Blacks and Jews*, is representative in this regard. Jewish funded, written and directed by Jews (Alan Snitow and Deborah Kaufman) – and asymmetry unacknowledged *within* the film – it offers the following facile précis: "Early in the 20th century, Black and Jewish Americans began to join forces against bigotry and for civil rights . . . In the 1960's, each group turned inward, and the coalition fell apart. Today the relationship is defined by the ritual of mutual blame and accusation . . . In spite of efforts to resolve the conflict there are no easy solutions." The documentary exactly recapitulates that narrative, along with the failures of encounter and misrecognitions which constitute it, by re-presenting, minus any critical mediation, only the most obvious flashpoints of recent Black–Jewish

conflict: Crown Heights, the Million Man March, the fracas over inner-city students ejected from a cinema for laughing during a showing of *Schindler's List*.

26 Anna Deavere Smith, *Fires in the Mirror* (New York: Anchor Doubleday, 1993), xvii.

27 As with "face," I give this word a fairly wide semantic latitude. In addition to the complementary analyses of face-to-face encounter from philosophical and sociological perspectives by Levinas and Erving Goffman, I would also mention Charles Taylor's *Multiculturalism and the Politics of Recognition: An Essay* (Princeton: Princeton University Press, 1992). Taylor links identity, specifically ethnic identity, to the experience of recognition in a shared world – the fact that one's identity is partly shaped or deformed by others' recognition of it.

28 Levinas, from "Meaning and Sense" in *Collected Philosophical Papers*, 96.

29 Alain Finkielkraut, *The Wisdom of Love*, 12–13. Finkielkraut, though not a Levinas "scholar," provides, I think, the most accessible and nuanced reading of the many complexities Levinas sediments in his phenomenalist body-language of face, skin, caress, etc.

30 Subjectivity, then, can be conceived paradoxically as a kind of substitution, held hostage, finding its justification and meaning in the ethical obligation it *already* owes to otherness *before* its bid for autonomy. As Finkielkraut puts it, "For my presence alone does not suffice when the Other turns his face toward me: he demands that I be there *for him* and not just *with him*." See Levinas's essay, "Substitution" in *Basic Philosophical Writings*, 79–95.

31 See the essay "Meaning and Sense" in *Collected Philosophical Papers* where he speaks of a "bareness without any cultural adornment." (96).

32 Finkielkraut, *The Wisdom of Love*, 99. Levinas writes, "The face is not the mere assemblage of a nose, a forehead, eyes, etc.; it is all that, of course, but it takes on the meaning of a face through the new dimension it opens up in the perception of a being. Through the face, the being is not only enclosed in its form and offered to the hand, it is also open, establishing itself in depth, and, in this opening, presenting itself somehow in a personal way. The face is an irreducible mode in which being can present itself in its identity. A thing can never be presented personally and ultimately has no identity. Violence is applied to the thing, it seizes and disposes of the thing. Things *give*, they do not offer a face." ("Ethics and Spirit" in *Difficult Freedom*, 9) The paragraph ends by recalling the problem I discuss in my preface: "Perhaps art seeks to give a face to things, and in this its greatness and its deceit simultaneously reside."

33 "Transcendence et Hauteur," *Bulletin de la Societé Francais de la Philosophie*, 56:3 (1962), 92.

34 On essentialism's role in criticism and theory see the short but illuminating study by Diana Fuss, *Essentially Speaking: Feminism, Nature and Difference* (NY: Routledge, 1989).

35 In addition to chapter 5 of my *Narrative Ethics*, see also the excellent

treatment of ethics and politics in Simon Critchley, *The Ethics of Deconstruction: Derrida and Levinas* (London: Blackwell, 1992).

36 Consult the models of "insurgent, critical multiculturalism" and "heterogeneity" advanced by David Theo Goldberg in the helpful introduction in *Multiculturalism: A Critical Reader* (London Blackwell, 1995), especially pp. 21–23 which emphasize the "diasporic politics" at the heart of such a construct.

37 Levinas, "Peace and Proximity," in *Basic Philosophical Writings*, 167. Levinas quotes a passage from Vassily Grossman's *Life and Fate* in which a woman waits on line: "[She] had never thought that the human back could be so expressive, and could convey states of mind in such a penetrating way. Persons approaching the counter had a particular way of craning their neck and back, their raised shoulders with shoulder blades tensed like springs, which seemed to cry, sob, and scream." The back, in this sense, discloses like a face, and both are figures for justice.

38 See Noel Ignatiev's *How the Irish Became White* (New York: Routledge, 1995), for an excellent example of how such choices emerge or are made. Nathan Glazer's *We Are All Multiculturists Now* (Cambridge: Harvard University Press, 1997) superbly documents the way in which African Americans, to take another instance, were deleted from the largely immigrant European program for American assimilation into the "melting pot." See also William Denis-Constant Martin, "The Choices of Identity," *Social Identities*, 1:1 (November 1995), 5–20; Daniel and Jonathan Boyarin, *Jews and Other Differences: The New Jewish Cultural Studies* (Minneapolis: University of Minnesota Press, 1997); and Norman L. Kleeblatt, "'Passing' Into Multiculturalism" in *Too Jewish? Challenging Jewish Identities* (New Brunswick: Rutgers University Press, 1996, 3–38.

39 In the prefatory essay to *The Nature and Context of Minority Discourse*, (New York: Oxford University Press, 1990) Abdul R. JanMohamed and David Lloyd ask the pertinent question, "toward a theory of minority discoursewhat is to be done?" Although the editors argue for the "transformative potential" of *all* minority discourse, any such potential depends on the *uses* of such discourse, as opposed to its functioning either as an intrinsic value or stable oppositionality. Perhaps it can stand as one more instance of the blackjewish uncanny that the editors' introduction moves seamlessly from a recycling of Marx's terms of analysis in "On the Jewish Question" to the critical possibilities of vernacular African American culture, without registering the missed opportunity, precisely here, for heterogeneity. See in this respect William E. Connoly's *Identity/Difference: Democratic Negotiations of Political Paradox* (Ithaca: Cornell University Press, 1991), and the dialectical continuum between "immanentist" and "contextualist" constructions of literary history proposed by David Perkins in *Is Literary History Possible?* (Baltimore: Johns Hopkins University Press, 1992).

40 Richard Brodhead, *The School of Hawthorne* (New York: Oxford University Press, 1986). See also Henry Louis Gates, Jr., *Figures in Black*

(New York: Oxford University Press, 1988), especially the chapter, "The 'Blackness of Blackness': A Critique of the Sign and the Signifying Monkey," 235–276.

41 See John Guillory, "Canon, Syllabus, List: A Note on the Pedagogic Imaginary," *Transition*, 52 (1991), 36–55.

42 See *Time and the Other*, trans. Richard Cohen (Pittsburgh University Press, 1987), *Totality and Infinity, Otherwise Than Being, Or Beyond Essence*, trans Alphonso Lingis (The Hague: Martinus Nijhoff, 1981), *Collected Philosophical Papers, The Levinas Reader*, ed. Seán Hand (Oxford: Blackwell, 1989), and Richard Cohen's helpful introduction to Levinas, *Elevations: The Height of the Good in Rosenzweig and Levinas* (Chicago: The University of Chicago Press, 1994).

43 Werner Sollors, *Beyond Ethnicity: Consent and Descent in American Culture* (New York: Oxford University Press, 1986), Henry Louis Gates, Jr., "Authenticity; or the Lesson of 'Little Tree'," *New York Times Book Review* (November 24, 1991), and David Theo Goldberg, ed. *Multiculturalism: A Critical Reader*.

44 Doris Sommer, *Foundational Fictions* (Berkeley: University of California Press, 1991), 45, 47.

45 Not surprisingly given their congruent personal histories as European Jews imperiled at mid-century, both Benjamin and Levinas coincide not only in their tragic sense of allegory, but also in a twin commitment to an anti-Hegelian notion of history as final end and arbiter. See especially Benjamin, *Illuminations*, 253–264, and Levinas's *Totality and Infinity*, 22–26 and 298–307.

46 Kelley, *Reinventing Allegory*, 260.

47 Yet from a more recent perspective, when Afrocentrist pedagogy claims Middle and Late Kingdom Egypt as specifically and recognizably Black or African cultural property, a dramatic rupture in the longitude of embedded cultural loyalties and collective identification has been announced, conspicuously inverting the historical analogy pairing not Black and Egyptian but Black and (Biblical) Jew as a deeply resonant moment of transcultural identification. Paul Gilroy notes, "This change betrays a profound transformation in the moral basis of black Atlantic political culture. Michael Jackson's repeated question 'Do you remember the time?' (of the Nile Valley civilisations) has, for example, recently supplanted *Burning Spear*'s dread inquiry into whether the days of slavery were being remembered at all." (207) See *The Black Atlantic: Modernity and Double Consciousness* (Cambridge: Harvard University Press, 1993), one of whose central themes is, in Gilroy's words, the "relation between tradition, modernity, temporality, and social memory." (198) (On a side note, Gilroy holds the work of Levinas at arm's length in his book, remaining skeptical of both its Eurocentrism and its Judeo-centrism.) In terms of empirical parallel, however, the travail of Blacks under slavery and in ghettos possesses a more precise socioeconomic counterpart in the Jews of Eastern Europe, however temporarily impoverished Jewish urban life may have been in America (see in this vein the Yiddish poet Berysh Vaynshteyn's "Negro" poems). The analogue for nineteenth-

century African Americans was not the Jewish merchant or occasional abolitionist but the scriptural Hebrew, as that distinction was preserved and instrumentalized in Gentile America.

48 Revelant in this connection is the religious tradition of depositing soil from *Eretz Yisrael* into Jews' coffins, no matter what country they may have lived and died in, thus affirming the link to a prior national consciousness. See also the Menachem Daum and Oren Rudavsky film, *A Life Apart: Hasidism in America* (USA, 1997).

49 See Michael Rogin "Black Face, White Noise: When the Jewish Jazz Singer Finds His Voice," *Critical Inquiry*, 18 (Spring, 1992), 417–453.

50 See Anna Deavere Smith, *Fires in the Mirror*, 32.

51 "Negroes are Anti-Semitic Because They're Anti-White," in Nat Hentoff, ed., *Black Anti-Semitism and Jewish Racism* (New York: Richard W. Baron, 1969), 9.

52 Kazin, *A Walker in the City* (New York: Harcourt, Brace, Jovanovich, 1973), 11.

53 See Rabbi I. Harold Sharfman, *The Frontier Jews: An Account of Jewish Pioneers and Settlers in Early America* (Seacaucus: The Citadel Press, 1977). For the converse case, communities of Black Jews, see Abraham D. Lavender, ed., *A Coat of Many Colors: Jewish Subcommunities in the United States* (Westport, CN: Greenwood, 1977), 209–232. Finally, see the slave narrative of Peter and Vina Still, *The Kidnapped and the Ransomed* (by Kate E. R. Pickard), ed., Maxwell Whiteman and Nancy Grant (Lincoln: University of Nebraska Press, 1995) for a singular case of Black–Jewish relations in the American South.

54 See the lapidary analysis of the stranger in Georg Simmel's 1908 essay "The Stranger" in *On Individuality and Social Forms*, ed. Donald N. Levine (Chicago: The University of Chicago Press, 1971), 143–149.

55 I am thinking particularly of a CBS *Face the Nation* broadcast on December 14, 1997, as hosted by Bob Schieffer, where the topic at issue was the veracity of *Amistad*'s screenplay as adapted for use in high schools. On opposite sides of the issue (and the split-screen) were Michael Medved, film critic and Jewish spokesman, and Congressional Black Caucus leader Kweisi Mfume, respectively denouncing and endorsing the educational booklet, and ironically closing the circle on the film's own collaboration between Jewish director Stephen Spielberg and Black producer Debbie Allen.

56 Philip Roth, *The Counterlife* (New York: Farrar, Strauss, Giroux, 1987), 146. Roth's most recent novel, *American Pastoral* (New York: Houghton Mifflin, 1997), read as a cautionary fable, strikes the counter-chord to such *chez-soi* assimilationism, however.

57 It may be no coincidence, then, that Fiedler's own story of Jewish annihilation through assimilation, "The Last Jew in America," is accompanied by a companion piece which features a Black man's affirmation, against all odds, of his "at-home-ness." Of the protagonist in that story, "The First Spade in the West," remarks the narrator, "Well, he didn't know about the rest of them,", "but *he* had a right . . . he had every right in the world." [*The Last Jew in America* (New York: Stein and Day, 1966), 191.]

58 Michael Rogin, *Blackface/White Noise: Jewish Immigrants in the American Melting Pot* (Berkeley: The University of California Press, 1996).

59 Compare, for example, Orlando Patterson's *Ethnic Chauvinism: The Reactionary Impulse* (New York: Stein and Day, 1977) and Nathan Glazer's *We Are All Multiculturalists Now* and the way each assigns an *exemplary* role to Jewish peoplehood, in Patterson's analysis, "Hebraism" (the quintessential ethnic condition) as the crisis of alienation, "of being cut off from time, from self, and from community," (272), and in Glazer's, Jewishness as archetypically successful, contented, assimilation. The former, that is, similar to Sartre's *Anti-Semite and Jew*, depends upon an exterior vantage point on postexilic Jewish life; the latter tends to collapse exteriority (Jewish particularity) into secular liberalism and bourgeois success (thus echoing Rosenfeld's analysis of Levinsky cited above).

60 One allegorical compression would position Leo Frank (the sole piece of Jewish American "strange fruit") in stark contrast to hundreds of lynched Blacks, a story framed by the Middle Passage at one end and Rodney King at the other. Demurrers on the other side could enlist the Maryland Jew Bill of 1826, the antisemitic police riot of 1902 in New York, the 1948 Displaced Persons Act, and the Jonathan Pollard trial. Of course the commensuration of American antisemitism and American racism is unhelpful at best and at its worst a vulger and ethically suspect exercise in identity politics. See on this point Laurence Mordekai Thomas's excellent *Vessels of Evil: American Slavery and the Holocaust* (Philadelphia: Temple University Press, 1993) and also "The Matrices of Malevolent Ideologies: Blacks and Jews", *Social Identities* 2:1 (February 1996).

61 "The Trace of the Other," in Mark Taylor, ed., *Deconstruction in Context: Literature and Philosophy* (Chicago: University of Chicago Press, 1986), 353.

62 "Enigma and Phenomenon," from *Collected Philosophical Papers*, 66. Levinas here as elsewhere in his work, alludes to the verse, *patachti ani l'dodi v'dodi chamak avar* (I opened for my beloved, but my beloved had departed) from *Shir ha'shirim* (The Song of Songs).

63 There occurs a stunning moment in Benjamin's *The Origin of German Tragic Drama* in which Levinas is, as it were, anticipated by default: "Everything about history, that, from the very beginning, has been untimely, sorrowful, unsuccessful, is expressed in a face – or rather in a death's head." (166) While the pivot-point of face or countenance may be merely fortuitous here, Benjamin and Levinas do converge in a mutual apprehension of history – ontologically and economically understood – as history of the victors, and of the barbarous. See Simon Critchley, *The Ethics of Deconstruction*, 30, 56. on this point.

1 Ellison and Roth

1 Ralph Ellison, *Invisible Man* (New York: Vintage Press, 1987), 5.

2 Henry Roth, *Call It Sleep* (New York: Avon Books, 1981), 441.

3 Mikhail Bakhtin, "Discourse and the Novel," *The Dialogic Imagination:*

Four Essays, ed. Michael Holquist (Austin: University of Texas Press, 1990). 367.

4 Ibid., 369.

5 See Hana Wirth-Nesher's new afterword to *Call it Sleep* (New York: Farrar, Straus, and Giroux, 1991), which attends to the novel's exemplary status as a Jewish novel with divided cultural and linguistic loyalties, as well as the pieces by Werner Sollers, Ruth Wisse, and Karen R. Lawrence in the volume edited by Wirth-Nesher, *New Essays on Call It Sleep* (Cambridge: Cambridge University Press, 1996), and the Roth anthology, *Shifting Landscapes*, ed. Mario Materassi (Philadelphia: Jewish Publication Society, 1987).

6 The phrase belongs to Paul de Man. See also Henry Louis Gates, Jr., "The Blackness of Blackness: A Critique on the Sign and the Signifying Monkey," from *Figures in Black: Words, Signs, and the "Racial" Self* (New York: Oxford University Press, 1987), which uses Bakhtin's construct of *dialogism* from "Dialogue and the Novel" to gloss Ellison's authorial mobility and his fiction's network of diversified loyalties.

7 "Faulkner at Nagano," in *Essays, Speeches, and Public Letters*, ed. J. Merriwether (New York: Random House, 1966).

8 Given the tendency to conflate discourses of universalism and universality (the one, as David Goldberg points out, a function of epistemological politics, and the other, of a political epistemology), the more inductive categories of general and specific may be more helpful for less constrictive approaches to literary history. Thus, one might see Roth's and Ellison's novels as specific (that is, idiosyncratic, self-allegorizing as well as self-selected) instances against the horizon of a general (that is, probabilistic, always approximate) literary "tradition," in addition to a generalized corpus of "literary values."

9 Bakhtin's phrase from "Discourse and the Novel," 365; see also his distinction between "authoritative" and "inner-persuasive" discourses, 341–349.

10 Henry Louis Gates, Jr. "Bad Influence" (review of Nathan McCall's *Makes me Wanna Holler*), *The New Yorker* 70:3 (March 7, 1994), 94–98.

11 Robert Alter, "Jewish Dreams and Nightmares," from *What is Jewish Literature?* ed. Hana Wirth – Nesher (Philadelphia: Jewish Publication society, 1994), 57.

12 See Nathan Huggins, *Harlem Renaissance* (New York: Oxford University Press, 1971), David Levering Lewis, *When Harlem Was in Vogue* (New York: Oxford University Press, 1989), and Ann Douglas's *Terrible Honesty: Mongrel Manhattan in the 1920's*.

13 See, however, the history narrated by Ramon A. Gutierrez, "Ethnic Studies: Its Evolution in American Colleges and Universities" in *Multiculturalism: A Critical Reader*, 157–167, and Cornel West's advocacy for "prophetic" or "demystificatory" criticism in "The New Cultural Politics of Difference," in *The Cultural Studies Reader*, ed. Simon Durang (New York: Routledge, 1993), 203–217.

14 Roth's resumption of his fictional output with the multi-part *Mercy in a Rude Stream* has not fared well as a continuation, even restaging, of

his earlier touchstone text; Ellison's magnum opus 2, *Juneteenth*, makes its long-awaited appearance in June, 1999; besides their previous joint reputation as one-novel authors, another uncanny convergence involves the authors' deaths within a year of each other in 1994 and 1995.

15 Wirth-Nesher, however, argues that as emblem for Roth himself, David's apotheosis in the end involves a dual linguistic patricide, leaving *mameloshn* (Yiddish) behind as well as *fotersprakh* (Hebrew) for "an English literary language that speaks through him." (458) Roth thereby slays the cultural father, this being the land, as David himself parrots, of liberty, the land "where our fodders died" (62). English, the language of "the other," of Christianity, thus "kills the kid who is reborn as Christ." (Wirth-Nesher, *What is Jewish Literature*, 460) "Christ, it's a kid!" a bystander's exclamation during the book's climax, recapitulates David's own self-identification with the "kid sold for two zuzim" from the Passover song, *Chad Gadya*, itself an image to be conflated with Christ-as-paschal-sacrifice. Compare Karla Lydia Schultz's "At Home in the Language: The Cases of an Exile and an Immigrant," *Yearbook of German-American Studies* 20 (1985):125–132.

16 No theorist but rather pragmatist, Ellison writes in the new introduction to *Invisible Man*: ". . . So my task was one of revealing the human universals (damning term!) hidden within the plight of one who was both black and American . . . as a way of dealing with the sheer rhetorical challenge involved in communicating across our barriers of race and religion, class, color, and region – barriers which consist of the many strategies of division that were designed, and still function, to prevent what would otherwise have been a more or less natural recognition of the reality of black and white fraternity (incriminated, again!)." (xxii)

17 For example, in its caricatural and picturesque form, the "Holy Family" tableau at the beginning of *Call It Sleep* could be said to pick up where *The Scarlet Letter* leaves off, with Chillingworth/Albert Schearl in the ascendant.

18 In *Call it Sleep*, Albert Schearl is recurrently associated with paranoid "looking." Invisible Man, obviously swells with sight and eye images too numerous to catalogue. That Ellison's text depends on the framing device of narration-in-retrospect, and that "looking back" motifs are prevalent in Roth's (94, for example) should also be noted.

19 See Bakhtin's "Forms of Time and Chronotope in the Novel," *The Dialogic Imagination*, 84–258.

20 Here, then, is probably the clearest difference between Roth's purposes and those of proletarian or realist writers like Gold and Fuchs.

21 Compare the conventional slave narrative trope, as found, for example, in Harriet Jacobs' brother's "A True Tale of Slavery,": "He left us the only legacy that a slave father can leave his child, his whips and chains." John S. Jacobs, "A True Tale," in *The Leisure Hour: A Family Journal of Instruction and Recreation* (London, 1861), 86. I thank Jean Fagan Yellin for this reference.

22 See Angelika Bammer's "Mother Tongue and Other Strangers," and compare Invisible Man when he reverts to home, family, and the past recaptured: "And why did I, standing in the crows, see like a vision my mother hanging wash on a cold windy day . . . ? (Ellison, 267) Look at that old woman, somebody's mother, somebody's grandmother, maybe. We call them 'Big Mama' and they spoil us and – you know, you remember . . . Look at them, they look like my papa and my grandma and grandpa, and I look like you and you look like me." (271)

23 See Levinas's essay, "Everyday Language and Rhetoric without Eloquence," from *Outside the Subject*, trans. Michael B. Smith (Stanford: Stanford California Press, 1994), 135–143, and for a very different approach to Invisible Man's rhetoric, John F. Callahan, "Frequencies of Eloquence: The Performance and Composition of Invisible Man," in *New Essays on Invisible Man*, ed. Robert O'Meally (New York: Cambridge University Press, 1988), 55–94.

24 Ellison's novel resists subtlety in this respect too. But the patent obviousness of its Freudianism, e.g., Trueblood's dream, the various sexual objective correlatives – the belch at the beginning of chapter 2, the "partly uncoiled firehouse" at the beginning of chapter 19 – the name and character of Supercargo, demonstrates its utility as one more class of "discourse" to be ranged within the novel's discursive taxonomy.

25 We discover later in the novel that Albert actually is a parricide (of sorts). "Didn't she tell you that my father and I had quarreled that morning, that he struck me, and I vowed I would repay him . . . I could have seized the stick when the bull wrenched it from my father's hand. When he lay on the ground in the pen. But I never lifted a finger! I let him be gored!" (390)

26 Each, moreover, taps into that capacious image-reservoir which is *the city*. See in this regard Georg Simmel's landmark essay, "The Metropolis and Mental Life," in *On Individuality and Social Forms*, ed. Donald Levine (Chicago: University of Chicago Press, 1971), 324–339, especially on the "specialization of self" and the "quantitative intensification" of things; the final chapter on "the Multicultural City" in Richard Sennett, *Flesh and Stone: The Body and the City in Western Civilization* (New York: W. W. Norton & Co., 1994); Benjamin's "On Some Motifs in Baudelaire" in *Illuminations*, 155–200, together with Susan Buck-Morss's study of Benjamin's Arcades project, *The Dialectics of Seeing* (Cambridge: MIT Press, 1991); and finally, Marshall Berman's *All that is Solid Melts Into Air: The Experience of Modernity* (New York: Penguin Books, 1982).

27 *Jeu* is one of William Boelhower's favored terms for postmodern ethnic shapeshifting in *Through a Glass Darkly: Ethnic Semiosis in American Literature* (New York: Oxford University Press, 1987). Invisible Man perhaps provides the titular hint: "Could this be the way the world appeared to Rinehart? All the dark-glass boys? 'For now we see through a glass darkly, but then . . . '" (480)

28 David, moreover, is obviously more vulnerable to psychological splitting: "Be two Davids, be two!" he says at one point. "One here, one

outside on the curb," (104) a specifically childhood version of duality.
29 Levinas, "Everyday Language and Rhetoric Without Eloquence," *Outside the Subject*, 142.
30 Ellison, "Hidden Name and Complex Fate" in *Shadow and Act*, 147.
31 Compare also, "Solidities baffled him now, eluded him with a veiling shifting of contour . . . The sunlight that had now been so dazzlingly before was mysteriously dulled now as though filtered by an invisible film. Something of its assertion had been drained from stone, something of inflexible precision from iron. Surfaces had hollowed a little, sagged, edges had turned. The stable lineaments of the mask of the world had overlapped, shifted configuration as secretly and minutely as clock-hands, as sudden as the wink of an eye." (274)
32 In addition to initiating the novel's constant drive towards mix and mosaic, the casual ethnic assemblage in the prologue is answered in the climatic rendering of mingled voices and ethnicities in the penultimate chapter of Book IV: "David opened his eyes. Behind, between them, and around them, like a solid wall, the ever-encroaching bodies, voices, faces at all heights, all converging upon him, craning, peering, haranguing, pointing him out, discussing him." (432)
33 The phrase used by John Murray Cuddihy to describe Old World intellectual and cultural passages to New in *The Ordeal Of Civility: Freud, Marx, Lévi-Strauss* (Boston: Beacon, 1987).
34 Another way to regard the circulation of music in the text, indeed of much of its traveling debris, is economically – as capital. When asked by a drunk member of the Brotherhood at the Cthonian club for a spiritual, "or one of those good ole Negro work songs," (304) Brother Jack is horrified – "The brother does not sing!" – the drunk insists – "Nonsense, all colored people sing." – but Invisible Man, after some initial amusement, is in fact perplexed: "Shouldn't there be some way for us to be asked to sing?" (307) The question is not easily answered by Ellison's text, posed at the end in another form, when Invisible Man wonders whether "we [blacks], through no fault of our own, were linked to all the others in the loud-clamoring semi-visible world . . . . Weren't we part of them, as well as apart from them . . . ?" (561–562) In *Call it Sleep*, the transformation of capital seems a lot simpler; the *cheder* rabbi's "pointers" are actually lollipop sticks, a gift from students. Before the sticks turn into pointers, however, they are gambled for – as lollipops – by the students. (My thanks to Michael Martin for this observation.)
35 Roth is not unique among his modernist Jewish contemporaries in fashioning a composite form out of distinct idiolects, be they Christian and Jewish, or Biblical and secular. But Roth could not have selected his scripture idly: the verses from Isaiah and the chapters from Exodus which they accompany climax in revelation, one of the novel's central themes. They also play off the text's (and David's) preoccupation with idolatry and mystified sexuality. Hana Wirth-Nesher rehearses the routine reading of Judeo-Christian syntheses in Roth's text, and provides a reliable framing overall for the novels' triadic hierarchization of languages: street English, Yiddish, and Aramaic

and Hebrew (though she omits the coded role of Polish for divulging adult secrets).

36 Compare the call-and-response in Isaiah 6:3: "And one called unto another, and said: Holy, holy, holy is the Lord of Hosts."

37 See Gilles Deleuze and Félix Guattari, *Kafka: Toward a Minor Literature*, (Minneapolis: University of Minnesota Press, 1984), 27.

38 Just as Roth's novel signifies on *Ulysses* and *Dubliners* in its own scene featuring the now-wandering cleric Reb Pankower's interior monologue (chapter 4, Book 4).

39 See the worrisome usage of the term in *Through a Glass Darkly*.

40 Sleep, as I suggest earlier, has illusory or sedative force in *Invisible Man*, as well: Invisible Man frequently speaks of having awakened out of a stupor, e.g., "I'd been asleep, dreaming," (433) or, as he says of himself in the prologue, "I . . . walk softly so as not to awaken the sleeping ones [for] there are few things as dangerous as sleepwalkers." (5) See also Alter's brief rendition of the text's dreaming motifs in "Jewish Dreams and Nightmares" in *What is Jewish Literature?* 53–66.

41 Deleuze and Guattari, *Kafka*, 17.

42 Ibid., 18.

43 Compare Theresa Kelley's analysis of Benjamin's *One-Way Street* in *Reinventing Allegory*, and also Paul de Man's "Aesthetic Formalization in Kleist" in *The Rhetoric of Romanticism* (Minneapolis: University of Minnesota Press, 1984).

44 Ibid., 21.

45 Ibid.

46 Delmore Schwartz, *Genesis* (New York: New Directions, 1943), 117.

2 Himes and Bellow

1 In his autobiography *The Quality of Hurt* (New York: Doubleday, 1972), Himes himself refers to his first novel as "my bitter novel of protest," (75) a description echoed a few pages later in a broadside against his publisher's less than enthusiastic marketing: "the whole episode left me very bitter." (77) A sample contemporary review of Himes's work from an editorial in *Ebony* confirms Himes's acrimony: "an invidious, shocking, incendiary . . . virulent, malicious book full of venom and rancor [that] substitutes emotions for intelligence, dictates thinking with the skin rather than the brains" *Ebony* (November, 1947), 44. See also E. Margolies and M. Fabre, *The Several Lives of Chester Himes*: Jackson (University of Mississippi Press, 1997). The reception for Bellow's *The Victim*, on the other hand, was highly favorable, though Bellow himself considers the work part of his juvenalia. It is, however, fortunately lacking that element of cultural self-inflation so prevalent in Bellow's later work, interrogated by the author perhaps only in *Humboldt's Gift*.

2 Harold Cruse, *The Crisis of the Negro Intellectual* (New York: William, Morrow & Company, 1967), especially the chapter, "Negroes and Jews – The Two Nationalisms and the Bloc(ked) Plurality," and Cyn-

thia Ozick, "Literary Blacks and Jews," in *Art and Ardor* (New York: Alfred A. Knopf, 1983). (See also Ozick's updated reflections on Malamud's "fiction of blows" in Paul Berman, *Blacks and Jews: Alliances and Arguments* (New York: Delacorte Press, 1994).

3 In *Multiculturalism and the "Politics of Recognition": An Essay* (Princeton: Princeton University Press, 1992), Taylor explicitly concerns himself with the competing claims of disparate constituencies, and the institutional structures that govern or mediate response to them. My sense of the "politics" in Taylor's "politics of recognition" conveys an unavoidable *surplus* of identity borne by actors in intersubjective dramas of recognition that italicize their particularity, i.e., "Blacks" and "Jews," the ethical, however, still being primary. Or, in terms Taylor himself uses, "we must be open to comparative cultural study of the kind that must displace our horizons in the resulting fusions," (73) where "displacement" signifies for me an ethical troubling of intact political "fusions."

4 See Critchley's admirable account of a "Levinasian Politics of Ethical Difference" in *The Ethics of Deconstruction*, where the ethical "takes place" within collective, that is (in the best sense) *political* space. Critchley rightly calls this passage between ethics and politics a "doubling of discourse" as opposed to a temporal progression. See Levinas's own discussion of "the third party" in the "The Ego and the Totality" from *Collected Philosophical Papers*, the section "The Other and the Others" in *Totality and Infinity*, and especially chapter 5 of *Otherwise Than Being*.

5 Roger Simon, "Face to Face With Alterity: Postmodern Jewish Identity and the Eros of Pedagogy," in Wendy Steiner, *Pedagogy and Impersonation* (New York: Routledge), 90–105. See also Goldberg's introduction to *Multiculturalism: A Critical Reader*, 1–41, and Peter Caws's essay in that same volume, "Identity: Cultural, Transcultural, and Multicultural," 371–387, for arguments about what Caws calls the "chosen aspects of identities" over and above the merely given.

6 Saul Bellow, *The Victim* (New York: Avon Books, 1975), 21.

7 Chester Himes, *If He Hollers Let Him Go* (New York: Thunder Mouth's Press, 1986).

8 "Choice," on the level of title at least, seems to be limited to which verse of the children's song it will select, and which it will exclude. Logically speaking, the novel could just as well have been called *Catch a Nigger By the Toe* – although titled the way it is, it does seem to assert at least a *narrative* autonomy, which cleverly, politically, forces us on our own "recognizance" to fill in the missing word . . . and pronounce it.

9 "How it Feels to be Colored Me" is the title of a short essay by Zora Neale Hurston, reprinted in *I Love Myself When I Am Laughing . . . And Then Again When I Am Looking Mean And Impressive: a Zora Neale Hurston Reader* (Old Westbury, Connecticut: The Feminist Press, 1979).

10 From the essay "Attack Words" in Canetti's *The Conscience of Words*, trans. Joachim Neugroschel (New York: Seabury Press, 1976). As

these are discursive as much as experiential categories, see again the relevant analyses of race prejudice by Sartre, Fanon, and Alain Finkielkraut, and the essays in *The Anatomy of Racism*, ed. David Theo Goldberg (Minneapolis: University of Minnesota Press, 1990).

11 Critchley on Levinas's *Otherwise Than Being*: "From the first, my ethical discourse with the Other is troubled and doubled into a political discourse with all the other others: a double discourse. The immediacy of the ethical is always already mediated ethically . . . *Le tiers* [the third party] has always already entered into the ethical relation, troubling and doubling it into a political discourse." (231) Another way to put this would be Benedict Anderson's notion of the simultaneously closed and open character of the nationalist imaginary, where the ethno-racially marked person lies in an ironic echo of *Invisible Man* "outside history," and comradeship takes place therefore at his expense. "[N]ation-ness," writes Anderson, "is virtually inseparable from political consciousness." (135) And in this sense, politics – as nationhood or group-consciousness – maintains a direct, necessary, and causal link to ethics. See "Patriotism and Racism" in *Imagined Communities*, 141–154.

12 Compare Levinas: "Justice is necessary, that is, comparison, coexistence, contemporaneousness, assembling, order, thematization of the *visibility* of faces . . . in a society where there is no distinction between those close and those far off, but in which there also remains the impossibility of passing by the closest." (*Otherwise Than Being*, 157, 159)

13 Himes, 129, 59, 39, 127.

14 Bellow, 31, 33, 99, 151. The interesting thing is that the Jew here, as if proving Sartre, almost requires the antisemite for his own Jewish identity to surface – something Allbee (as Sartre predicts) identifies with in the very act of stigmatizing. "[Albee] fingered Leventhal's hair, and Leventhal found himself caught under his touch and felt incapable of doing anything." (198) When Allbee lectures Leventhal on the arbitrary distribution of luck and quotes the Catholic catechism about the world being created for man – and by implication, "for everybody who repeats 'For man' it means 'For me,'" (172) – he only mirrors Leventhal's own urgently personal concern with fate and happenstance ("I was lucky. I got away with it"), and unconsciously echoes the identical theory of personal responsibility in Jewish tradition: "Therefore everyone is in duty bound to say, 'For my sake is the universe created.'" (*Mishna Sanhedrin* 4.5)

15 Emmanuel Levinas, *Totality and Infinity*, 89 (my italics).

16 John Rawls, *A Theory of Justice* (Cambridge: Belknap Press of Harvard University Press, 1971) and *Justice as Fairness* (New York: Irvington Publishers, 1991). Seyla Benhabib's *Situating the Self* (Routledge: New York, 1992) provides a helpful summary of the debate Rawls's work has prompted.

17 Emmanuel Levinas, "From Ethics to Exegesis," *In the Time of Nations*, 100–111.

18 Compare the following critique of politicized pluralism: "the sara-

band of innumerable and equivalent cultures, each justifying itself in its own context, creates a world which is, to be sure, deoccidentalized, but also disoriented. To catch sight, in meaning, of a situation that precedes culture, to envision language out of the revelation of the other . . . in the gaze of man aiming at a man precisely as abstract man disengaged from all culture, in the nakedness of the face . . . is to find oneself able to judge civilizations on the basis of ethics." "Phenomenon and Enigma" in *Collected Philosophical Papers*, 101. See also "The Rights of Man and the Rights of the Other," in *Outside the Subject*; the essays on nationalism and Jewish identity in *Difficult Freedom*; and my own *The Fence and the Neighbor: Levinas, Leibowitz, and Israel Among the Nations* (forthcoming), which addresses Jewish particularism in the context of religious praxis and textuality.

19 "Demanding Judaism," in *Beyond the Verse: Talmudic Readings and Lectures*, 4.

20 For Levinas Jewish particularism cannot be other than historicized particularism, oscillating (as does Jewish self-understanding generally) between two legitimating grounds: a nationhood founded on sacred responsibility ("You shall be holy for I am holy"), *and* responsibility which ensues from continued travail suffered as, or in, peoplehood. The *particular* particularism, of Jewish peoplehood, in this sense, derives from its being absolutized both from within and from without. However, this issue really demands the depth focus of its strictly philosophical contextualization as spelled out in Levinas's dense and idiosyncratic versions of kinship relations – paternity, filiality, fraternity, and the like – in his early work, and their implications for *Otherwise Than Being* and the essays on Judaism in *Difficult Freedom*, *Beyond the Verse*, and *In the Time of Nations*.

21 For an informative and sensible discussion of the Biblical and Rabbinic genealogy of these issues, see Gordon Lafer, "Universalism and Particularism in Jewish Law: Making Sense of Political Loyalties," in *Jewish Identity*, eds. David Theo Goldberg and Michael Krausz (Philadelphia: Temple University Press, 1992), 177–211; Jacob Katz, *Exclusivism and Tolerance* (New York: Oxford University Press, 1961; and Marvin Fox, ed., *Modern Jewish Ethics: Theory and Practice* (Columbus: Ohio State University Press, 1975.

22 See the talmudic essay, "Judaism and Revolution, in *Nine Talmudic Readings*, 94–119, especially the section, "Politics and Violence"; the essays grouped under the section *Politics* in *The Levinas Reader*, and David and Jonathan Boyarin, "Diaspora: Generation and the Ground of Jewish Identity," in *Critical Inquiry* 19 (Summer 1993), 693–725, where the authors claim "that Diaspora, and not monotheism, may be the most important contribution that Judaism has to make to the world." In "Beyond Memory," Levinas speaks of a Judaism that "overflows memory . . . and senses an unforeseeable future," a future perhaps like our diasporized and disaggregated present. Yet paradoxically or not, it is "in Israel's destiny," that "human universality transpires and is being accomplished." (96)

23 I refer back to David Theo Goldberg's substitution of the terms "gen-

eral and specific" for "universal and particular" as one possible definitional solution to the seeming difficulties here. But perhaps these must simply remain difficult.

24 These matters certainly warrant more than cursory attention, since even within the strict confines of Levinas's *oeuvre*, they pose real structural difficulties. The overriding cultural distinction for Levinas, for instance, opposes Jewishness to the West, "Hebrew" to "Greek." The "orient," in other words, denotes Israel. His diasporic identity as Lithuanian Jew, his political loyalties as a French national, his directorship of the westernizing *Ecole Normale Israélite Orientale*, and his resolute Europocentrism all underscore a significant bias in the terms he dignifies for argumentation, as well as the ideological assumptions by which he proceeds. The "other" in Levinas is thus not entirely pre- (or even post) cultural; alterity, I think it is fair to say, is explicitly Western and masculine.

25 See chapter 5, "Face and Monstration in Crane, Melville, and Wright."

26 Compare Roland Barthes's analysis of verbal precision in *The Pleasure of the Text*, trans. Richard Howard (New York: Hill and Wang, 1975): "The exactitude in question is not the result of taking greater pains, it is not a rhetorical instrument in value, as though things were *increasingly well* described – but of a change of code: the (remote) model of the description is no longer oratorical discourse (Nothing at all is being 'painted'), but a kind of lexicographical artifact." (26–27) In Bellow's case, by contrast, the language of text in fact *does* take greater pains.

27 See the chapter "The Fact of Blackness," trans. George Lam Maskman (New York: Grove Press, 1967) in *Black Skin, White Masks*. Compare also the passage in Himes where being looked at produces "a blinding explosion [that] went off just back of my eyes as if the nerve centres had been dynamited. I had the crazy sensation of my eyes popping out of my head." (33–35).

28 Levinas, of course, would insist on the necessary subordination of politics to ethics in this sense, cultural difference being overridden by the demands of pure alterity. See Finkielkraut's *The Wisdom of Love* and also his interview with Levinas reprinted in *The Levinas Reader*, 289–295.

29 The relevant passage from Fanon can be found on pp. 160–161 in Fanon, *Black Skin, White Masks*. At moments like these, Fanon unfortunately recirculates what one wants him to transcend.

30 Real victimization predicated on ethnic or racial hatred almost surely serves as an implicit model for the recasting of terms Levinas introduces in *Otherwise Than Being* where subjectivity is now defined as a persecution and a wounding by the Other, and the self as held hostage in a steady state of unwilled substitution.

31 That both novels traffic in victimization does not necessarily make them congruent anatomies of race-hatred and distinguishes them from the more simpleminded rhetoric of injury.

32 The only times in the novel that "letting go" does not squeeze and render the narrator into "the accusative" are when he vomits at a party – "I let it go into the sink," (67) – and when he backs off

argumentation with Alice – "I'm willing to let it go, why in the hell aren't you?" (91)

33 Compare Alfred Kazin's similar – and self-conscious – predicament: "It troubled me that I could speak in the fullness of my own voice only when I was alone on the streets, walking about. There was something unnatural about it; unbearably isolated. I was not like the others! I was not like the others!" (*A Walker in the City*, 24)

34 I also think it significant that unlike Bellow's various ethnic supernumeraries, the cameo roles played by a Jewish labor unionist and the "two Mexican youths" at novel's end betray Himes's keener sense of co-ethnic implicatedness: "[The Mexicans] fell in beside me and we went out . . . the three of us abreast and the cop in the rear," the latter also being the narrative's last exercise in the poetics of physiognomy: "They were both brown-skinned, about my colour, slender and slightly stooped, with Indian features and thick curly hair." (203)

35 Of the cleft without and the fissure within, Julia Kristeva writes, "Strangely, the foreigner lives within us: he is the hidden face of our identity, the peace that wrecks our abode, the time in which understanding and affinity founder. By recognizing him within ourselves. we are spared detesting him in himself. A symptom that precisely turns 'we' into a problem, perhaps makes it impossible, The foreigner comes in when the consciousness of my difference arises, and he disappears when we acknowledge ourselves as foreigners, unamenable to bonds and communities." *Strangers to Ourselves*, 1. Levinas goes even further: citing Numbers 11:12 where Moses speaks of himself as father-nursemaid, he calls responsibility "maternity," in the sense of carrying the other and our responsibility for him/her. Charles Taylor's *Multiculturalism and the "Politics of Recognition"* comes at this dialectic of interiority and exteriority less figurally, but no less relevantly: "What has come about with the modern age is not the need for recognition but the conditions in which the attempt to be recognized can fail." (35)

36 As cited above, one of Levinas's favorite tropes for the Other's unanswerable claim as his intrusion into selfhood and immediate departure is the Biblical verse fortuitously echoed here: *Song of Songs* 5, 2–6. See *Otherwise Than Being*, 141–142, and also Derrida's "At This Very Moment in This Work Here I Am," in *Re-Reading Levinas*, which begins, *"He will have obligated* . . . as after the passing of some singular visitor, you are no longer familiar with the places, those very places where nonetheless the little phrase – Where does it come from? Who pronounced it – still leaves its resonance lingering." (11)

37 Compare the scene in *Invisible Man*, described in an endnote to the previous chapter, where Invisible Man becomes a similar target for such stereotypic race-baiting, 303–307.

38 Bellow, 34, 44, 131, 179.

39 Genre considerations are not unimportant in regard to this text, part crime novel, part detective fiction, part social (proletarian) realism, part "protest novel." For a helpful taxonomy and guide to the kinds of popular literature within which we can situate Himes's novel, see

Tony Hilfer, *The Crime Novel: A Deviant Genre* (Austin: The University of Texas Press, 1992). Also relevant here are Himes's authorial persona and his implied readership(s) – that is, his relationship to other writers (Hemingway, Wright, Sartre), and his position in the marketplace. The author of *If He Hollers Let Him Go* began his writing career while serving jail-time for jewel theft. Consider also in this context John Edgar Wideman's introduction to *Live From Death Row* by Mumia Abdul Jamal (New York: Addison Wesley, 1995), where, in contrast to contemporary "neoslave narratives" of black triumph over "system," he wonders aloud on behalf of imprisoned black men, "Isn't one of the lessons of African-American culture the reality of an unseen world, below, above, around what is visible?" (xxxv)

40 Fanon, 160.

41 During one of his "miraculous and transforming" moments – really, a scene of acting – Invisible Man speaks of having become *"more human,"* (Ellison, 337) but by novel's end, one can, with Leventhal, contrast this state with something more scaled down, just tough enough: "why should an old slave use such a phrase as, 'This or this or this has made me more human,' as I did in my arena speech? Hell, he never had any doubts about his humanity – that was left to his 'free' offspring. He accepted his humanity just as he accepted the principle." (567)

42 See Erving Goffman, *Interaction Ritual: Essays in Face-to-Face Behavior* (Garden City, NY: Anchor Books, 1967), and *The Presentation of Self in Everyday Life* (Garden City: Doubleday Books, 1959).

43 "Reality and its Shadow," *Collected Philosophical Papers*, 6.

44 "Freedom and Command," *Collected Philosophical Papers*, 21.

45 In a perceptive review, "Ozick Seizes Bellow" in *The Nation* (February 26, 1996),34–36, Lee Siegel shows how Ozick's determination to read Bellow through the rose-colored glasses of moral essentialism and thematic truth-value misses the "beast" in Bellow. "Fetishizing *Seize the Day* as one of the last expressions of 'higher consciousness' and the 'human essence,'" Siegel writes, ignores the novel in its capacity as *"social protest* simply as part of its own intangible motion into the material world" (36, my italics) – the very public place, I have argued, where Saul Bellow and Chester Himes keep company.

46 *The Imaginary Jew*, 71.

47 Tickets of admission form a motif in their own right in the text. Compare pp 27, 30, 112, 150, 155, 186.

48 Lyrics taken from the song "They Don't Care About Us" by Michael Jackson, from his 1994 CD, *HIStory*. They read in full, "Sue me, Jew me, everybody do me/Kick me, Kike me, don't you black or white me," and have subsequently been altered for a second (revised) pressing.

3 Bradley and Roth

1 David Bradley, *The Chaneysville Incident* (New York: Harper and Row, 1981).

2 In order to distinguish Roth, the author, from Roth, the narrator, I place quotation marks around the latter.

3 Philip Roth, *Operation Shylock* (New York: Simon & Schuster, 1993), 346.

4 Friedrich Nietzsche, *The Use and Abuse of History* (New York: Macmillan Publishing Company, 1986), 8.

5 *The Counterlife* (New York: Farrar, Straus, Giroux, 1986), 323.

6 The only other unfictionalized element in the novel comprises conversations between "Roth" and the Israeli writer and Holocaust survivor Aharon Appelfeld, published by *The New York Times* in January, 1988. As recorded by "Roth," Appelfeld appeals to a formal principle of "naiveness" in his own work as the only possible response to the implacable reality of the Holocaust, which "surpassed any imagination" (86); art must, perhaps can only, *reconstruct* History, even – and especially – when it is inhuman. See the volume by Appelfeld, *Beyond Despair: Four Lectures and a Conversation with Philip Roth*, trans. Jeffrey M. Green (New York: Fromm International, 1994).

7 *The Facts: A Novelist's Autobiography* (New York: Penguin Books, 1988), 162. Compare *The Counterlife*, 321.

8 See Alan Cooper's *Philip Roth and the Jews* (Albany: State University of New York, 1996), especially the chapter, "Biography versus the Biographical," and *Conversations with Philip Roth* (Jacksonville: University Press of Miss., 1992).

9 Ellison, 428. Compare, also, Benedict Anderson's fate for the objects of race-hatred, refractory to historical destiny, and thus "outside history," (*Imagined Communities*, 149), and Bakhtin's description of the perceptually self-distorted self and its "mask-face[s]" as being "absolutely extrahistorical." ("Author and Hero," 32.)

10 *The Counterlife*, 147. Compare Daniel and Jonathan Boyarin's "Diaspora: Generation and Ground of Jewish Identity" together with James Clifford's guarded review of that essay in his "Diasporas," and Kobena Mercer's "Diaspora Culture and the Dialogic Imagination," in *Blackframes: Celebration of Black Cinema*, M. Cham and C. Andrade-Watkins, eds. (Massachusetts: MIT Press, 1988), 50–61.

11 Cahan's novel ends with a paean to Irving Berlin, left unnamed. As if in confirmation of Roth's fictional axiom that reality arrives already garbed in allegory before the novelist has said a word, a letter to the editor in *The New Yorker* (July 24, 1995) ends with the following, "In a showdown between Israeli and Christian fundamentalists, on the one hand, and Islamic fundamentalists, on the other, we could witness the unthinkable – another Masada, another destruction of the Temple, [sic] and another Diaspora, with the tattered remnants drifting back to the land of their fathers: Warsaw, Vilnius, and Vienna." (6)

12 One of the novel's allegorical set pieces describes Washington's Hemingwayesque stalking of a deer.

13 Michel Foucault, *The Archaeology of Knowledge*, trans. A. M. Sheridan-Smith (New York: Pantheon Books, 1972), 7.

14 Compare the Ojibwa chief Nanapush's metaphor at the end of Louise Erdrich's Native-American chronicle, *Tracks* (New York: Harper and

Row, 1988), lamenting the documentalization of his history and culture: "a tribe of file cabinets and triplicates, a tribe of single-space documents, directives, policy. A tribe of pressed trees. A tribe of chicken-scratch that can be scattered by a wind, diminished to ashes by one struck match." (225)

15 Benedict Anderson, "The Angel of History," in *Imagined Communities,* 162. Compare Nietzsche, the "weight of the past ... presses him down and bows his shoulders; he travels with a dark invisible burden that he can plausibly disown ... And so it hurts him, like the thought of a lost paradise, to see a herd grazing, or nearer still, a child that has nothing yet of the past to disown ... (5–6) with Benjamin: "But a storm is blowing from Paradise; it has got caught in his wings with such violence that the angel can no longer close them." ("Theses on the Philosophy of History," from *Illuminations,* 258.)

16 See Kelley again on an allegorical conception of history in *Reinventing Allegory,* 258–261.

17 "Because what it all means is that those of us who count black people among our ancestors ... must live forever with both our knowledge and our belief; the quandary is that there is no comfort for us either way. Somewhere here with us, in the very air we breathe, all that whipping and chaining and raping and starving and branding and maiming and castrating and lynching and murdering – all of it – is still going on." (213) Compare Jonathan Boyarin's preface to *Storm from Paradise,* cited earlier.

18 Consider Roth's own short story "I Always Wanted You to Admire My Fasting; Or, Looking at Kafka," in *Reading Myself and Others* (New York: Bantam, 1977) with Deleuze and Guattari's observation on the disjunction between sense and language in *Kafka: Toward a Minor Literature.*

19 The whiskey in Bradley's novel is always hot, as stories are told or learned by firelight, the warming and intoxicating effects correlative with stories themselves. And yet, storytelling is just as palpably haunted by death, either of the story's subject or imagined narrator, or of the decimated ranks of enslaved Africans killed in the middle passage or on plantations. That is to say, Bradley knows his Benjamin, knows not only that the storyteller is "the figure in which the righteous man encounters himself," but also that "Death is the sanction of everything that the storyteller can tell." "The stories were breaking up inside him," writes John Washington of his elderly, dying friend; "he coughed out fragments. I listened to him, sitting by the roaring stove, sipping whiskey and feeding the fire." (112)

20 Benjamin, *The Origin of German Tragic Drama,* 178.

21 On dueling public intellectuals, see Irving Howe's essayistic address to Ralph Ellison in "Black Boys and Native Sons" in *Dissent* (Autumn, 1963), Ellison's response in "The World and the Jug" in *Shadow and Act,* and Ozick's updating of that debate in her discussion of Malamud's *The Tenants* in "Literary Blacks and Jews"; Harold Cruse's *The Crisis of the Negro Intellectual: From its Origins to the Present;* "Public Academy" by Michael Berube in *The New Yorker* (January 29, 1995),

73–80; Robert Boynton, "The Intellectuals" in *The Atlantic Monthly* 275.3 (March, 1995), 53–65; Stanley Crouch's *Notes of a Hanging Judge: Essays and Reviews 1979–1989* (New York: Oxford University Press, 1990); Michael Henchard's "Intellectual Pursuit" in *The Nation* (February 19, 1996), 22–24; Adolph Reed, Jr.'s "What Are the Drums Saying, Booker? The Current Crisis of the Black Intellectual," *The Village Voice* (April 11, 1995): 31–37, and Leon Wieseltier's critique of Cornel West in *The New Republic*, discussed in the next chapter.

22 In West's words, "From the bourgeois model, it recuperates the emphasis on human will and heroic effort. Yet the insurgency model refuses to conceive of this will in individualistic and elitist terms [Washington's genealogical and cultural answerability]. From the Marxist model, it recovers the stress on structural constraints, class formations and radical democratic values . . . yet it acknowledges the latter's naivete about culture [Washington in his capacity as cultural critic]. Lastly, from the Foucaultian model, the insurgency model recaptures the preoccupation with worldly skepticism, the historical constitution of 'regimes of truth,' and the multifarious operations of 'power/knowledge' [Washington as theorist of History]," 83. Cornel West, *Keeping Faith: Philosophy and Race in America* (New York: Routledge, 1993), 67–85. See, however, Adolph Reed Jr.'s skeptical and scathing critique of such academic models for black public intellectuality in "What are the Drums Saying, Booker?"

23 See Jacques Lacan, *The Four Fundamental Concepts of Psychoanalysis*, trans. Alan Sheridan (New York: W.W. Norton, 1981), 185–187; and Slavoj Žižek, *Looking Awry: An Introduction to Jacques Lacan Through Popular Culture* (Cambridge: Massachusetts Institute of Technology Press, 1991), and the explanation of the Lacanian "symptom" in Žižek's *The Sublime Object of Ideology* (London: Verso Press, 1989).

24 Compare the following passage of mimetic transfer where Washington recalls his youth: "I began to be really frightened, recalling the stories about how once Old Jack and Snakebelly White reached the far side of the Hill they became something other than human. Boogeymen. But I thought it out, and reasoned that if being there changed them, then it ought to change me too. Now *I* was a boogeyman, and it would serve everybody well to stay out of my way." (29)

25 Consult Appelfeld's collection of essays, *Massot Beguf Rishon* (Essays in the First Person) (Jerusalem: Zionist Library, 1979), as well as the essay by Nurit Govrin, "To Express the Inexpressible: The Holocaust Literature of Aharon Appelfeld," *Remembering for the Future* (Oxford: Pergamon Press, 1988), 580–594.

26 William Faulkner, *Light in August* (New York: Random House, 1959), 449.

27 Primo Levi, *The Periodic Table*, trans. Raymond Rosenthal (New York: Schocken Books, 1984), 233.

28 Obviously, I cannot do any kind of justice here to the complexity of commentary and argument that such a problem has posed for modernity. "The limits of representation," for example, is a phrase forming part of the title for a dense 1992 anthology about the Holo-

caust and its representational vicissitudes – in confessing which I
merely acknowledge that it is often and especially the catch-phrases
that beckon careful and deliberate analysis. See Saul Friedlander, ed.,
Probing the Limits of Representation: Nazism and the "Final Solution"
(Chicago: University of Chicago Press, 1992). Among its more important pieces are those by Geoffrey Hartman, Amos Funkenstein, Martin
Jay, Eric Santer, and Hayden White. As I say, the literature in the
many subtensive fields addressed by these issues is vast. A highly
selective list confined to the specifically literary domain of Roth's and
Bradley's texts might include Sidra Dekoven Ezrahi, *By Words Alone:
The Holocaust in Literature* (Chicago: University of Chicago Press,
1980); Berel Lang, ed., *Writing and the Holocaust* (New York: Holmes
and Meier, 1988); Jean-François Lyotard, *Heidegger and "the jews"*,
trans. Andreas Michel and Mark S. Roberts (Minneapolis: University
of Minnesota Press, 1990); Hayden White, *Metahistory* (1973), *Tropics
of Discourse* (1978), and *The Content of the Form* (1987), all published by
Johns Hopkins University Press; James E. Young, *Writing and Rewriting the Holocaust: Narrative and the Consequences of Interpretation* (Indiana: Indiana University Press, 1988).

29 As antiphony, competition, or creative appropriation (depending on
one's viewpoint) the Black–Jewish relationship here has not gone
unnoticed. See, for example, Emily Budick, *Blacks and Jews in Literary
Conversation* (Cambridge: Cambridge University Press, 1998), and
Carol Kessner, "Motherhood in Extremis: Ozicks' *The Shawl* and
Morrison's *Beloved* in the light of Laurence Thomas's *Vessels of Evil*,"
in *Literary Encounters: African Americans and American Jews* (forthcoming). Thematic, imagistic, and structural-stylistic parallelisms between the two texts abound. A very selective list might include:
configured space (buildings, women's bodies, interiors, exteriors);
orality (mouths that suck, speak, smell); thresholds (topographic,
personal, intersubjective, narrative); motherhood (as, severally, adoration, murder, pacification, servitude, ownership, authorship); twin
sets of ghosts, axes, colors, marks, women, and invasive men; com-
pact, layered, loaded, polysemous prose; "one's own" (language,
body, history) as opposed to "another's"; the body language of beat-
ing, smashing, rubbing, choking, whipping, coupling (by choice and
through rape); the discourses of telling, showing, publishing, writing
and reading.

30 Yiddish (also Hebrew) for "destruction" as compared with the more
recent "*Shoah*').

31 Toni Morrison, *Beloved* (New York: Plume, 1988), 274; Cynthia Ozick,
The Shawl: A Story and Novella (New York: Alfred A. Knopf, 1989), 44.
Morrison's sentence, however, aside from a declaration against transmission, can just as easily lend itself to imply a pledge not to ignore as
well as not to let die. (In this third sense, incidentally, Bradley reminds
us in *Chaneysville* that against the background of Africanisms (an-
throplogists, he reminds us, call them "survivals") black persons will
typically say "passed away" or "passed on" instead of "died," (213)
highlighting a difference about the fundamental nature of death be-

tween Western-Christianized and indigenous African belief systems.)

32 In *Storm from Paradise: The Politics of Jewish Memory* (Minneapolis: University of Minnesota Press, 1992), Daniel Boyarin puts Benjamin's allegory of history to idiosyncratic use by offering the trope of "forgetting," not in the sense of the ghostly counterpart of memory (the *absence* to the other's *presence*), but rather as bearing a weight and spatiality all its own; forgetting "inhabits" a place, so to speak; it can be localized. Forgetting is *willing* something or someone into oblivion, forgotten places are those whose absences have been *made*, selected. Echoing Roth and Bradley, Boyarin explains, "Part of the import of Benjamin's image is the lesson that we are once again being driven out, that something eternally precious is eternally being lost." (xvi) Compare the more ironic diatribes against remembering in *The Counterlife* and against "Jewish history" in Haim Azaz's "The Sermon," cited by Y. H. Yerushalmi in *Zakhor: Jewish History and Jewish Memory* (New York: Schocken, 1989).

33 An authorial decision that might be analyzed with reference to the programmatic theory, along with a representational strategy can be found in Hayden White's essay in Friedlander's *Probing the Limits*. The narrative voice of *Beloved*, in White's view, by blurring the simple distinction between agency and passivity does greater (linguistic) justice to the enormous tragedy and loss of Black American history by thus obliquely speaking "unspeakable things unspoken," or again, from Morrison's essay of the same name, by "keeping the reader preoccupied with the nature of the incredible spirit world while being supplied a controlled diet of the incredible political world." (32) White himself makes reference to Primo Levi's metaphor of the atom as an exemplary case of modernist style, but that is the very opposite use to the one I make of that metaphor here, which leads me from Levi back to Levinas. In "Reality and its Shadow," Levinas fears that such style *qua* style, is precisely what compromises a diet of the political world – the "spirit world," as Morrison calls it, being dangerously suited to what Levinas regards with skepticism as "magic." "The world to be built is replaced by the essential completion of its shadow. This is not the disinterestedness of contemplation but of irresponsibility. The poet exiles himself from the city. From this point of view, the value of the beautiful is relative. There are times when one can be ashamed of it, as of fasting during a plague." ("Reality and its Shadow," 12)

34 Strangely, Morrison, in "Unspeakable Things Unspoken," asserts the absence of "painterly language" in *Beloved* as compared with her other fiction. For "the urgency of what is at stake" for the characters (with whom she wants her readers to identify, to be "there as they"), "the work of language is to get out of the way." (33) But that it often doesn't, even in *Beloved*, may be Morrison's distinguishing flaw as a novelist – what James Wood, in a penetrating review of her most recent novel *Paradise*, isolates as the consolations of magic over the "measured unreality" of fiction and its consequent demands on belief, or the preference for evasive opacity over narrative's "flat

stealth." Ultimately, argues Wood – and I agree – the problem lies with the sovereignty of the author's own voice whose signature lyricism is left uncriticized *in* the fiction, and allows Morrison to "love her own language more than she loves her characters." (31) See "The Color Purple," *in The New Republic* (March 2, 1998), 29–32, and compare Sandra Adell's review of Morrison's *Playing in the Dark: Whiteness and the Literary Imagination* in "Writing About Race," *American Literary History* (1996), 559–571, and Dwight McBride's "Speaking the Unspeakable: On Toni Morrison, African Intellectuals, and the Uses of Essentialist Rhetoric," *Modern Fiction Studies* 39 (Fall, Winter, 1993), 755–780, both of which locate a disturbing equivocality either within Morrison's fiction or between it and her more programmatic criticism.

35 Or to put it another way, where Morrison's novel funnels its meaning into word-as-object, Ozick's stops at objects themselves, junk, antiques, paraphernalia, together with the figural suitcases and packing material that transport them, and elects poor, intimate, human converse instead.

36 See "Of Plots, Witnesses, and Judgments," 99, and the chapters on a hermeneutics of agency, and narrative identity in Paul Ricoeur's *Oneself as Another*, trans. Kathleen Blamey (Chicago: University of Chicago Press, 1992).

37 From Y. H. Yerushalmi's *Zakhor*, 11–12, where Yerushalmi offers the narrative kernel of Deuteronomy 25:5–9 (the basis for the exfoliating structure of the Passover seder) as a model of "capsule history at its best."

38 Jonathan Boyarin, *Storm from Paradise*, xvi.

4 Wideman and Malamud

1 Ian Hacking's phrase from his essay of the same name about the posthoc construction of social "types" (usually in terms of linked behaviors) in *Reconstructing Individualism*, ed. Thomas Heller (Paolo Alto: Stanford University Press 1986): 222–236.

2 The phrase belongs to Gilles Deleuze and Félix Guattari in *Kafka: Toward a Minor Literature*, 41.

3 See the essay "Author and Hero in Aesthetic Activity" in *Art and Answerability: Early Philosophical Essays by M.M. Bakhtin*, trans. Vadim Liapunov (Austin: University of Texas Press, 1990).

4 Saul Bellow, *Mr. Sammler's Planet* (New York: Penguin, 1977), 48–49.

5 Bellow's comments were made in the course of a speech about the Western canon, but were, as he later explained, misunderstood when taken out of context.

6 See McBride cited in the previous chapter on racialized discourse as allegory in Paul de Man's sense, the fictivity of representations that purport to portray an entirely abstract category like "race." Kelley explains a parallel view on the dissonance between emblem and reality in *Reinventing Allegory*, 260.

7 The noun used is *gavrah* ("man," from a root denoting strength), not *golem* (lump, or lifeless substance). But in the midrash to the verse

"And he breathed into his nostrils the breath of life," we read, "This teaches us that He set him up as a lifeless mass [*golem*] reaching from earth to heaven, and then infused a soul into him," *(Genesis Rabbah 14:8)* so the two denominatives, by usage, tend to converge.

8 The Talmud is glossing a *mishna* (Tractate *Sanhedrin* 7.7) that reads, "A *ba'al ov* [A necromancer] is a sorcerer that makes [the dead] speak from his armpit, and a *yid'oni* [a soothsayer] is he that speaks with his mouth. These [must be executed] by stoning." Compare the focus on speech – sorcerers being those who work as *ventriloquists*, the concomitant possibility being their capacity to, in the Talmud's words, *achizat einayim* ("mesmerize," lit. "deceive the eyes") – with the self-conscious "conjuring" I subscribe to in the preface.

9 "The person created, while animated, was not alive. He lacked the *nishmat chayim* [the ability to speak]"; and indeed, the verb for "create" here is *barah*, not *yitzer*. See the relevant comments by Rav Ahron Soloveichik in his *The Warmth and the Light* (Jerusalem: Genesis Press, 1992), 6–8, and 147.

10 "'In the Image of God,' According to Rabbi Hayyim Volozhiner," from *Beyond the Verse*, 161. Levinas cites precisely this verse from Genesis as paradigmatic for the connection in his own philosophy between discourse (language, expression) and the ethical relation. See also "Judaism and Kenosis" in Levinas's *In The Time of Nations*.

11 From "Yiddish in America" in *The Pagan Rabbi and Other Stories* (New York: Dutton, 1983), 94.

12 In "Imaginary Others: Blacks and Jews in New York," *Partisan Review* (1992),573–582, Leonard Kriegel writes, "To become an imaginary other is to assume the weight of the other's fantasies, even when those fantasies are conspiratorial . . . Obsessed with the imaginary other, Jews and blacks nurture not the actual other but the other's image. A curious legacy of looking in the mirror to see how the other carries his pain. By now, the reflection in that mirror has grown distorted." (582–583)

13 "The Jewbird," from *The Magic Barrel* (New York: Farrar, Straus, and Giroux, 1958), 150.

14 See the essays by Gabriel Josipovici, "Going and Resting," 309–321, and Richard Shusterman, "Next Year in Jerusalem? Postmodern Jewish Identity and the Myth of Return," 291–308, in *Jewish Identity*, eds. David Theo Goldberg and Michael Krausz (Philadelphia: Temple University Press, 1993).

15 "Literary Blacks and Jews," in Berman, *Blacks and Jews*, 43.

16 *A Lover's Discourse*, 43.

17 "America: Toward Yavneh," in *What is Jewish Literature?*, ed. Hana Wirth-Nesher (Philadelphia: Jewish Publication Society, 1994), 20–35. In the introduction to *Bloodshed and Three Novellas* (New York: Knopf, 1976), she writes, "the story-making faculty itself can be a corridor to the corruptions and abominations of idol worship, of the adoration of the magical event." (11) See also "Literature as Idol: Harold Bloom" in *Art and Ardor*, 178–199, and "Bialik's Hint" in *Metaphor and Memory: Essays* (New York: Alfred Knopf, 1989), 223–39. Rael Meyerowitz's

Transferring to America: Jewish Interpretations of American Dreams (Albany: State University of New York Press, 1995), 113–124 and 140–142, cogently analyzes the contradictions at work here.

18 See, for instance, the introduction and epilogue to Ze'ev Chafets, *Devil's Night: And Other True Tales of Detroit* (New York: Random House, 1990), 3–16 and 234–240.

19 Malamud, *The Tenants* (New York: Farrar, Straus, and Giroux, 1971), 211.

20 John Edgar Wideman, "Valaida" in *The Stories of John Edgar Wideman* (New York: Pantheon, 1992).

21 Grace Paley deserves at least footnoted attention for her several stories in which Jews commune with Blacks. By the time of "The Long-Distance Runner" from her second collection of short fiction (1974), and "Zagrowsky Tells" from her third (1985), the moment of coalition between real-life Jewish American and African American constituencies that Malamud's stories presuppose, has already crested and begun its downturn. When one of Paley's characters exclaims to her daughter in "Dreamer in a Dead Language" from *Later the Same Day* (New York: Farrar, Straus, and Giroux, 1985), "'Faith, what do you think? The war made Jews Americans and Negroes Jews.'" Ha Ha. What do you think of that for an article? 'The Negro: Outside in at Last,'" a signal has been sent that Jews have themselves moved on, or that at least theirs is an inside-out, not the Negro's outside-in; Jews can now afford the fiction of "imaginary Negroes" (Leslie Fiedler's term), while the reverse condition remains an irrelevancy. See also Fiedler's *Waiting for the End* (Harmondsworth: Penguin, 1984).

22 Compare Wideman's stories with *The Nature of Blood* (New York: Knopf, 1997), by Caryl Phillips, four parallel, intersecting, and trans-historical stories of Black-cantilevered-with-Jew, and also James C. MacBride's *The Color of Water: A Black Man's Tribute to His White Mother* (New York: Riverhead Books, 1996), where an alternation of typeface underscores interwoven narratives by Jewish American mother and African American son.

23 Wideman cites Linda Dahl's *Stormy Weather: The Music and Lives of a Century of Jazzwomen* (New York: Pantheon, 1984) for the factual information on Valaida Snow. See also John Chilton, *Who's Who of Jazz: From Storyville to Swing* (London: Bloosmbury Book Shop, 1970), 383; D. Antoinette Handy, *Black Women in American Bands and Orchestras* (Metuchen, NJ: Scarecrow Press, 1981), 132; and Harrison Smith, "Valaida's Gone," *Record Review* (May–June, 1965). Either Valaida was interned somehow in Scandinavia or deported to a concentration camp; the sources conflict. (A side note: Handy quotes a 1950 New York newspaper article reporting that Valaida Snow "played the Waldorf for the benefit of the Hebrew Home for the Aged.")

24 "Bobby" is Bobby Short, and Wideman has borrowed the "orchid" line from Short's *Black and White Baby* (New York: Dodd, Mead, and Co., 1971), 99.

25 See Wallace Martin, *Recent Theories of Narrative* and Dorrit Cohn, *Transparent Minds: Modes For Presenting Consciousness in Fiction* (Prin-

ceton: Princeton University Press, 1979), for the narratological distinctions here.

26 See Bakhtin, "Author and Hero," 138–155.

27 Ozick, 74.

28 Bakhtin, "Author and Hero," 112.

29 See again Cohn's *Transparent Minds*.

30 The storytelling motif in "Fever" assumes several other explicit guises, the most obvious being Allen's account in general as an act of testimony. Contra the bogus medical opinions he's forced to obey, Allen remarks, "What I know of the fever I've learned from the words of those I've treated, from stories of the living that are ignored by the good doctors. When lancet and fleam bleed the victims, they offer up stories like prayers." (252) But as in Morrison's *Beloved*, Allen's reportage passes narrative on as cultural inheritance, just as the freedom/slavery motif does not exclusively bear on political realities. See 257–258, 261, and 265.

31 Bakhtin, "Author and Hero," 36.

32 Ibid., 42.

33 Ibid., 79.

34 Wideman has André Schwartz-Bart's famous novel, *The Last of the Just*, in mind here. The legend itself can be found in its original form in the Talmud, tractates *Sanhedrin* 97b and *Sukkot* 45b.

35 The "hostage" in his late work becomes a figure for the self ethically bound, answerable and substitute *for* the other. See *Otherwise Than Being*, chapters 4–6.

36 George Eliot, *Silas Marner: The Weaver of Raveloe* (Harmondsworth: Penguin Books, 1967), 101.

37 Leon Wieseltier, "All and Nothing at All: The Unreal World of Cornel West," *The New Republic*, 212.10 (March 6, 1995), 31–36. A more positive contribution by Wieseltier to blackjewishrelations can be seen in *Time* magazine's "The Rift Between Blacks and Jews," 143.9 (February 28, 1994), 28–32, where Wieseltier advocates "celebrating individual experience even as you celebrate collective memory; acknowledging the changes of the present in full, learned sight of the unchanging cruelties of the past; believing in politics and pitting politics against the lachrymosities of culture." (29). I would also like to see Wieseltier's most recent publication, a deeply moving account of his father's death entitled *Kaddish* (New York: Alfred Knopf, 1998) as a kind of corrective exercise in rhetorical probity.

38 Lest I seem overly metaphorical, *The New Republic* made its partisanship and incitement of this nonfiction of blows unmistakable through the cover headline, *The Decline of the Black Intellectual*, and underneath, *Leon Wieseltier Rakes Over Cornel West*.

39 See Henchard, "Intellectual Pursuit," in *The Nation* (February 19, 1996), 22.

40 Malamud, *The Magic Barrel*, 144.

5 Mamet and O. J.

1 Anthony Drazan's *Zebrahead* (1992) and Mattieu Kassovitz's *Café Au*

Lait (1994) are films that also suggest rich possibilities for genuine play with Black/Jewish identity politics. But these films, one American, the other French, are curiously compromised by a shared and unfortunate dynamic: a culturally Jewish, deraciné young man in love with a fetishized, ethnically dominant Black woman, Jewishness thus cathected onto Blackness.

2 Borges, "From Allegory to Novel," in *Other Inquisitions*, trans. Ruth L. C. Simms (Austin: University of Texas Press, 1964), 126.

3 As Philip Roth says of a similar parade of objects in *Operation Shylock*, "The Smilesburger million-dollar check. The Lech Walesa six-pointed star. Now the Leon Klinghoffer travel diaries. What next, the false nose worn by the admirable [nineteenth-century British Shylock] Macklin? Whatever Jewish treasure isn't nailed down comes flying straight into my face!" (280)

4 For example, "We need to *take* him, but we need him *alive*. That's the job we're given to do. That's why they gave it to the cops, 'stead of the F.B.I. Our job's to bring him down alive. Listen to me. I know it stinks. I know there's so much death in the world. I know that it's full of hatred, Momma. I know it all turns out wrong Here we are; here we are, we're the garbage men. You think I don't know that? I know that. Looking for something to love. You *got* something to love. You got your boys. That's something. Look in my eyes." (49)

5 Much of Mamet's work turns on the manipulation of this purely linguistic *savoir*, an enormously sophisticated procedure belied by its colloquialism. "Our *'plan'*? Our *'plan'* is to serve and protect – can I get back to you?" (15); "that sounds like an interesting case, and what did you do, *apprehend* him" (16); "garner some of them 'kudos' and all, that they got."(22); "Yeah. Some of that 'police' work that people talk about." (23) Plan, apprehend, kudos, police work: all words estranged by their quotation marks, formulaic discourse, as it were, publicly embarrassed and deflated. Gold's "to serve and protect" finds its way a few beats later into the mouth of the man on the way to the holding cell explaining why he murdered his family: "to protect them." (17) Gold's partner sardonically echoes him, "Someone was shooting at them, the Jew family," (79) only for Gold seconds later to say, "You're like my family, Tim." (80)

6 Mamet also peppers the film with antisemitic slurs like so many gunshots or stab wounds perpetrated by Gold and non-Jews alike. His most recent novelistic work, *The Old Religion* (New York: The Free Press, 1997), besides supplying one last accidental Black–Jewish pivot-point – to, of all texts, Reed's *Reckless Eyeballing* – fully metastasizes the inner burden of Jewish identity in the person of Leo Frank as he sits alone in his prison cell, and in the "tiny tub" of the mystified Jewish self (and Mamet's latest trio of one-act plays, *The Old Neighborhood*, gives its own twist to "the Jewish problem," as well).

7 Toni Morrison's word from her introduction to *Birth of a Nation'hood: Gaze, Script, and Spectacle in the O.J. Simpson Case*, eds. Toni Morrison and Claudia Brodsky Lacour (New York: Pantheon Books, 1997), xiii.

8 "The Bad News: The Good News" (with Jimmy Breslin), *Esquire*, 124.6

(December 1995), 108–116. Also see Robert Boynton's "The Professor of Connection," in *The New Yorker*, 71.35 (November 6, 1995), 95–108, where Crouch constructs a similar disanalogy-within-an-analogy between Blacks and Jews.

9 Ishmael Reed, *Reckless Eyeballing: A Novel* (New York, Athenaeum, 1988).

10 Reed himself contributes an essay to the *Birth of a Nation'hood* collection in which he uses Richard Wright's *Native Son* as the uncanny precursor text for the trial. (Although he mentions Bigger's lawyer in the novel, who is quite prominently a Jew, Reed lets any Black/Jewish correlations between novel and trial go unremarked.) See "Bigger and O. J.," 169–195, Morrison's introduction, "The Official Story: Dead Man Golfing," vii–xxviii, Kimberlé Williams Crenshaw, "Color-blind Dreams and Racial Nightmares," 97–168, and Patricia Williams's "American Kabuki," 273–292. As neither Reed's nor any of the other incisive essays – almost all of them drawing numerous parallels between discursive arenas like theater or literature and the trial itself – broaches the accidental allegorization of Black–Jewish relations within the context of the trial, this last section of my book assumes the role of Derrida's supplement: additional but intrinsic.

11 I am reminded of the famous experiment by the psychologist Simon Gaertner in 1970 when members of the New York Liberal party were asked over the phone for assistance by a "black-sounding" voice and a "white-sounding" voice: the differential results were decidedly illiberal. Would a similar argument have been entertained if region, not race had been the operative variable, say the difference between a speaker from Georgia and one from Northern Maine?

12 Jeffrey Rosen, "The Bloods and the Crits: O. J. Simpson, Critical Race Theory, the Law, and the Triumph of Color in America," *The New Republic*, December 9, 1996, 27–42. Compare the essay by Claudia Brodsky Lacour, "The Interest of the Simpson Trial: Spectacle, Judgment, and the National Interest," 367–413, in *Birth of a Nation'hood* which invokes not only Kant's critique of judgment, but also Arendt's analysis of the Eichmann trial (and in passing, the Dreyfus trial), but makes no reference to Cochran's own invocation of National Socialist ideology and genocide by analogy.

13 See Philip Brian Harper, *Framing the Margins: The Social Logic of Postmodernity* (New York: Oxford University Press, 1994).

14 *Time*, June 27, 1994.

15 Jorge Luis Borges, Tlön, Uqbar, Tertius," *Ficciones*, ed., Anthony Kerrigan (New York: Grove Press, 1962), 24.

Post-face: *Fires in the Mirror*

1 From the text version of *Fires in the Mirror: Crown Heights and Other Identities* (New York: Anchor Books, 1993).

2 *Studies in Ethnomethodology* (Cambridge: Polity Press, 1984).

3 One can hardly deny a racist component in the way many (perhaps most) of Crown Heights' Jews perceive African Americans, but I still

want to underscore that the primary frame of reference here differenti-
ates Jews from non-Jews *tout court*. (On a side note, since arriving in
their new Jewish homeland many of the Ethiopian Jews in Israel have
been subjected to an ad hoc racism, blood donations being refused
because of the purported likelier possibility of AIDS transmission. This
community continues to fit into Israeli society with difficulty. See
Ruben Schindler, *The Trauma of Transition: The Psycho-social cost of
Ethiopian Immigration to Israel* [Brookfield, VT: Averbury Press, 1997].)

4 Moreover, they comprise one Hasidic sect in a not-at-all amicable
relation to other Hasidic sects only a few miles away. In her later work
about the Los Angeles riots, a carelessness about Korean has been the
impetus for complaint from the Korean American community. In response to such complaints, Smith dismissed any claim on her to be
scrupulous in rendering such basic nuances – this, despite her avowed
dedication to the "intervention of listening," to "inhabit the words of
those around me."

5 Boelhower makes a similar point in *Through a Glass Darkly*, 21–28. A
more pragmatic postmodern account of ethnicity can be found in
Michael Fischer, "Ethnicity and PostModern Arts of Memory," in
Writing Culture: The Poetics and Politics of Ethnography (Berkeley: Uni-
versity of California Press, 1986). See, again, Diana Fuss's *Essentially
Speaking*, the essays in Goldberg's *Multiculturalism*, and Walter Benn
Michaels's *Our America: Nativism, Modernism, and Pluralism* (Durham:
Duke University Press, 1995), with its indictment of cultural theories
that do not acknowledge the racial essentialism to which their use of
"culture" or "ethnicity" necessarily appeals.

Bibliography

Adell, Sandra. *Double Consciousness/Double Bind: Theoretical Issues in Contemporary Black Literature*. Urbana: University Of Illinois Press, 1994.

Adorno, Theodor. *Aesthetic Theory*. Trans. C. Lenhardt. London: Routledge, 1984.

Negative Dialectics. Trans. E. B. Ashton. New York: Continuum, 1983.

Anderson, Benedict. *Imagined Communities: Reflections on the Origin and Spread of Nationalism*. London: Verso, 1983.

Anonymous. *The Secret Relationship Between Blacks and Jews*. Chicago: Latimer Associates, 1991.

Appelfeld, Aharon. *Massot Beguf Rishon*. Jerusalem: Zionist Library, 1979.

Beyond Despair: Four Lectures and a Conversation with Philip Roth. Trans. Jeffrey M. Green. New York: Fromm International, 1994.

Appiah, K. Anthony. "The Multiculturalist Misunderstanding." *The New York Review Of Books*. xliv:15, October 9, 1997.

Bakhtin, Mikhail. *Art and Answerability: Early Philosophical Essays*. Trans. Vadim Liapunov. Austin: The University of Texas Press, 1990.

The Dialogic Imagination: Four Essays. Trans. Caryl Emerson and Michael Holquist. Austin: The University of Texas Press, 1981.

Problems of Dostoevsky's Poetics. Trans. Caryl Emerson. Minneapolis: University of Minnesota Press, 1984.

Speech Genres and Other Late Essays. Trans. Vern W. McGee. Austin: The University of Texas Press, 1986.

Toward a Philosophy of the Act. Trans. Vadim Liapunov. Austin: University of Texas Press, 1993.

Bammer, Angelika. *Displacements: Cultural Identities in Question*. Bloomington: Indiana University Press, 1995.

Barthes, Roland. *The Pleasure of the Text*. Trans. Richard Miller. New York: Hill and Wang, 1975.

Bellow, Saul. *Mr. Sammler's Planet*. New York: Penguin, 1977.

The Victim. New York: Avon Books, 1975.

Benjamin, Walter. *Illuminations*. Trans. Harry Zohn. New York: Schocken Books, 1968.

The Origin of German Tragic Drama. Trans. John Osborne. London: *NLB,* 1977.
Reflections. Ed. Peter Demetz. New York: Schocken Books, 1986.
Berlin, Sir Isaiah. *The Sense of Reality: Studies in Ideas and their History.* London: Chatto and Windus, 1996.
Berman, Marshall. *All that Is Solid Melts Into Air: The Experience of Modernity.* New York: Penguin Books, 1982.
Berman, Paul. *Blacks and Jews: Alliances and Arguments.* New York: Delacorte Press, 1994.
Berube, Michael. "Public Academy." *The New Yorker.* January 29, 1995.
Bhabha, Homi. *Nation and Narration.* London: Routledge, 1990.
Blanchot, Maurice. *The Writing of the Disaster.* Trans. Ann Smock. Lincoln: University of Nebraska Press,1986.
Bloom, Harold. *Kabbalah and Criticism.* New York: Continuum, 1984.
Boelhower, William. *Through a Glass Darkly: Ethnic Semiosis in American Literature.* New York: Oxford University Press, 1987.
Borges, Jorge Luis. *Ficciones.* Ed, Anthony Kerrigan. New York: Grove Press, 1962.
"From Allegory to Novel." In *Other Inquisitions.* Trans. Ruth L. C. Simms. Austin: University of Texas Press, 1964.
Boyarin, Daniel. *Storm from Paradise: The Politics of Jewish Memory.* Minneapolis: University of Minnesota Press, 1992.
Boyarin, Daniel and Boyarin, Jonathan. *Jews and Other Differences: The New Jewish Cultural Studies.* Minneapolis: University of Minnesota Press, 1997.
"Diaspora: Generation and the Ground of Jewish Identity." *Critical Inquiry,* 19. Summer 1993.
Boynton, Robert. "The Intellectuals." *The Atlantic Monthly.* 275.3 March, 1995.
"The Professor of Connection." *The New Yorker.* 71.35 November 6, 1995.
Brackman, Harold. *Farrakhan's Reign of Terror: The Truth Behind The Secret Relationship Between Blacks and Jew.* Los Angeles: Simon Wiesenthal Center, 1992.
Bradley, David. *The Chaneysville Incident.* New York: Harper and Row, 1981.
Brodhead, Richard. *The School of Hawthorne.* New York: Oxford University Press, 1986.
Brown, Claude. *Manchild in the Promised Land.* New York: New American Library, 1965.
Buck-Morss, Susan. *The Dialectics of Seeing: Walter Benjamin and the Arcades Project.* Cambridge: MIT Press, 1991.
Budick, Emily. *Blacks and Jews in Literary Conversation.* Cambridge: Cambridge University Press, 1998.
Canetti, Elias. *The Conscience of Words.* Trans. Joachim Neugroschel. New York: Seabury Press, 1976.
Cave, Terence. *Recognitions: A Study in Poetics.* Cambridge: Cambridge University Press, 1988.
Chafets, Ze'ev. *Devil's Night: And Other True Tales of Detroit.* New York:

Random House, 1990.

Chilton, John. *Who's Who of Jazz: From Storyville to Swing.* London: Bloomsbury Book Shop, 1970.

Clifford, James. "Diasporas." *Cultural Anthropology.* 9:3, August, 1994.

Cohen, Richard. *Elevations: The Height of the Good in Rosenzweig and Levinas.* Chicago: The University of Chicago Press, 1994.

Cohn, Dorrit. *Transparent Minds: Modes For Presenting Consciousness in Fiction.* Princeton: Princeton University Press, 1979.

Connoly, William E. *Identity/Difference: Democratic Negotiations of Political Paradox.* Ithaca: Cornell University Press, 1991.

Cooper, Alan. *Philip Roth and the Jews.* Albany: State University of New York, 1996.

Critchley, Simon. *The Ethics of Deconstruction: Derrida and Levinas.* London: Blackwell, 1992.

Crouch, Stanley. *Notes of a Hanging Judge: Essays and Reviews 1979–1989.* New York: Oxford University Press, 1990.

with Breslin, Jimmy. "The Bad News: The Good News." *Esquire.* 124.6 December 1995.

Cruse, Harold. *The Crisis of the Negro Intellectual.* New York: William, Morrow & Company, 1967.

Cuddihy, John Murray. *The Ordeal Of Civility: Freud, Marx, Levi-Strauss and the Jewish Struggle With Modernity.* Boston: Beacon, 1987.

Deleuze, Gilles and Guattari, Félix. *Kafka: Toward a Minor Literature.* Trans. Dana Polan. Minneapolis: University of Minnesota Press, 1984.

De Man, Paul. *The Rhetoric of Romanticism.* Minneapolis: University of Minnesota Press, 1984.

Diner, Hasia. *In the Almost Promised Land: American Jews and Blacks 1915–1935.* Westport: Greenwood Press, 1977.

Dinnerstein, L. *Uneasy at Home: Antisemitism and the American Jewish Experience.* New York: Columbia University Press, 1987.

Douglas, Ann. *Terrible Honesty: Mongrel Manhattan in the 1920's.* New York: Farrar, Straus, and Giroux, 1995.

Drazan, Anthony. *Zebrahead.* (Film.) 1992.

Du Bois, W. E. B. *The Souls of Black Folk.* New York: Penguin Books, 1989.

Eliach, Yaffa, ed. *Hasidic Tales of the Holocaust.* New York: Oxford University Press, 1982.

Ellison, Ralph. *Invisible Man.* New York: Vintage Press, 1987.

Shadow and Act. New York: Random House, 1994.

Erdrich, Louise. *Tracks.* New York: Harper and Row, 1988.

Ezrahi, Sidra. *By Words Alone: The Holocaust in Literature.* Chicago: University of Chicago Press, 1980.

Fanon, Frantz. *Black Skin, White Masks.* Trans. George Lam Markman. New York: Grove Press, 1967.

Faulkner, William. *Essays, Speeches, and Public Letters*, ed. J. Merriwether. New York: Random House, 1966.

Fiedler, Leslie. "The Jew in American Literature," New York: Stern and Day, 1970. In *The Collected Essays of Leslie Fielder.*

The Last Jew in America. New York: Stein and Day, 1966.

Waiting for the End. Harmondsworth: Penguin, 1984.

Finkielkraut, Alain. *The Imaginary Jew*. Trans. Kevin O'Neill and David Suchoff. Lincoln: University of Nebraska Press, 1992.

The Wisdom of Love. Trans. Kevin O'Neill and David Suchoff. Lincoln: University of Nebraska Press, 1984.

Fischer, Michael. "Ethnicity and PostModern Arts of Memory." In James Clifford and George Marcus, eds. *Writing Culture: The Poetics and Politics of Ethnography*. Berkeley: University of California Press, 1986.

Foucault, Michel. *The Archaeology of Knowledge*. Trans. A. M. Sheridan-Smith. New York: Pantheon Books, 1972.

Fox, Marvin, ed. *Modern Jewish Ethics: Theory and Practice*. Columbus: Ohio State University Press, 1975.

Fredrickson, George. *The Black Image in the White Mind*. New York: Harper and Row, 1971.

Friedlander, Saul, ed. *Probing the Limits of Representation: Nazism and the "Final Solution"*. Chicago: University of Chicago Press, 1992.

Fuss, Diana. *Essentially Speaking: Feminism, Nature and Difference*. New York: Routledge, 1989.

Garfinkel, Herbert. *Studies in Ethnomethodology*. Cambridge: Polity Press, 1984.

Gates, Jr., Henry Louis. "Authenticity; or the Lesson of 'Little Tree'." *New York Times Book Review*. November 24, 1991.

"Bad Influence." *The New Yorker*. 70:3, March 7, 1994.

Figures in Black. New York: Oxford University Press, 1988.

Gilman, Sander. *Jewish Self-Hatred: The Secret Language of the Jews*. Baltimore: Johns Hopkins University Press, 1986.

Gilroy, Paul. *The Black Atlantic: Modernity and Double Consciousness*. Cambridge: Harvard University Press, 1993.

Glazer, Nathan. *We Are All Multiculturists Now*. Cambridge: Harvard University Press, 1997.

Goffman, Erving. *Interaction Ritual: Essays in Face-to-Face Behavior*. Garden City, NY: Anchor Books, 1967.

The Presentation of Self in Everyday Life. Garden City, NY: Doubleday Books, 1959.

Goldberg, David Theo. *Multiculturalism: A Critical Reader*. London Blackwell, 1995.

The Anatomy of Racism. Minneapolis: University of Minnesota Press, 1990.

with Krausz, Michael, eds. *Jewish Identity*. Philadelphia: Temple University Press, 1992.

Govrin, Nurit. "To Express the Inexpressible: The Holocaust Literature of Aharon Appelfeld." In *Remembering for the Future*. Oxford: Pergamon Press, 1988.

Guillory, John. "Canon, Syllabus, List: A Note on the Pedagogic Imaginary." *Transition*. 52, 1991.

Hacking, Ian. "Making up People." In Thomas Heller, ed. *Reconstructing Individualism*. Palo Alto: Stanford University Press, 1986.

Handy, D. Antoinette. *Black Women in American Bands and Orchestras* Metuchen, NJ: Scarecrow Press, 1981.

Bibliography

Henchard, Michael. "Intellectual Pursuit." In *The Nation*. February 19, 1996.

Hentoff, Nat, ed. *Black Anti-Semitism and Jewish Racism*. New York: Richard W. Baron, 1969.

Higham, John. *Strangers in the Land: Patterns of American Nativism 1860–1925*. New York: Atheneum, 1968.

Hilfer, Tony. *The Crime Novel: A Deviant Genre*. Austin: The University of Texas Press, 1992.

Himes, Chester. *If He Hollers Let Him Go*. New York: Thunder Mouth's Press, 1986.

The Quality of Hurt. New York: Doubleday, 1972.

Howe, Irving. *A World More Attractive: A View of Modern Literature and Politics*. New York: Horizon Press, 1963.

World of Our Fathers. New York: Harcourt, Brace, Jovanovich, 1976.

Huggins, Nathan. *Harlem Renaissance*. New York: Oxford University Press, 1971.

Hurston. Zora Neale. *Novels and Stories*. New York: Library of America, 1995.

Idel, Moshe. *Kabbalah: New Perspectives*. New Haven: Yale University Press, 1988.

Ignatiev, Noel. *How the Irish Became White*. New York: Routledge, 1995.

Jackson, Michael. *HIStory*. CD, 1995.

James, Henry. *The American Scene: Together with Three Essays From "Portraits of Places"*. New York: Charles Scribner's Sons, 1946.

The Art of the Novel: Critical Prefaces. New York: Charles Scribner's Sons, 1962.

Essays, Selections, Literary Criticism. New York: Viking, 1984.

JanMohamed, Abdul R. and Lloyd, David. *The Nature and the Context of Minority Discourse*. New York: Oxford University Press, 1990.

Kassovitz, Mattieu. *Café Au Lait*. (Film.) 1994.

Katz, Jacob. *Exclusivism and Tolerance*. New York: Oxford University Press, 1961.

Kaufman, Jonathan. *Broken Alliance: The Turbulent Times between Blacks and Jews in America*. New York: Charles Scribner's Sons, 1988.

Kazin, Alfred. *A Walker in the City*. New York: Harcourt, Brace, Jovanovich, 1973.

On Native Grounds: An Interpretation of Modern American Prose Literature. New York: Doubleday, 1952.

Kelley, Theresa. *Reinventing Allegory*. London: Cambridge University Press, 1997.

Kleeblatt, Norman L., ed. *Too Jewish? Challenging Jewish Identities*. New Brunswick: Rutgers University Press, 1996.

Klein, Marcus. *Foreigners: The Making of American Literature 1900–1940*. Chicago: The University of Chicago Press, 1981.

Kriegel, Leonard. "Imaginary Others: Blacks and Jews in New York." *Partisan Review*. 60:4 Fall, 1993.

Kristeva, Julia. *Strangers to Ourselves*. Trans. Leon S. Roudiez. New York: Columbia University Press, 1991.

Lacan, Jacques. *The Four Fundamental Concepts of Psychoanalysis*. Trans.

Alan Sheridan. New York: W. W. Norton, 1981.

Lang, Berel, ed. *Writing and the Holocaust*. New York: Holmes and Meier, 1988.

Lavender, Abraham. *A Coat of Many Colors: Jewish Subcommunities in the United States*. Westport, CN: Greenwood, 1977.

Lester, Julius. "The Outsiders." *Transition*. 68, Winter 1995.

Levi, Primo. *The Periodic Table*. Trans. Raymond Rosenthal. New York: Schocken Books, 1984.

Levi Yitzkhakh Berdichiver. *Kedushat Levi Ha Shalem*. Jerusalem: *Ha mosad l'hotsa'at sifre musar va'hasidut*, 1964.

Levinas, Emmanuel. *Basic Philosophical Writings*. Bloomfield: Indiana University Press, 1996.

Beyond the Verse: Talmudic Readings and Lectures. Trans. Gary D. Mole. Baltimore: Johns Hopkins University Press, 1990.

Collected Philosophical Papers. Trans. Alphonso Lingis. The Hague: Martinus Nijhoff, 1987.

Difficult Freedom. Trans. Seán Hand. Baltimore: Johns Hopkins University Press, 1990.

In the Time of Nations. Trans. Michael B. Smith. Bloomington: Indiana University Press, 1994.

The Levinas Reader. Ed. Seán Hand. Oxford: Blackwell, 1989.

Nine Talmudic Readings. Trans. Annette Aronowicz Bloomington: University of Indiana Press, 1990.

Other wise Than Being; Or Beyond Essence. Trans Alphonso Lingis. The Hague: Martinus Nijhoff, 1978.

Outside the Subject. Trans. Michael B. Smith. Stanford: Stanford California Press, 1994.

Time and the Other. Trans. Richard Cohen. Pittsburgh University Press, 1987.

Totality and Infinity: An Essay on Exteriority. Trans. Alfonso Lingis. Pittsburg: Duquesne University Press, 1969.

"The Trace of the Other." In Taylor, Mark, ed. *Deconstruction in Context: Literature and Philosophy*. Chicago: University of Chicago Press, 1986.

"Transcendence et Hauteur." *Bulletin de la Societé Francais de la Philosophie*. 56:3, 1962.

Lewis, David Levering. *When Harlem Was in Vogue*. New York: Alfred Knopf, 1981.

Lindemann, Albert S. *Esau's Tears: Modern Anti-Semitism and the Rise of the Jews*. Cambridge: Cambridge University Press, 1997.

Luria, Rabbi Yitzkhakh. *Peri etz hayim*. Jerusalem: Hotsa'at kivenu Rabenu Ha-Ari, 1965.

Lyotard, Jean-François. *Heidegger and "the jews"*. Trans. Andreas Michel and Mark S. Roberts. Minneapolis: University of Minnesota Press, 1990.

MacBride, James C. *The Color of Water: A Black Man's Tribute to His White Mother*. New York: Riverhead Books, 1996.

McBride, Dwight. "Speaking the Unspeakable: On Toni Morrison, African Intellectuals, and the Uses of Essentialist Rhetoric." *Modern Fiction Studies*. 39, Fall, Winter, 1993.

Malamud, Bernard. *The Magic Barrel*. New York: Farrar, Straus, and Giroux, 1958).
    The Tenants. New York: Farrar, Straus, and Giroux, 1971.
Mamet, David. *Homicide*. (Film.) 1992.
    The Old Religion. New York: The Free Press, 1997.
Margolies, Edward and Fabre, Michael. *The Several Lives of Chester Himes*. Jackson: University of Mississippi Press, 1997.
Martin, Tony. *The Jewish Onslaught: Dispatches From the Wellesley Battlefront*. Dover: The Majority Press, 1993.
Martin, Wallace. *Recent Theories of Narrative*. Ithaca: Cornell University Press, 1986.
Martin, William Denis-Constant. "The Choices of Identity." *Social Identities*. 1:1, November 1995.
Melnick, Jeffrey. *Right to Sing the Blues: The Uncanny Relationship of American Blacks and Jews*. Cambridge: Harvard University Press, 1998.
Mercer, Kobena. "Diaspora Culture and the Dialogic Imagination." In M. Cham and C. Andrade-Watkins, ed. *Blackframes: Celebration of Black Cinema*. Massachusetts: MIT Press, 1988.
Meyer, Adam. *Cooperation and Conflict: Cross Ethnicity in Contemporary Jewish American and Afro-American Literature*. Diss. Vanderbilt University, 1991.
Michaels, Walter Benn. *Our America: Nativism, Modernism, and Pluralism*. Durham: Duke University Press, 1995.
    "Race Into Culture: A Critical Genealogy of Cultural Identity." *Critical Inquiry*. 18:4, Summer 1992.
Morrison, Toni. *Beloved*. New York: Plume, 1988.
    "Unspeakable Things Unspoken." *Michigan Quarterly Review* 28:1, Winter, 1989.
    with Lacour, Claudia B. *Birth of Nation'hood: Gaze, Script and Spectacle in the O. J. Simpson Case*. New York: Pantheon Books, 1997.
Newman, Naomi and O'Neal, John. *Crossing the Broken Bridge*. A Traveling Jewish Theater and Junebug Productions, 1994.
Newton, Adam Zachary. "Call Me/It Ishmael: The Sound of Recognition in *Call it Sleep* and *Invisible Man*." In *Prospects*, Ed. Jack Salzman, New York: Cambridge University Press, 1996.
    "From Ethics to Exegesis: Recognition and Its Vicissitudes in Saul Bellow and Chester Himes." *South Atlantic Quarterly* 95:4, Fall, 1996.
    "Incognito Ergo Sum: Riding the Hyphen in Cahan, Johnson, Larsen, and Yezierska," Eds. Jarab and Melnick. *Race and the Modern Artist*. New York: Oxford University Press, 1999.
    Narrative Ethics (Cambridge: Harvard University Press, 1995.
Nietzsche, Friedrich. *The Use and Abuse of History*. New York: Macmillan Publishing Company, 1986.
O'Meally, Robert, ed. *New Essays on Invisible Man*. New York: Cambridge University Press, 1988.
Ozick, Cynthia. *Art and Ardor*. New York: Alfred Knopf, 1983.
    Bloodshed and Three Novellas. New York: Alfred Knopf, 1976.
    Metaphor and Memory: Essays. New York: Alfred Knopf, 1989.
    The Pagan Rabbi and Other Stories. New York: Alfred Knopf, 1983.

The Shawl: A Story and Novella. New York: Alfred Knopf, 1989.
Patterson, Orlando. *Ethnic Chauvinism: The Reactionary Impulse*. New York: Stein and Day, 1977.
Peck, Abraham J. *Blacks and Jews: The American Experience*. Cincinnati: The American Jewish Archives, 1988.
Perkins, David. *Is Literary History Possible?* Baltimore: Johns Hopkins University Press, 1992.
Phillips, Caryl. *The Nature of Blood*. New York: Alfred Knopf, 1997.
Pinkney, Darryl. *High Cotton*. New York: Farrar, Straus, and Giroux, 1992.
Proust, Marcel. *On Reading Ruskin*. Trans. J. Autret, W. Burford, and P. J. Wolfe. New Haven: Yale University Press, 1987.
Reed, Jr., Adolph. 'What Are the Drums Saying, Booker? The Current Crisis of the Black Intellectual.'' *The Village Voice*. April 11, 1995.
Reed, Ishmael. *Reckless Eyeballing: A Novel*. New York: Athenaeum, 1988.
Richter, David. *Narrative Theory*. White Plains, NY: Longmans, 1996.
Ricoeur, Paul. *Oneself as Another*. Trans. Kathleen Blamey. Chicago: University of Chicago Press, 1992.
Rogin, Michael. *Blackface, White Noise: Jewish Immigrants in the Melting Pot*. Berkeley: University of California Press, 1996.
"Black Face, White Noise: When the Jewish Jazz Singer Finds His Voice." *Critical Inquiry*. 18, Spring, 1992.
Rose, Jeffrey. "The Bloods and the Crits: O. J. Simpson, Critical Race Theory, the Law, and the Triumph of Color in America." *The New Republic*. December 9, 1996.
Rosenfeld, Isaac. *An Age of Enormity*. Cleveland: World Publishing Co., 1962.
Passage From Home. New York: Dial Press, 1946.
Roth, Henry. *Call It Sleep*. New York: Avon Books, 1981.
Mercy in a Rude Stream (3 vols.). New York: St. Martin's Press, 1994.
Roth, Philip. *American Pastoral*. New York: Houghton Mifflin, 1997.
The Counterlife. New York: Farrar, Strauss, Giroux, 1987.
The Facts: A Novelist's Autobiography. New York: Penguin Books, 1988.
Operation Shylock. New York: Simon & Schuster, 1993.
Reading Myself and Others. New York: Bantam, 1977.
Rubin, Barry. *Assimilation and Its Discontents*. New York: Random House, 1995.
Salzman, Jack. *Bridges and Boundaries: African Americans and American Jews*. New York: George Braziller, Inc., 1992.
with West, Cornel. *Struggle in the Promised Land: Towards a History of Black-Jewish Relations in the United States*. New York: Oxford University Press, 1997.
Sartre, Jean-Paul. *AntiSemite and Jew*. Trans. George J. Becker. New York: Schocken Books, 1948.
Scholem, Gershom. *Major Trends in Jewish Mysticism*. New York: Schocken, 1961.
On the Kabbalah and its Symbolism. New York: Schocken, 1965.
Schwartz, Delmore. *Genesis*. New York: New Directions, 1943.
Segal, Lore. *Her First American*. New York: Alfred A. Knopf, 1985.
Sennett, Richard. *Flesh and Stone: The Body and the City in Western Civiliza-*

tion. New York: W. W. Norton & Co., 1994.

Shankman, Alfred. *Ambivalent Friends: Afro-Americans View the Immigrant*. Westport, Conn: Greenwood Press, 1982.

Sharfman, Harold J. *The Frontier Jews: An Account of Jewish Pioneers and Settlers in Early America*. Seacaucus, NJ: The Citadel Press, 1977.

Shell, Marc. *Children of the Earth: Literature, Politics, and Nationhood* (New York: Oxford University Press, 1993.

Siebers, Tobin. *The Ethics of Criticism*. Ithaca: Cornell University Press, 1988.

Simmel, Georg. *On Individuality and Social Forms*. Ed. Donald Levine. Chicago: University of Chicago Press, 1971.

Simon, Roger. "Face to Face With Alterity: Postmodern Jewish Identity and the Eros of Pedagogy." In Jane Gallop, ed. *Pedagogy: The Question of Impersonation*. Bloomington: Indiana University Press, 1995.

Smith, Anna-Deavere. *Fires in the Mirror: Crown Heights, Brooklyn, and Other Identities*. New York: Anchor Books, 1993.

Smith, Theophus. *Conjuring Culture: Biblical Formations of Black America*. New York: Oxford, 1994.

Sollors, Werner. *Beyond Ethnicity: Consent and Descent in American Culture*. New York: Oxford University Press, 1986.

Neither Black Nor White Yet Both: Thematic Explorations of Interracial Identity. New York: Oxford University Press, 1997.

Sommer, Doris. "Allegory and Dialectics: A Match Made in Romance." *Boundary 2*. 18:1, 1991.

Foundational Fictions: The National Romances of Latin America. Berkeley: University of California Press, 1991.

Starke, Catherine Juanita. *Black Portraiture in American Fiction*. New York: Basic Books, 1971.

Stein, A. and Weisbord, R. *Bittersweet Encounter: The Afro American and the American Jew*. Westport: Negro University Press, 1970.

Still, Peter. *The Kidnapped and the Ransomed* (Kate E. R. Pickard). Ed. Maxwell Whiteman and Nancy Grant. Lincoln: University of Nebraska Press, 1995.

Suchoff, David. *Critical Theory and the Novel: Mass Society and Cultural Criticism in Dickens, Melville, and Kafka*. Madison: University of Wisconsin Press, 1994.

Sundquist, Eric. *To Wake the Nations: Race in the Making of American Literature*. Cambridge: Belknap Press of Harvard University Press, 1993.

Taylor, Charles. *Multiculturalism and the Politics of Recognition: An Essay*. Princeton: Princeton University Press, 1992.

Thomas, Laurence Mordekai. "The Matrices of Malevolent Ideologies: Blacks and Jews." *Social Identities*. 2:1, February, 1996.

Vessels of Evil: American Slavery and the Holocaust. Philadelphia: Temple University Press, 1993.

Thompson, Robert Farris. *The Flash of the Spirit*. New York: Random House, 1983.

Washington, J. R., ed. *Jews in Black Perspectives: A Dialogue*. Rutherford: Farleigh Dickinson Press, 1984.

West, Cornel. *Keeping Faith: Philosophy and Race in America.* New York: Routledge, 1993.

"The New Cultural Politics of Difference," in *The Cultural Studies Reader.* Ed. Simon Durang. New York: Routledge, 1993.

and Lerner, Michael. *Jews and Blacks: Let the Healing Begin.* New York: G. P. Putnam's Sons, 1995.

Wideman, John Edgar. *The Stories of John Edgar Wideman.* New York: Pantheon, 1992.

Introduction to Mumia Abdul Jamal. *Live From Death Row.* New York: Addison Wesley, 1995.

Wieseltier, Leon. "All and Nothing at All: The Unreal World of Cornel West." *The New Republic.* 212:10, March 6, 1995.

"Letting Go." *The New Republic.* 209:14, October 4 1993.

"The Rift Between Blacks and Jews." *Time.* 143:9, February 28, 1994.

Wirth-Nesher, Hana. *What is Jewish Literature?* Philadelphia: Jewish Publication Society, 1994.

Yerushalmi, Yosef Haim. *Zachor: Jewish History and Jewish Memory.* New York: Schocken, 1989.

Young, James E. *Writing and Rewriting the Holocaust: Narrative and the Consequences of Interpretation.* Indiana: Indiana University Press, 1988.

Žižek, Slavoj. *Looking Awry: An Introduction to Jacques Lacan Through Popular Culture.* Cambridge: Massachusetts Institute of Technology Press, 1991.

The Sublime Object of Ideology. New York: Verso Press, 1989.

Index

Index

Index